BEYOND CLASS IMAGES

SOCIAL ANALYSIS

A Series in the Social Sciences

Edited by Richard Scase, University of Kent

BEYOND CLASS IMAGES

EXPLORATIONS IN THE STRUCTURE OF
SOCIAL CONSCIOUSNESS

HOWARD H. DAVIS

CROOM HELM   LONDON

© 1979 Howard H. Davis

Croom Helm Ltd, 2-10 St John's Road, London SW11

British Library Cataloguing in Publication Data

Davis, Howard H
   Beyond class images.
   1. Social classes – Scotland – Central Region
   2. Social classes – Case studies   3. Occupations
   I. Title
   301.44'4'094131   HN398.S3

ISBN 0-85664-801-9
   0-7099-0030-9 Pbk

Printed in Great Britain by
Biddles Ltd, Guildford, Surrey

CONTENTS

PREFACE

The research for this book was carried out at the University of
Edinburgh and the Centre d'Etude des Mouvements Sociaux, Paris,
with financial support from the Social Science Research Council
and the Centre National de la Recherche Scientifique. The results
were presented earlier in a different form as a PhD thesis: 'Elements
of Workers' Consciousness: Images of Society among Manual and
Clerical Workers', University of Edinburgh, 1978.

I am deeply indebted to the workers, supervisors and managements
of the three companies who made the empirical part of this study
possible. For obvious reasons they have to remain anonymous. Thanks
are also due to colleagues at the Universities of Edinburgh, Glasgow
and Kent for their comments and encouragement. I have particularly
valued the friendly criticisms made by Professor T. Burns and
Professor A. Touraine of earlier versions of this work. Of course they
take no responsibility for the outcome.

Where quotations from French and German sources appear in the
text in English, the translations are my own unless otherwise indicated.

Howard Davis
May, 1978

INTRODUCTION: THE ANALYSIS OF IMAGES OF SOCIETY

The term 'image of society' has had currency in sociology for two decades. During this time, however, few researchers have succeeded in elaborating the concept itself, to give it a sound theoretical base and make it more rigorous empirically. In fact, as a medium in the exchange of ideas it has become devalued through uncritical use or perhaps through overuse. Renewed interest in recent years has conspicuously failed to give the notion greater strength or clarity.[1] The aim of this study is to critically assess the progress of research in Britain and Europe and to make an empirical contribution to the understanding of images of society through the analysis of interviews with maintenance craftsmen, steel workers and clerical workers from three locations in Central Scotland.

'Image of society' was adopted as a sociological concept by H. Popitz, H.P. Bahrdt *et al.* in their seminal study *Das Gesellschaftsbild des Arbeiters*[2] and was used by Alfred Willener at about the same time.[3] It then became current in British sociology largely through the work of Lockwood, whose early attempt at a typology of working class images of society inspired a great deal of the subsequent debate.[4] In the course of this debate the term has unfortunately been put to such a variety of uses that it has become more a figure of sociological speech than a usable analytical term. The first chapter is therefore an attempt to clear some of the original insights of their confusions and pave the way to a more rigorous, analytical approach to the further study of these 'images' of class, hierarchy and social order in general. Images are particularly important in the conceptual apparatus of macro-sociology because they provide a means of entry into the empirical problems posed by ideas about workers' consciousness and class awareness – or the lack of it – that have dominated British sociology in the last ten years.

In the detailed study of workers in three industries reported in Chapters 4-7 we have attempted to take these ideas a stage further by looking at images of society in the light of a general theory of social action. To the extent that it derives from the theoretical work of Alain Touraine, this general theory can be called 'Actionalism'.[5] The general relevance of this theory is discussed in Chapter 2 and its particular advantage in viewing consciousness as a relation rather than an object is explained. In our view it is the absence of a systematic sociology of action rather than the inherent complexity of social imagery which has caused such doubts about the consistency, stability and content of images of society.

'Actionalism' provides a theoretical alternative to those approaches which — implicitly or explicitly — are forced to choose between people's awareness of society and the structural sources of this awareness. Too often, the description and analysis of images of society have failed to grasp the complex relations that are involved, preferring an over-simplified division of social experience into 'subjective' or 'objective' components of a crude base-superstructure model. To consider inequality and social differentiation exclusively, or even preponderantly, from either an 'objective' or a 'subjective' point of view must be inadequate, even where some shorthand account of the 'other' is included. Concentration on the 'objective' leads ultimately to a version of mechanistic materialism which dispenses with human agency in the construction of social reality and meaning. Exclusive concentration on the 'subjective' cannot amount to anything more than descriptive reporting. The reductionist tendencies involved in both of these approaches should be avoided.

We therefore propose a definition of an 'image of society' which is close to that used by Popitz, Bahrdt *et al.*, since theirs is made explicit and does not give way to this restrictive and unhelpful dichotomy. They do not presuppose a correspondence between images of society and class relations defined in terms of market or economic criteria, as many observers have. Instead they draw attention to the workers' experience (including experience only shared by small groups as well as the common experience of the working class) and attribute an important role to the image in actively making sense of this experience of work, institutions and social relations in their particular as well as their general aspects. According to this view, an image of society is a collection of themes, which may or may not constitute a comprehensive framework for understanding society, but which nevertheless provide a means for understanding the fragments of personal experience and collating them in such a way as to postulate a movement between past and present and between present and future. This definition makes use of the tension to be found within the word 'image' itself, which conveys both the idea of reflection and the idea of projection. We argue that the concept must be dissociated from a naive 'reflection' or 'transcription' view and must be re-applied sociologically. It should be understood to refer to complex phenomena of consciousness whose ambivalence is accepted; not as something to be explained away as a form of adaptation to given circumstances but as something which is integral to the relation between man as a producer and his products.

There are some signs that the openness and fluidity of images of society are being more widely acknowledged. The development of the concept over the past few years has shown increasing recognition of the inadequacy of closed typologies to grasp the complex and sometimes apparently contradictory evidence.[6] Yet obscurity and ambiguity continue to flourish because images are thought to be consistent and complete, representative of an existing social order, as though they were in some way analogous to the social theories of the investigator. The accumulation of empirical evidence bears few signs of any serious questioning of this assumption and the theories of social experience and consciousness which it implies.

One response to the impoverished state of research in this area has been to deny that images of society have any systematic social basis and to maintain that any images of society which are identified simply represent a pattern imposed by the sociologist either in the process of interviewing or in the selective reinterpretation of results.[7] This is a damaging criticism for those who have thought of images of society as simplified mirror images of social structure. However, we have not assumed that images of society are systematically related to occupational groups or social strata in such a way that work or class position are the only criteria or description. The definition we have used simply makes a twofold assumption about consciousness: that its structures are not independent of the structures of social relations and that the ordering of these relations will at least sometimes become the object of conscious awareness. Because this awareness is not constant, the term 'image of society' has seemed unsatisfactory when there is little evidence that 'abstract' social relations (i.e. those which are not directly experienced) are brought to mind in any coherent or stable pattern. As an alternative, the term 'social consciousness' is used in a general sense to refer to any awareness of the ordering of society, whether this is static and complete or unstable and fractured. We have continued to use 'image of society' when its meaning is clear from the context and where its static connotations are not misleading.

Notes

1. See for example the papers presented to the SSRC Conference on *The Occupational Community of the Traditional Worker* (Durham, September 1972). These papers are available in M. Bulmer (ed.), *Working-Class Images of Society*, (London, 1975).

2. H. Popitz, H.P. Bahrdt, E.A. Jueres and A. Kesting, *Das Gesellschaftsbild des Arbeiters* (Tübingen, Mohr, 1957).

3. A. Willener, *Images de la société et classes sociales* (Bern, 1957).

4. D. Lockwood, 'Sources of Variation in Working Class Images of Society', *Sociological Review*, 14 (1966).

5. See A. Touraine, *Sociologie de l'action* (Paris, 1965); *Production de la société* (Paris, 1973).

6. See for example the contribution by J. Cousins and R. Brown to the SSRC Durham Conference, 1972. They conclude 'that shipbuilding workers do not all have one unambiguous "image of society" which is relevant whatever the context of speech or action', in M. Bulmer (ed.), *Working-Class Images*, p.79.

7. See for example A.P.M. Coxon's review of M. Bulmer (ed.), *Working-Class Images of Society*, (London, 1975), in *Quantitative Sociology Newsletter* No.17. (Autumn 1976). The suggested alternative, which draws on the disciplines of cognitive psychology, artificial intelligence and ethnosemantics, is well represented by the work of the Project on Occupational Cognition, Dept. of Sociology, University of Edinburgh. See A.P.M. Coxon and C.L. Jones, *The Images of Occupational Prestige* (London, 1978).

1 SOCIETY IN THE MIND: REFLECTIONS AND PROJECTIONS

The use of the term 'image' in the social sciences to refer to a complex of ideas about the social world and representations of it, has its origins in the 1950s, the term having been borrowed from psychology and market research. Initially, it was made to signify the representation of society as a whole which, as was then thought, had to be presupposed in any study of normatively orientated behaviour but which (like the brand image of a product) might be only indirectly related to reality. This can be regarded as a development of technique within the general framework of tne perennial problem of stratification. Given the inescapable fact of social differentiation and evidence that these differences are not necessarily destructive, many functional theorists and others were inclined to regard one of the sources of cohesion as being a consistent, shared image of the society. Thus, for example, Louis Wirth could write that 'a society is possible in the last analysis because the individuals within it carry around in their heads some sort of picture of that society'.[1] It is hard to disagree with this simple statement as it stands; but it can be questioned whether the implication that there is general agreement about the composition and meaning of the picture has any basis in fact.

It is clear that our world is both the scene of our actions and the object of our actions. But empirical studies have been preoccupied with evidence of a correspondence between social consciousness and class or status within society without providing theoretical grounds for such a correspondence. Despite their apparent dissimilarity, 'objectivist' approaches to social relations (usually class relations defined in terms of market or economic criteria) and 'subjectivist' approaches (which interpret tnese relations in terms of group awareness, perceived status, etc.) share the same framework of interpretation although each element is evaluated differently.

Early Studies of Images of Society

The first European studies of images of society, while they did not stem directly from the work on stratification and social class by American social scientists like Warner and Centers, certainly have to be seen against the background of this earlier work in order to judge their

significance.[2] Warner's achievement was the 'discovery' of class structure
in America and Centers followed this up in the late forties. However,
the introduction to American social science of one of the basic facts of
social life was accompanied by lasting conceptual confusion. Warner
identified the concept of class completely with that of status or rank,
so that a class was said to consist of people who have similar rankings
in a community and associate on equal terms. Centers, however, whilst
agreeing that the views of participants were crucial in any study of
social differentiation, wished to distinguish status from class despite
their close relationship because common interests and values often
unite people of different statuses and do not always depend on close
association. He returned to a consideration of older theories of class,
including that of Marx, and tried to direct attention away from rank
and hierarchy by re-defining class as a psychological phenomenon, as
part of a man's ego, 'a feeling on his part of belongingness to something,
an identification with something larger than himself'.[3] His study
concluded that classes, which are essentially psychologically or
subjectively based groupings corresponding approximately to socio-
economic groupings, can be regarded as groups with political and
economic interests which are a function of the given 'life situation' in
both objective and subjective aspects.[4]

Thus the terms social stratification and social class were used almost
interchangeably with the result that subsequent authors in America and
Europe often failed to distinguish between psychologically or
subjectively based categories of inequality and socio-economic
groupings.

This was not recognised as a problem and the confusion it led to is
well illustrated in Willener's early study.[5] He set out to define classes
by means of the representations held by people with society. Calling
these representations 'images of society', his stated intention was to
'provide a concrete definition of classes *from the inside*, from the
consciousness which is explicitly and implicitly expressed in the replies
of an aggregate of individuals placed in a variety of social situations'.
From the results of a sample survey of the adult male population of
Lausanne in 1955, Willener made inferences from general statements
about life chances, success, wealth and inequality, marriage etc., as well
as using explicit information about individual's actual income, social
situation and behaviour. He argued that despite the great diversity of
replies there were consistencies of response with respect to the theme
in question (income or occupation, for example) and the 'objectively'
defined categories of the respondents. The most important of these

regularities were: (1) that lower categories of respondents (classified by income and occupation) replied more frequently in terms of 'classes' than the higher categories who tended to refer to 'levels' or a hierarchy; (2) that the higher the income and occupational category, the greater the number of respondents who defined 'success' in individualistic as opposed to collective social terms. Willener concluded that the pattern of images varied according to two main dimensions: the 'them' and 'us' duality, apparently universal among manual workers, which Dahrendorf was to interpret as a function of enduring structural inequalities in industrial society,[6] and which Popitz seemed to regard as the residue of the vulgarised version of Marxist tradition among the working-class movements of all Western European countries; and, secondly the graduated scale or pyramid favoured by middle class respondents, which functionalist sociologists across the Atlantic, with their newly awakened interest in social stratification, found too obvious a model of social structure to be worth discussing. The other dimension of the variation was, of course, the particular aspect of respondents' location within the social structure which was salient for them, and the concordance between those aspects and their personal experience. Thus, in these early studies, 'images of society' are no more than a reflection of what are the felt occupational realities of the class structure among different groups — in which case, the assertion that any study of class or stratification must take account of the point of view of the participants ceases to carry much conviction.

Although published in the same year as Willener's monograph, Popitz and Bahrdt's study stands out as of lasting importance largely because it addresses itself to the problem of the relation between variations in images and the concrete work and life situations of groups of workers. Popitz demonstrates that within a single stratum, within a single occupational group in fact, there can exist wide differences of imagery which can neither be dismissed as the products of personality structure nor accounted for by contrasts in work situation and skill. He shows that diversity of personal experience is not to be regarded as an obstacle to interpretation; it is the function of images, not to provide a uniform orientational framework for behaviour, but to provide a framework for the articulation of varied elements from personal experience and from a collective supply of themes and ideas. The heterogeneity of images is therefore no less important than their homogeneity. Resisting the temptation to create inflexible categories and crude characterisations, Popitz can be said to have at least partly succeeded in his attempt to be free of the 'notion that the industrial worker is a unified "type figure" or Gestalt who plays a martyr's or Oedipus role on the horizon of bourgeois mythology'.[7]

Since the individual can only experience a small fraction of social reality, it is the 'objectifying' capacity of institutions which makes unity in diversity possible. 'There is a discrepancy between the vast complex of interrelated action which provides the conditions for a person's identity, and the narrow field which is actually open to him through perceptions and experience' and 'it is in the nature of social institutions to objectify this discrepancy.'[8] Institutions and norms are the means by which the infinite variety of individual experiences can have apparently 'objective' meaning, but this is at the cost of concealing the socially constructed nature of these norms. Nor are they the only source of images, which are regarded by Popitz as the outcome of a person's social experience in a much broader sense.

In the extended interview study of iron and steel workers operating under similar conditions it was found that nearly all workers had some unified image of society and of their place within it, and that these images could be classed in six categories built around the notions of ordered social structure and social class. Perspectives were found to vary from that of the compliant workers who regarded the social order as composed of two distinct formations in which change was neither necessary nor desirable, to the view of a small minority of workers who adopted the classical marxist interpretation of society made up of classes in conflict. Despite these apparent extremes, however, the authors claimed that two common features occur in all the views expressed and that the images of society of these workers are formulated in an awareness of their collective position.

> All the workers with whom we spoke and who do develop an image of society. . .see society as a *dichotomy* — whether this is changeable, unchangeable, bridgeable or to be mediated by means of a 'partnership' — and they answer the question concerning their personal social position by reference to a *workers' consciousness* (Arbeiterbewusstsein) which enables them to understand themselves as part of the working class within the total society.[9]

Two elements comprise this common consciousness: awareness of achievement (*Leistungsbewusstsein*) and an awareness of collectivity (*Kollektivbewusstsein*). The claim to achievement (which implies the notion of a 'professional' or craftsman's pride in workmanship), clearly more important among skilled workers, was found to relate directly to the feeling that physical, value-creating work is an essential pre-condition for the existence of all members of society and to the feeling that non-manual workers are less obviously engaged in productive activity.

Thus the various dichotomous images which Popitz found can all be seen as variations on a common theme; they were all put to use in the context of a more general awareness of collectivity or |workers' consciousness (*Arbeiterbewusstsein*) comprising an awareness of achievement in physical work as well as the sense of shared experience. But Popitz avoids interpreting this consciousness in terms of a work situation, not even that of the foundry, where strength, skill and judgement are highly valued. Instead he maintains that images of society are only indirectly related to the work situation; they refer 'independently of the features of the individual occupational groups, to the common features of work'. Similarly, the awareness of collectivity does not derive simply from the immediate context of work — similar tasks, work groupings, styles of supervision, etc. — but from this together with an awareness that this personal social position is part of the working class within the total society. Popitz suggests that a person's location in society can be summarised in the ordering of phenomena, allocation of status or prestige and the means of association or distancing between individuals. Going beyond the functional account, he suggests that 'these very formal features of location are completed by a fourth: the attempt of the individual to relate himself to the world in which he lives can never be restricted to what is palpable and immediately accessible. Perspectives which extend beyond the range of immediate, particular experiences must be constructed'. The practical consequences, according to Popitz, are threefold: at certain points an evaluation of experiences as such will not lead to an explanation of workers' images; it is therefore necessary to ascertain which are the potential sources of information concerning social questions, and the degree of openness to such sources; and thirdly there is the question of how workers use these opportunities to inform themselves and to create representations of society which go beyond personal experiences. The method of looking for 'Topoi' or themes and stereotypes conveyed in recurring forms of speech is related to the second of these consequences (see below Chapter 3). It rests on the assumption that, for the majority of people, the most accessible source of information about society is the collectively owned stock of ideas, themes and cliches which is specific to their social group, which for these purposes can be likened to a 'speech community'.

Two years later, also in Germany, Moore and Kleining carried out a study of images of society making use of a rather different approach. Like the Popitz study, it does begin to acknowledge the partial independence of images from the social circumstances in which they are to be found.[10] But this lesser-known investigation further illustrates the difficulty of escaping from the dualist perspective, this time within the context of a functionalist theory of society. Moore and Kleining sought first to analyse the structure of images, that is to say their capacity to define society as a totality, and secondly to describe the 'social self image' of each stratum defined by a status evaluation procedure similar to Warner's.[11] The emphasis on the functional importance of images was a preliminary step away from simple dualism and focused attention on the characteristics of images themselves; the image being regarded as subject to different laws from that which it signifies.

From their survey investigation, Moore and Kleining concluded that except for a tiny minority (5 per cent) either unwilling or unable to reply to open-ended questions on class and strata, there exists a definitely structured image with recurring features. It is constituted from distinct but varied perceptions of social differences which are ordered along a vertical axis defined by common criteria. The common criteria can be conceived as symbols chosen according to need from a relatively limited repertoire. It is claimed that the vertical axis or dimension is based on a 'behavioural ideal' represented by the highest level: the ideal of freedom of action, a culturally conditioned form which is implied in occupational, income, educational and status symbols. Regardless of whether the most elevated group is called the upper class, the rich, the elite or by any other name, the symbols used can all be seen to imply independence, choice and the possibility of development in contrast to the restricted possibilities and dependence of those 'below'. The social strata, whatever their names or number, are dependent on a 'continuum which leads from external compulsion to human freedom, self-determination, responsibility, choice and the enjoyment of the good things of life'.[12] The way in which groups are allocated to this continuum, according to the authors, is by symbols which define complex behaviour, the most frequently used symbols being occupation, status and wealth or possessions.

However, as might be expected in a functional interpretation, the variations in imagery (particularly in the number of social strata identified and the descriptive vocabulary) were regarded as functions of personality and not as functions of structurally distinct elements in society. Moore and Kleining supported their case by showing that — given a general propensity to identify three levels — the actual number of strata identified is partly an artifact of the interviewing method: the more persistent the question, the greater the subtlety and differentiation of the reply. But an exclusively functional account fails to give a reason for the persistent tendency to define social groups or classes (a phenomenon which these authors dismiss without explanation as an expression of the 'natural' human tendency to order the world in discrete units) rather than points on a continuum. It likewise fails to account for the variations in theme pointed out by Willener. The relative emphasis given to 'success', marriage or wealth, for example, among different strata are overlooked in the stress upon the normative aspects of images.

The earliest phase of studies of images of society which includes the contributions mentioned can be regarded in some measure as a response to a more general question about changes in the class structure of contemporary western societies. The question assumed different forms in different countries, but whether it was spelt out in terms of the 'economic miracle' in Germany, or the long run of Conservative governments in Britain with substantial support from the working class, the basic question was the same: were theories of class and class conflict still applicable in post-war European societies which seemed to be less divided than ever before?

One answer to this question led Dahrendorf to make a synthesis of the results of several of the above studies in support of his thesis in *Class and Class Conflict in Industrial Society*.[13] Having previously established the need for some modification of traditional views of class and stratification in the light of developments in industrial societies, he appealed to 'socio-psychological' evidence to lend weight, if not confirmation, to his analysis of political conflict. He argued that the evidence produced independently by Centers, Willener and Popitz *et al.*, together with Hoggart's autobiographical account of working class culture in Britain,[14] points to two major conclusions: that very many, though not all, people do have an image of society as a whole which amounts to a more or less coherent interpretation of social reality and their place within it, and that these images differ in a systematic way according to class divisions. Particularly important is the recurrence of dichotomous images among the working class — although Dahrendorf would have had more difficulty in incorporating the conclusions of Moore and Kleining into his synthesis, had they been available. However, Dahrendorf's assessment that there is substantial agreement between sociological and popular images of society is an unambiguous statement of the motif which finds its way into all the studies mentioned in this section. Two models of society reappear: a continuous hierarchical system of stratification and a dichotomous model, each with several varieties of meaning. But they correspond in general form to sociological interpretations of society which emphasise order and consensus or conflict and coercion respectively. The theme of social conflict is not an intrusion into a basically integrated and harmonious social reality; it finds an echo in the views of at least some members of society. 'The dichotomies of post-capitalist society have very little to do with those asserted by Marx: there is no disagreement here between sociological and public opinion. But there are still dichotomies, and they are very real to those who experience society in terms of them.'[15] It was partly thus that the question of images of society came to be regarded as important, not simply as an element in the functional description of social stratification but as a 'solid and, probably, powerful social fact', equally relevant to theories of conflict and coercion.

Images and Their Social Milieux

Whatever their theoretical inadequacies, one tentative conclusion can be drawn from all the studies carried out before 1960. The 'image of society', 'social self-image' and dichotomous workers' consciousness which Popitz identified had the appearance of a comprehensive framework for interpreting complex social situations. Workers used it as a scanning device for locating and clarifying individual experiences in their social context. Whether the evidence pointed to a dichotomy or a hierarchy of social groups, the idea of a more or less cohesive society provided a reference point. More recent evidence shows some decline in the coherence of this idea as an organising framework. It suggests that the influence of the dichotomous scheme has diminished and that individual experience is replacing collectivity as the dominant reference point in the social consciousness of workers.[16] In an increasingly differentiated world of work, consciousness of both achievement and collectivity are found to have declined, leaving very little in the way of uniform structures of social thought. Particularly important is the reduced significance of the physical aspect of work which was a defining characteristic for the workers studied by Popitz. Other factors are the changing role of the unions (which have ceased, particularly in Germany, to be the chief mediators of marxist-socialist theory which is behind the interpretation of society as composed of antagonistic groups) and an increasingly uniform commodity consciousness. The attributes which are now appealed to by workers for their self interpretation are individualistic attributes which are just as likely to be based on roles in consumption as on performance at work.

In work on images of society in the 1960s, however, less attention was paid to the evolution of work than to 'milieux', or, more specifically, to experience of social relationships within occupational communities. The idea that common elements of life and experience will give rise to similar types of image of society was formulated by Lockwood[17] in a way which provided the stimulus for quite a number of studies which shared the premise that 'the individual's social consciousness is to a large extent influenced by his immediate social context' rather than by the broader features of social structure. Images, according to this view and despite the occasional use of the term 'social consciousness', are still perceptions, the way in which people 'visualise the class structure of their society from the vantage points of their own particular *milieux*'. As we have already pointed out, the use of the word 'image' in this figurative sense can only be misleading because society can never be an object of direct perception, however concrete its institutional systems may appear to be. It does not, however, prevent the construction of ideal types of representation, which is in effect Lockwood's procedure.

His presentation of three main variants in working class images is widely known and need not be described in detail here. Making the assumption that there will be a connection between images and social context, he anticipated that the diversity of industrial and community milieux of manual workers would account for differences of imagery. Thus a dichotomous image, a hierarchical image based on prestige and a hierarchical image based on income are said to be associated with structurally different occupational groups. For example, the experience of solidarity and isolation and the overlap of patterns of work and leisure association in mining communities is said to engender a 'traditional proletarian' consciousness of society as a dichotomy of power. There is another form of 'traditional' image which is said to be most common among workers exposed to paternalistic forms of authority as in small firms or among agricultural workers. It is recognition of a status hierarchy which legitimises the worker's position and thus accounts for his 'deference' towards or, more strictly, endorsement of the status quo. In modern industrial situations involving routine, specialised and 'alienating' work and a home-centred and socially isolated existence, the dominant relationship is identified as the cash nexus with a corresponding image of society as an arrangement

according to income and patterns of consumption. This latter type,
of course, is the one connected with the condition described as
'privatisation' by Lockwood and his associates in the *Affluent Worker*
studies.[18] It is important to understand this general setting of the
'embourgeoisement' debate and the somewhat more limited debate
concerning the 'technological implications' approach to attitudes and
behaviour. It helps to account for the otherwise unjustifiable stress on
working-class images and the oversimplified typology which, although
it provides useful support for the critique of embourgeoisment and the
thesis of 'normative convergence', has done little to directly further
an understanding of images as such.[19]

For this reason it is particularly necessary to look more closely at
the presuppositions which have conditioned this and so much other
work on images of society. Lockwood acknowledged his debt to Bott,
whose observations concerning reference groups and ideology in the
context of a detailed study of family relationships have been assumed
by many to carry more weight than they actually do. The statement
which has provided so much impetus is worth quoting again:

> . . .the ingredients, the raw materials, of class ideology are located
> in the individual's various primary social experiences, rather than in his
> position in a socio-economic category. The hypothesis advanced
> here is that when an individual talks about class he is trying to say
> something, in a symbolic form, about his experiences of power and
> prestige in his actual membership groups and social relationships
> both past and present.[20]

The equivocal notion here, of course, is that of 'experience', with its
implications of personal knowledge and modification of consciousness
brought about by specific events. Quite correctly, 'class ideology' or
images are interpreted within a framework of social relations — relations
at work, in the home, in leisure activity and relations with educational,
legal and other authorities — but since the image itself is regarded as a
'symbol' or static representation, its relation to this realm of experience
can only be interpreted as the relation of the reflected image to its
source. The logic of the study of images thus defined must therefore
be to identify the common elements of experience in a variety of
milieux (elements which may be related of course to much more general
systems of production, distribution and consumption) and relate these
to 'corresponding' symbolic forms. However, in what can be regarded
as an attempt not unlike that of Dahrendorf to develop an alternative

to the functional account of values and representations as a normative whole, Lockwood scarcely avoided the pitfall of explaining 'social facts' by non-social facts.

A number of more recent studies can be quoted by way of illustration. The majority of those already referred to have stemmed from the debates of industrial sociology and can for the most part be seen as a critical response to the human relations approach and the continuing debate about the influence of technology on attitudes and behaviour at work. This is certainly true of more recent studies which have considered it necessary to broaden the framework of reference in view of the inconclusive results of a 'variable-centred' approach which creates a false dichotomy between work and non-work life. This broader frame of reference, which is said to include 'orientations' and the 'expectations which people bring to their work' became widely known as an 'action frame of reference'. (The merits of this phrase are dubious in view of the variety of possible meanings of the term 'action' and it is certainly not to be confused with the action theory of Touraine.) Its main assumption is that man is to a certain extent his own master: the consciousness which people have of a situation is a feature of that situation insofar as it provides evidence both of goals and the choice of means for achieving them. In the context of an industrial plant or occupational group, therefore, an understanding of attitudes and behaviour will embrace both the technological and formal organisational aspects of work and the way in which this concrete situation is experienced. Whereas the Luton study of affluent workers had left some ambiguity as to the source and relative importance of the 'meaning which workers give to their work' and sometimes appeared to point to variations in ego-involvement without explaining how they are generated and sustained, Beynon and Blackburn[21] attempted to go beyond this and inject an active ingredient into the 'action' approach.

They argued that perceptions of work (in the broadest sense of people's understanding of their position within the social structure as well as within an organisation) depend on an interaction between orientations and situations but that orientations are not random. Any explanation must take account of the 'whole range of social characteristics of the workers in that situation' and 'experience within the social structure of the work situation must be related to the individual's position within the social structure of the wider society'. 'Experience' of course has a past dimension and in this view is composed of whole sets of interrelated experiences within the world at work. Thus we return to the major theoretical link with the notion of 'occupational community' which promises an alternative to the sterile juxtaposition of concrete work situations and attitudes.

In a useful summary of the components and determinants of occupational communities, Salaman has said that members of such communities

> see themselves in terms of their occupational role: their self-image is centred on their occupational role in such a way that they see themselves as printers, policemen, army officers or whatever, and as people with specific qualities, interests and abilities. Secondly, members of occupational communities share a reference group composed of members of the occupational community. Thirdly, members of occupational communities associate with, and make friends of, other members of their occupation in preference to having friends who are outsiders, and they carry work activities and interests into their non-work lives.[22]

In such communities, in other words, a person's self-image will be inseparable from his occupational role and he will associate with others who share and support this image. Most striking, according to Salaman, is that 'members of occupational communities live in their own separate world composed of assumptions, attitudes, knowledge, expectations and shared history'.[23] There is substantial evidence from Salaman's own study and those he quotes that there are occupational groups which approximate to the model described. The steelworker's sample in our own study has such patterns of association and a shared world of work and non-work experience that it can usefully be described as an occupational community.

However, Salaman's statement that members of occupational communities share a world of assumptions and attitudes requires qualification, which he in fact gives, although he still considers that central to the concept of occupational communities is a concern 'with images, definitions and assessments in as far as these derive from and are used to categorise and evaluate the nature of work and the meaning of occupation and colleagueship'.[24] As we have pointed out, the thesis as formulated by Lockwood, that the common elements of life and experience will give rise to similar types of image of society in occupational communities, has only partly been confirmed in subsequent research. In fact, studies by Cousins and Brown,[25] and Bell and Newby,[26] for example, have stressed the diversity and variability of images of society which, it is argued, are as much an expression of the tension between different aspects of a complex work situation as a sign of shared experience. The former, in a study of shipbuilding workers, state that

> the social situation of workers in a traditional industry and their images of society are more varied than has been allowed for; and that the links between social context and social consciousness are looser than has been suggested, that workers faced by similar market and work situations may interpret them differently and have some choice as to the strategies they may pursue. This is not to reject the basic proposition of Bott, Lockwood and others, but to suggest that it demands both the specification of a much wider range of typical possibilities and the introduction of a greater element of indeterminacy into the assumed relationship of social context and social consciousness.[27]

It is abundantly clear from this and other accounts of 'traditional proletarian' communities that such milieux are not necessarily a source of radical views or class-specific images of society. They can just as easily provide the context for an identity and solidarity (admittedly based on separateness or dichotomy) which are fundamentally conservative. The category of the traditional but 'deferential' worker also dwindles to very little under close scrutiny. Here Bell and Newby's study of agricultural workers is conveniently complementary to the work of Brown *et al.* among shipbuilding workers. These authors also concentrate on the variations *within* a single occupational community and conclude that agricultural workers make use of a variety of images according to the characteristics of the local social situation, particularly the degree of urbanisation and the degree of bureaucratisation in the work situation. 'Deferential' images which approximate to Lockwood's ideal type are to be found, but only among the relatively few workers who live in tied housing in farm communities where personal interaction between the farmer and farm employees is at a maximum. Among most other groups there is 'ambivalence' of imagery, that is 'a multiplicity of class images or meaning systems from which|[workers] will draw upon the one most appropriate to explain a particular situation with which they are confronted'.[28]

The impact of these studies is not limited to their detailed description of particular communities nor even to their refinement of the essentially heuristic typology of Lockwood. Either implicitly or explicitly they call into question the assumed one-to-one relationship

between images and milieux. There is more than a hint that workers
not only *have* an image but that they *make use* of a set of images in
response to situations which form the context of action — milieux
which are apparently becoming more rather than less differentiated
through the evolution of technique in production and organisation.
Thus the attempt to relate images to a common basis of experience
in community has, ironically, led back to a closer consideration of
work differences and the tensions involved in industrial development.

The postulate that a common experience of inequality (dependence
and subordination in the case of the working class) will account for
social consciousness, is open to criticism on the same grounds. This
theme frequently recurs in the literature and was elaborated by Andrieux
and Lignon in particular, who argued that it was the 'social situation'
of the worker rather than the objective circumstances of work which
was responsible for workers' consciousness.[29] But the conclusion of
this and any other study which seeks the lowest common denominator
of experience is bound to ignore the specific conditions of the
production of images: consciousness thus conceived is an expression
of an undifferentiated class condition defined *a priori* which can only
be analysed as a form of adaptation in the same manner as the simple
confrontation of a 'concrete work situation' and 'subjective reactions'
only allows an analysis in terms of satisfaction and dissatisfaction.

The study which has gone to the greatest lengths to examine and to
relate processes of technical innovation and the evolution of industrial
work as a whole to workers' consciousness is that carried out by Kern
and Schumann in a wide range of German industries.[30] They reaffirm
the importance of work, the thesis that 'man concretises and represents
society' precisely through 'the *specific* conditions of his work under
which he reproduces himself socially'.[31] They consider, however, that
the relatively obvious relationship between the sphere of work and the
social and political consciousness of workers in the early stages of
capitalism has become more complex: instead of the process of levelling
and homogenisation of the labour force (which, it can be argued, Marx
predicted) modern industrial work is increasingly differentiated. This
has had repercussions in workers' consciousness and it helps to account
for significant changes in the thinking of industrial workers.

The empirical method adopted by Kern and Schumann was to
develop a typology of industrial work based on extended observation
of technical innovation and production processes in eight sectors of
industry in order to make comparisons with the responses of the 981
workers interviewed. As they rightly point out, detailed knowledge of

work situations has been generally lacking or has been subsumed under crude classifying schemes, such as craft, assembly and automated work, with the result that the full significance of workers' attitudes and orientations has been lost. There is no doubt that the types mentioned do represent major breaks in technical development. They do not occur in a strict temporal sequence, however, so Kern and Schumann argue that the increasing diversity of work situations in advanced industrial societies must be taken into account if the present state of workers' consciousness is to be properly understood.

Like Popitz, they believe that 'it is the way in which workers appropriate and evaluate technical change which provides a clear indication of workers' social thinking'. But one of their concerns was to re-open the question of whether industrial workers have an image of society which is based in the experience of workers *as a whole* (the collective experience of being producers in a direct physical sense) or whether workers still have a serviceable image of society at all. Although there was no substantial empirical evidence against the conclusions of the Popitz study, its limitations in time and space and the continuous evolution of industrial work made continued generalisation hazardous.

In the section of their study which deals with attitudes and orientations, Kern and Schumann conclude that expressions of satisfaction or dissatisfaction can be accounted for by the relation between two main variables: the worker's current work situation and his occupational history, particularly his experience of technical and organisational changes. As far as assessments of technical progress as a whole and its significance for the social situation of working people is concerned, responses showed a high degree of ambivalence, even among those for whom technology had meant the abolition of the onerous and restrictive aspects of work. It was shown that workers with comparatively skilled and rewarding occupations relate quite uncritically to their work, whilst a low degree of involvement was found to exist among other groups. Even the frequently quoted workers in process or automated industries did not develop an occupational consciousness or pride in their role as producers. In all groups there was a minimum of identification with social conditions, a failure to make work a pretext for the endorsement of the social order. To this extent the findings of Kern and Schumann run counter to those of Popitz and, as we shall see, question the importance of collective experience in the formation of images.

The outstanding characteristic of workers' consciousness in the groups studied by Kern and Schumann, which were representative of the entire range of production processes, was a predominantly negative orientation towards the social context and a prevalent uncertainty and inconsistency of judgement about social questions. This, they argue, is an accurate reflection of the contradictory nature of individual worker's experience. There is no longer a comprehensive framework of interpretation of complex social situations such as that provided by the dichotomous scheme identified by Popitz in the 1950s. This scheme, regardless of individual variations, was used as a general device for locating and interpreting individual experiences in their social context. Now, the attributes which workers appeal to in constructing an identity are individual attributes which are most likely to be based on roles in consumption — i.e. private rather than public or occupational attributes.

It is conceivable that diminished consciousness of collectivity may be superseded by a new awareness, as Mallet[32] predicted and as Goldthorpe, Lockwood *et al.* pointed out might be the case among 'instrumentally' oriented and privatised workers.[33] This is also suggested by Kern and Schumann, who see uncertainty as the common factor of experience — a factor which relativises individual experiences and directs attention to the dependency of all workers on a wage which is threatened by 'progress', which makes workers replaceable and potentially superfluous. This uncertainty in a situation of dependency may, they suggest, be expressed in a dichotomous image which 'signifies distrust of the motives of those who rule. . .which runs counter to the identity of interests between labour and the social system'.[34]

In itself, therefore, the private experience of the individual (experience which has no principle by which to relate to society) can never give rise to an image of society; the image implies recognition of an object of action which is collective and social. The need to structure the world of experience in this way is not so much a basic fact of human nature as an integral part of the desire to accommodate to, or change, the world in the realisation of particular interests. The groups of workers studied by Kern and Schumann can be regarded as the victims of relatively rapid social change which has shattered the former awareness of collectivity without providing a substitute except the consciousness of indeterminacy and individualistic variation in the realm of consumption — a consciousness which is rarely translated into the language of social relations.

Images and Movement

The capacity of 'images' to grasp society as it is and as it could be is therefore far from uniform. This is to be expected for most of the studies discussed above provide scant evidence for images of society which, as it were, mirror social structures. There is, however, a readily accessible theoretical distinction between structure and process which can help to bring some order to the complex variations of imagery through time and between social groups. An image of society is for the most part a projection of the process of social construction rather than a depiction of social structure. As a projection of the processes in which the individual is caught up, it can no longer be seen as a representation with a precise content but as a creative act, as an exercise of the imagination.

This has been recognised and it has led to a certain amount of methodological rather than theoretical discussion. For instance, in a postscript to his work on class images and 'affluent' workers, Goldthorpe defends himself against the argument that few people apart from sociologists and intellectuals have an image of society at all and that so-called images of class and society are an artifact of the interview method.[35] He argues that in 'non-directed' interviews, most people are capable of expressing ideas (often quite complex ideas) about the nature of social stratification and that these ideas form a more or less logical whole. There is a great deal of internal evidence from such interviews that these ideas are consistent in the short term at least. But Goldthorpe does not deny that images are subject to change in the longer term, as is clear from the discussion of the 'new' image of society held by the 'affluent' workers. On the question of consistency he states that

> most individuals, in one way or another, are 'marked' in their daily life with certain 'objective' features of social stratification. It follows that most people have an ensemble of operational ideas which allow them to grasp and interpret this aspect of their social environment. . . In general, these ideas are organised in a model whose consistency is such that it enables individuals to reach *the point* at which their *need* to give meaning to their experience can be satisfied.[36]

With this, we encounter the difficulty, particularly evident in the light of recent findings, that ambivalence and uncertainty are no less characteristic of many images than coherence around a common theme or experience. The 'need' of which Goldthorpe speaks is clearly relative. It is not a datum against which to measure the adequacy of an image but is a function of two sets of circumstances: the character of an individual's social context, which may become larger or smaller or may undergo transformation; and the individual's own project or conception of an alternative. Sources of inconsistency are therefore twofold: firstly, new elements (technical innovation, new forms of social organisation or the formation of social groups) may confront an image with a problem which cannot be resolved, although the capacity of images to absorb novelties and experiences should not be underestimated; and secondly, the project (a 'retreatist' one for example) may be such that consistency at the level of society as a whole is unnecessary because meaning does not depend on shared experience.

On the question of stability, Goldthorpe replies to the criticism that certain types of image (including the 'pecuniary' image) are unstable because they distort the 'objective' aspects of social structure. Such criticisms, which assume that a lack of correspondence between image and reality will necessarily bring about a transformation of the image, have little foundation and refuse to acknowledge that consciousness is the attribution of meaning. But Goldthorpe's conclusion fails to give the reader a clear idea of the conditions which may render images unstable or the experiences which are involved in the formation of a new image. There is no doubt that this is a major lacuna still waiting to be filled.

In general terms, the evidence from studies of student, ethnic and political movements suggests that images as projections — 'social imagination' — function most authentically at times of social crisis or within a social movement. Willener's study of participants in the May movement in France in 1968 claimed to illustrate a new kind of image based on a critical understanding of society and complemented by a utopian vision of the society of the future.[37] Although the study does little more than reproduce the thoughts and aspirations of the students and others involved without demonstrating their relationship to the complex political and cultural movement, it is a useful description of an image of society which is for the most part a projection of social processes rather than a description of social structures.

The situation depicted in this study of the May events (which is partly complemented by accounts of the student movement in Germany by Habermas and others) is the complete antithesis of the breakdown of group experience and consciousness among industrial workers described by Kern and Schumann. This contrast between two de-structured social situations suggests that images are linked to action in a far more complex way than has been admitted previously. Even in relatively structured situations (such as industrial bureaucracies) the relationship is complex. Managers and white-collar workers have traditionally been regarded as having a self and social identity of an individualistic, hierarchical kind, with a stress on self-determination. However, as Willener *et al.* point out in their study of *cadres* at the time of the May movement, they too can be considered as having a collective social consciousness under certain conditions. But their common search for autonomy remains not so much a plan or project in the sense of a programme of consciously and systematically structured action as a negation of existing states of affairs beyond which it is difficult to venture even in imagination.[38]

Having examined the tradition of research in images of society we conclude that any further progress will depend on an understanding of their relationship not only to society as a system but also to movements within society, whether political movements, the evolution of work or movements aiming to conserve a particular state of affairs. What is required is a theory of the constitution of meaning and a method to establish the underlying unity between the analysis of social situations on the one hand and the knowledge of opinions and attitudes on the other. Much of the material we have referred to (especially within British sociology) has served only to show the irreconcilable nature of these two aspects in the study of images of society. We have found that it uses a framework of explanation (as with the study of attitudes and orientations to work) which can best be described in terms of adaptive responses towards a given organisational or social system — an approach perhaps best exemplified in studies of 'work satisfaction'. In place of this we will employ a framework which combines principles of analysis deriving from Touraine's 'actionalist' theory and a method of interpretation which, following Popitz, assumes that the 'image' is a bricolage of symbols, concepts and expressions which may be governed by personal experience, hearsay, knowledge, an ideology or (as is most likely) by a combination of all four.

Notes

1. Quoted in C. Madge, *Society in the Mind* (London, 1964), p.13.
2. W. Lloyd Warner *et al.*, *Social Class in America* (Chicago, 1949), and R. Centers, *The Psychology of Social Classes* (Princeton, 1949).
3. Centers, *Psychology of Social Classes*, p.27.
4. Ibid., pp.210-11.
5. A. Willener, *Images de la société et classes sociales* (1957).
6. R. Dahrendorf, *Class and Class Conflict in Industrial Society* (Stanford, 1959), especially the final chapter.
7. H. Popitz *et al.*, *Das Gesellschaftsbild des Arbeiters* (1957), p.8.

8. Ibid, pp.1-2.
9. Ibid, p.237. This is a slightly altered version of C. Ryan's translation in T. Burns (ed.) *Industrial Man* (Harmondsworth, 1969), p.320.
10. H. Moore and E. Kleining, 'Das Bild der Sozialen Wirklichkeit', *Kölner Zeitschrift für Soziologie und Sozialpsychologie,* 11 (1959), pp.354-76 and 'Das Soziale Selbstbild der Gesellschaftsschichten Deutschlands,' *K.z. für Soz. und Sozialpsych.,* 12 (1960), pp.86-119.
11. H. Moore and E. Kleining, 'Das Soziale Selbstbild' (1960). As stated earlier, Warner developed two techniques for measuring 'social class': Evaluated Participation and the Index of Status Characteristics. They begin with the subjective judgements of people within a community and with 'objective' socio-economic categories respectively. But both form part of a concept which identifies class as a property of people who have similar rankings in a community and associate on equal terms. Moore and Kleining, instead of providing 'class' categories, worked with symbols linked to occupational categories.
12. Ibid, p.370. It is interesting to note that confirmation of the importance of this continuum was to emerge later in Kohn's studies of values and social class. For his discussion of 'conformity', 'self-direction' and their relation to class, see M.L. Kohn, *Class and Conformity* (Dorsey Press, 1969).
13. R. Dahrendorf, *Class and Class Conflict*, especially Chapter VIII.
14. R. Hoggart, *The Uses of Literacy* (Harmondsworth, 1957).
15. R. Dahrendorf, *Class and Class Conflict*, p.289.
16. There is almost certainly an affinity here with the themes of 'pluralisation', 'modernisation' and 'abstraction' in contemporary cultural analysis on a much more general level. See for example P.L. Berger, B. Berger and H. Kellner, *The Homeless Mind* (Penguin, 1974) and A.C. Zijderveld, *The Abstract Society* (Allen Lane, 1972).
17. D. Lockwood, 'Sources of Variation in Working Class Images of Society', *Sociol. Rev.,* 14, 3 (1966).
18. J. Goldthorpe, D. Lockwood, F. Bechhofer, J. Platt, *The Affluent Worker in the Class Structure* (Cambridge University Press, 1969).
19. This was acknowledged by Lockwood himself in his own contribution to the Durham Conference, see M. Bulmer (ed.), *Working-Class Images*, pp.239-50.
20. E. Bott, *Family and Social Network* (London, 1957), p.163. It is interesting to note that this is contemporary with the work of Willener, Popitz and Hoggart on images of society.
21. H. Beynon and R.M. Blackburn, *Perceptions of work, variations within a factory* (Cambridge University Press, 1972).
22. G. Salaman, *Community and Occupation* (Cambridge University Press, 1974), p.21.
23. Ibid, p.24.
24. Ibid, p.129.
25. J. Cousins and R. Brown, 'Patterns of Paradox: Shipbuilding Workers' Images of Society', in M. Bulmer (ed.), *Working-Class Images*. See also R. Brown and P. Brannen, 'Social Relations and Social Perspectives amongst Shipbuilding Workers: a Preliminary Statement', *Sociology*, 4 (1970) 1 and 2.
26. C. Bell and H. Newby, 'The Sources of Variation in Agricultural Workers' Images of Society', in M. Bulmer (ed.), *Working-Class Images*. Also in *Sociol. Rev.,* 21 (1973), pp.229 ff.
27. J. Cousins and R. Brown, 'Patterns of Paradox', in M. Bulmer (ed.), *Working-Class Images*, pp.79-80.
28. C. Bell and H. Newby, 'Sources of Variation', *Social. Rev.* 21 (1973), p.246.
29. A. Andrieux and J. Lignon, *L'ouvrier d'aujourd'hui* (Paris, 1960).

30. H. Kern and M. Schumann, *Industriearbeit und Arbeiterbewusstsein*, 2 vols., Europaische Verlagsanstalt (Frankfurt, 1970).

31. Ibid, p.34.

32. S. Mallet, *La Nouvelle Classe Ouvrière* (Paris, 1963).

33. J. Goldthorpe, D. Lockwood *et al., The Affluent Worker in the Class Structure* (1969), pp.179 ff.

34. H. Kern and M. Schumann, *Industriearbeit und Arbeiterbewusstsein*, p.276.

35. J.H. Goldthorpe, 'L'image des classes chez les travailleurs manuels aisés', *R. franc. sociol.*, IX (1970), pp.334-8.

36. Ibid, p.335 (author's italics).

37. A. Willener, *The Action Image of Society* (London, 1970).

38. A Willener, C. Gajdos, G. Banguigiu, *Les Cadres en mouvement* (Paris, 1969), especially pp.206 ff.

2 SOCIAL ACTION AND SOCIAL CONSCIOUSNESS

Within the general framework of his theory of social action, one of Touraine's achievements has been to develop a theoretical understanding both of the meaning that class relations have for people and the grounds and ultimate goals for social action. It differs radically from the cruder forms of theory which assume only that people relate to their environment as a material circumstance and respond to it in determinate ways. Its distinctiveness lies in the attempt to take full account of the phenomenon of consciousness and show how it is instrumental in the creation of social values, that is, in the production of society itself.

Thus the notion of 'consciousness' (*conscience*, with its connotations of knowledge, moral consensus or conscience as well as awareness) is used analytically rather than descriptively in Touraine's theory. It is not to be regarded as a descriptive term with direct reference to a person's orientation towards a social situation, nor his recognition of the social system and his place within it. It does not denote the feelings of inclusion or exclusion which may accompany people's experience in social groups, nor the sense of subordination or marginality which may be part of such experience. Rather, as a way of defining the constitution of meaning, it is 'the central notion which makes it possible to establish the underlying unity between the analysis of social situations and knowledge of opinions and attitudes', the two aspects which, in the study of images of society to date, have proved virtually irreconcilable.[1] The study of images of society in this perspective ceases to be either a description of the 'cognitive' component in social thinking or a survey of complex attitudes towards social questions. It looks beyond the categories which people may use to visualise and order social classes. It is the study of the evidence — provided by members of society themselves — of their response to the twofold need to create and control, a response to 'non-reality' (in the sense of an alternative) as well as to 'reality'. This evidence can never be taken for granted, even when it is clearly articulated. There is always a certain distance between an expression of attitude or feeling and the object of the expression. Even though it may be possible to regard the evidence as signifying a system of normative orientations (as in functional accounts) this still leaves a question to be answered: how does this system come about, how is it transformed and what is its relation to the evaluation of work? This is the problem which Touraine addresses in *La conscience ouvrière.*

The starting point of the analysis is the observation that the feature which sets industrial civilisation apart from all others is a qualitatively different mode of social knowledge. Essentially this knowledge is no longer meta-social (based on religion, the state or economic laws) but is an understanding of society as a system of action. The consciousness of workers, salaried employees, managers or any other group provides evidence of this. The evolution of social consciousness, as Touraine describes it, is most clearly seen in the development of work organisation; in production programmes and development plans society appears directly as a system of action. But if new forms of consciousness are not a 'product' of scientific and technical progress, neither are they the cause of these developments; they are the expression of a relationship *both* to the means of production *and* to the system of social control.

Since Touraine's image of society is relatively unfamiliar to English readers and his work remains inaccessible because untranslated, we will outline the theory, paying particular attention to its relevance to the question of the nature of social consciousness and its role in social action.[2]

Touraine stands in the French post-liberation intellectual tradition with its liberal optimism and framework of ideas strongly dominated by a blend of marxism and existentialism in which Sartre remains a towering influence, whether as example or as opponent. At least one commentator regards Touraine's work as having close affinity to the major themes of existential thought.[3] For example, the term 'project' is taken up and the definition of 'consciousness' owes much to this tradition. Fortunately, the particular concerns which have motivated much of his work — workers' attitudes and workers' consciousness, changes in industry, the labour movement and the nature of industrial societies — correspond to some of the themes of our present concern with images of society. We will therefore examine Touraine's theory by way of his industrial sociological writings, acknowledging that his method is quite capable of being illustrated and understood in terms of social movements of a different kind, especially in societies undergoing rapid change and development.[4]

The Meaning of Action

At first sight, Touraine's definition of action, or the conditions of social action, is scarcely novel: 'a social action exists if, in the first place, it is *oriented* towards certain ends (an orientation which. . .must not be defined in terms of conscious individual intentions), if, secondly, the actor is placed within a system of *social relations* and, thirdly and finally, the interaction becomes communication by means of *symbolic systems* of which the most important is language'.[5] The first element corresponds closely to the Parsonian idea of social action as motivated, goal-directed behaviour. But if for Parsons action was to be interpreted within the framework of a social system and as a relation between means and ends, or as adaptive behaviour, Touraine is concerned to go beyond roles and values to study the processes of their actual creation. The novel element in Touraine is that he tries at all costs to avoid explaining action as a function of other circumstances, whether material or ideal. Although he does not deny that society can be studied both from the point of view of functional systems of social relations and from the point of view of its symbolic structures, he argues that values are socially created and that the study of their processes of creation is at least as important (more so in industrial societies which have learned to question their own existence) as the study of the values themselves. He insists that 'the meaning of action can be reduced neither to the actors' adaptation to a more or less institutionalised system of social norms nor to the operation of the mind which is evident in all social activity.'[6]

The Importance of Labour

Although the logic of the method allows any form of action (any process of the creation of values) to be used for illustration, the analysis of labour (*travail*) is the most appropriate means of elucidating the basic problem: how to get beyond the fundamental opposition between action which manifests itself as a response to a given situation or as historical necessity and action which is an innovative process, creating meaning. Labour, conceived here as a means of transforming both the material world and (following Marx) 'human nature', provides a key. It can be defined as the relation between man and his products in a very general sense and as such it is not simply a situation or a fact but a source of meaning.[7] 'The notion of labour would cease to have any sociological value if products appeared as things, as the workings of nature or robots. . .its existence cannot be conceived without also admitting that the behaviour of workers can be analysed as the manifestation of a double exigency: the creation of products and the control of these products, i.e. the struggle against the alienation of

labour.'[8] This double orientation, according to Touraine, takes
different forms in different societies yet it is particularly visible in
industrial societies on account of their relative freedom from material
necessity and greater capacity for self-determination. It is by nature
dialectical. In the process of labour, man creates products which exist
apart from him and which may therefore confront him as something
beyond his control. But he perpetually seeks to regain control over
what has been externalised. It would be possible to interpret the two
moments in the labour process as two sources of meaning, subjective
and objective, but Touraine insists on the notion of labour as a relation,
as a means of interpreting what is a unified experience which cannot be
decomposed into infra- and super-structure, or objective and subjective
components. 'There is no way of passing from the material
circumstances of labour to social organisation and to the form of social
life as a whole if labour has not already been defined as a relation,
charged with meaning, between the worker and his products.'[9]

This is a conception of social action as 'totalising activity'[10] and it
leads us to a consideration of the basic unit of analysis in action
sociology, the 'historical subject'. Although, according to Touraine,
the materials of action analysis are the intentions and conduct of
individual actors, social relationships or institutions, the task of action
sociology is to use these materials to construct an historical subject
which is neither to be identified with particular individuals nor with
a collective consciousness; on the contrary, society is a 'text' to be
critically analysed to demonstrate the complex origins and internal
tensions which are behind its apparent coherence. The historical subject
is thus a sociological construct, an analytical tool which defines the
relationship of society to itself. In short, to use Touraine's concise but
puzzlingly abstract formulation, the historical subject is never a given
totality but 'the emergent structure of a totalizing activity, the unity
of the dialectical movements of historical action'.[11] In this perspective
the 'how is society possible?' question which has been taken as central
to sociology from Hobbes to Simmel becomes 'how is it that man
continually makes and remakes society?'.

Before giving a more precise indication of the meaning of the
'subject', some remarks are necessary on Touraine's concept of
'historicity'. By this he does not simply imply the unique sequences
of events which are the material of descriptive history nor historical
'laws' (whether economic, geographical or any other) as in supposedly
objective historical accounts; historicity is neither a material situation
nor an idea which makes activity meaningful, but the capacity of

society to produce its own social and cultural sphere, 'it is the attribute of social action which constitutes its experience by the meaning given to it'.[12] More precisely, historicity is 'action exerted by society, arising from its activity, upon its social and cultural practices, by the combination of three components: the mode of knowledge, which constitutes an image of society and of nature, accumulation, which sets apart a proportion of the disposable product, and the cultural model which grasps and interprets society's capacity for action upon itself'.[13] The first of these is the most elementary, describing man's need to distance himself from his own activity, his capacity to create an image of the world and social relationships which confronts reality at a distance, not merely reflecting it but generalising, simplifying it and generating alternatives. Accumulation is seen as the activity which defines social class relations and the cultural model is the manner in which society represents its own creativity — through an idea of 'progress' or 'development' for example.

Touraine's intention in using this notion of historicity is not therefore to construct a new philosophy of history. This would be to place society within history, not to 'place historicity at the heart of society'.[14] It is a means of sociological analysis which makes it possible to go beyond appearances. The way is now clear to return to the notion of the historical subject: it is simply another name for the range or scope of historicity (*champ d'historicité*) in a society and is not to be confused with any concrete person, collectivity or law such as the law of the market.[15] The manner in which the historical subject is to be grasped is therefore sociological; it very rarely, if ever, corresponds directly with the interests of an individual or a group of individuals.

Classes and Class Consciousness

As we have seen, the study of labour with its emphasis on the double exigency of creation and control is the key to the concept of action. The key to historical action, i.e. the movement of the historical subject, is also a relationship — the relationship of social classes. Here, as at the level of organisations, the double dialectic of creation and control is definitive. Class relationships cannot be analysed in terms of a single principle of differentiation such as division of labour or authority; there has always to be a principle of unity, which in class societies is the common language of 'industrial civilization'. The conceptual currency is that of 'progress', 'development' and 'growth'. It is primarily a notion of society as a system of control over work and a means for distributing its products. There are elements of both identity and opposition within it. Variations between industrial societies can to some extent be traced to the balance between the elements of identity (which is shown, for example, in the progressive but affirmative action of pressure groups) and the element of opposition (which is shown in movements of protest and reform which make demands upon society). Such demands are not to be conceived as a response to conditions of oppression or even as an assertion of values but as a principle of resistance, a recognition that industrial society contains within itself the possibility of self-transformation because of the contradictions inherent in such societies. These claims to create and control constitute the system of historical action, the element of historicity which has its counterpart in class relationships. In this Tourainian approach, therefore, the system of historical action (in industrial societies at least) and the system of class relationships are interdependent but analytically distinct.

The relevance of the three components of historicity (knowledge, accumulation and culture) which were introduced above should now be more apparent. They are a means to the definition of class relationships. It is accumulation which provokes the conflict between classes but the dominant class controls the cultural model, thus bringing a measure of unity to the system of historical action as a whole. The mode of knowledge or 'image of society' is in one sense dependent on the other two components in that it expresses the distancing from society which is a feature of all activity; it is also, however, a basic 'force of production' since this distance is always grasped as an obstacle to be overcome. This is not to say that classes or class relationships are a function of consciousness or forms of knowledge:

the action of a class can never be analysed as a set of principles, as a 'world-view'. The action of each class is determined by the double dialectic of classes; it is simultaneously response to the opponent and orientation towards the cultural model. According to the circumstances, one or other aspect of the action of one class or another is more or less pronounced and it is one of the main tasks of sociology to study the modifications brought about in the system of actors as a whole when one of the elements undergoes certain modifications. Class relationships constitute a field of historical actors (*champ des acteurs historiques*) such that each one of its elements and the relationships between these elements are everywhere affected by change intervening at any point within this field. These transformations as a whole, whatever their origin or nature, are explained by the structure of the field, i.e. in the most general form by the double dialectic of social classes.[16]

It should by now be clear that the action analysis of class relations is far removed from any analysis of these relations in terms of non-social 'forces of production' or analyses which conceive of each social class in terms of a particular milieu with its own forms and values. It should also be clear why social movements (or collective action directed towards the control or transformation of the system of historical action) as opposed to roles, value systems or normatively oriented behaviour are so central to action analysis — theoretically central, that is, because 'social movement' in this highly abstract and general sense has proved difficult to translate into specific social and historical contexts.

There remains a further important question concerning the role of consciousness, individual and collective (and indeed unconsciousness) in the analysis of class relations. The term 'consciousness' which Touraine adopts in his answer to this question has, like so many other terms, a specific but abstract meaning.[17] In common with many marxists, Touraine does not use it in a descriptive manner. It is not simply a way of describing what actors in a given situation happen to think. The *conscience ouvrière* or workers' consciousness (which is not to be equated with class consciousness) is

> the manifestation of the historical subject which can only be grasped by way of [workers' consciousness] and the consciousness of those who direct or rule. . .it is a principle of analysis of empirical data, not an assessment which actors make of their situation. . .
> It is always defined by a combination of three elements. Firstly a consciousness of self, *a principle of identity* which provides the rationale for demands. . .Secondly, a consciousness of the adversary, *a principle of opposition* to the owner who exercises both economic and personal power, to the director or the manager. Finally a definition of the field of social conflict, *a principle of totality*.[18]

There is an apparent but misleading similarity between workers' consciousness thus defined and the readily accessible empirical reality of the interpretations which actors give of their own situation and the categories by which they grasp their own environment. Explanation of such accounts have been constantly drawn into the dualism of opposing consciousness to structure. However, if the analysis of action begins with social relations, as Touraine intends, consciousness can also be interpreted as a relation: not just the recognition by an actor of his place in a social situation but a property of social action at the highest social level (the system of historical action), the consciousness of labour in seeking to recognise itself and to be recognised through its products, the 'will to freedom and the struggle against alienation, against the opaqueness of a society which is forgetful of its own process of constitution'.[19] Just as the notion of social action is an instrument of analysis and not a way of describing behaviour, 'workers' consciousness' is an analytic and not a descriptive term.

Of course the notion is not without empirical referents. In *La conscience ouvrière*, Touraine situates the results of a study of transformation in the consciousness of workers in a wide range of French industries in the context of production and organisational technique. But he, unlike most other students of the problem, does not presuppose that workers have a well-organised conception of their own situation nor of their potential for collective action: even less does he assume that variations in consciousness are directly tied to particular milieux. Instead, workers' consciousness or the consciousness of conflict between capitalists and wage-earners for the orientation of industrial society, is a way of defining the labour *movement*. It includes both a representation of the conflict and a project which may be utopian or ideological, arising from the inclination to create and control. This is very far from being a 'psychological' definition. But it does allow the subjectivity of conduct to become apparent at different levels. In general the analysis of systems of action is made easier when these systems are disrupted, usually resulting in the elevation of the project of individual actors.

Consciousness and the Individual Project

The insistence that workers' consciousness is the meaning attached to the relation between man and his products including society and is not to be identified with a particular set of attitudes, does not preclude a study of the participation of individuals (personal subjects) in the process of constitution of meaning and values. In 'actionalist' terms, the object of study at the level of the individual is the project or the person's orientation towards and implication in the system of historical action. The place of the project in action analysis is analogous to that of the role in functional analysis: *an individual's project does not locate him within a social system but situates him in relation to historical action.*

Since historical action has already been defined as action within a system of class relationships and oriented towards the control (*emprise*) exerted by historicity upon social and cultural practices, it is to be expected that the objectives of individual actors will sometimes give the appearance of adaptation to a given social situation. Workers' attitudes and behaviour have not infrequently been interpreted as such. But there are many situations in which the logic of action is at odds with the organisational system or with class relations and, moreover, there can be a variety of adaptive responses to a single work situation. Instead of trying to reduce action to a technical and social situation or the workings of a socio-technical system, the study of projects 'is from the point of view of the concrete actor and seeks to discern in his action that which is *constitutive of a field of action* and not adaptation to a given field'.[20] This is not to say that all actors participate equally in social movements or in systems of historical action. At the lowest level, a project may be purely individual and retreatist. To deny this would be to ignore the fact that sociological surveys regularly encounter apathy and indifference to anything outside a narrow private sphere.

The notion of project and some of its implications with regard to migrant workers were explored in an earlier study by Touraine and Ragazzi.[21] In the first instance they identified the project of *displacement*, corresponding to the situation in which an individual, unable to find work or make a living in his own village or town is caught up in the general movement towards industrial cities. Secondly, there is the project of individual mobility or *departure* involving a deliberate intention to seek the rewards of promotion and personal advancement. And thirdly, there is a project which recognises the value of a social movement, the project of *collective mobility*, which incorporates values which are properly speaking social, such as 'industrialisation'. Each of these projects may be found in the same work context: their explanation cannot derive from this context but, in action theory terms, must begin with the assumption that the project is to a greater or lesser extent the incorporation within an individual of the historical subject. In other words 'every specific actor, at least in principle, participates in the historical subject, in the sense that his action has a certain *charge subjectale*'.[22]

Just as workers' consciousness is not to be identified with any existing totality of orientations, the project must not be confused with an intention or with a particular psychological state of affairs. Far from being a system of expectations or a set of concrete attitudes 'it is a principle of analysis which makes it possible to recombine the *event* which is an attitude'.[23] Hence Touraine's more recent definition of the project as 'the level of integration of the principles of identity, opposition and totality within a social movement'.[24] It must be admitted that his 'principle of analysis' has a certain ambiguity. As critics of Touraine have pointed out,[25] concepts such as 'action', 'historical subject', 'social movement' and 'project' do sometimes have a content which can be directly grasped empirically (in the sense of the May movement and certain mobility projects for example) but for the most part they are intellectual constructs which have no immediate relationship to observable phenomena. This is a criticism with important implications for our own study which seeks to develop certain aspects of the study of projects in the light of empirical evidence of workers' understanding of themselves and their situation. At one level it is a criticism which can be answered quite simply: like many other sociological constructs those employed by Touraine often resemble the terms in popular discourse but are abstractions which necessarily adopt a certain distance from reality if they are to have any analytic value. The problem is rather one of expression: the movement (which has to be constant) between observable phenomena and the analytical principles for grasping these phenomena must be made explicit. In the work of Touraine, the movement is predominantly from the latter to the former.

Principles of Analysis

The steps in Touraine's breakdown, analysis and re-constitution of workers' consciousness are based on the principles of totality, identity and opposition and the first part of *La conscience ouvrière* is an account of the changing relationship between these three principles based on a sample of workers representative of all levels of skill in seven industrial sectors. In this perspective, the most significant change in consciousness in the process of industrialisation has been the increasingly direct reference of the principle of totality to 'industrial society', to its economic and social development as being the common basis of evaluation. The development of technique has made this all the more true, so that 'the nearer one gets to modern forms of production, the less are social modes of work organisation determined by the technological character of work; on the contrary, they translate all the more accurately the totality of orientations of a society'.[26] An important implication is that, among certain occupations at least (refinery, gas and power station workers, for example), representations of society become relatively independent of occupational experience. Rather than being based on the defence of a particular status or role in the sphere of work as is often the case among miners or steelworkers, for instance, these representations consist of more general social attitudes tied to a societal value system.

Alongside this consciousness of society and related to it is the consciousness of being in possession of a factor of production which is labour. This 'self consciousness' in the modern context is a self definition in terms of a role in production and is to be inferred from statements about remuneration, skill, effort and qualifications, for example. According to Touraine, there has also been a change of emphasis with regard to this principle. For instance, 'whereas the miners defined the fair wage in terms of the effort contributed, workers in the most modern industries defined it with respect to qualification and particularly the cost of living. Here we pass from self- to society-centred judgements'.[27] This is the principle of identity which corresponds to the actor's own definition of the situation. To stop at this point, whether the definition is in terms of qualities or attributes (skill or strength, an 'awareness of achievement') or in terms of a model of the social system (rationalisation, for example), is clearly inadequate. The meaning of this definition only becomes clear in the broader context of the system of action at a particular state of development.

The principle of opposition, which is the third constituent of social consciousness, is a recognition of the other, the barrier to the realisation of the values embodied in the principle of totality. Within a system of action it has a necessity of its own: the principles of totality and identity together and without this third principle are utopian in the sense that a recognition of normative orientation is not transformed into decisions and other expressions. Likewise the principle of opposition on its own can only be ideological because it lacks a conception of society as an entity and has no positive means whereby to transform it. There is a consciousness of this kind which is a consciousness of being excluded from any positive participation in social action. This 'proletarian' form, to use Touraine's term, is found to a greater or lesser extent in several of the samples he studied.

It is clear that workers' consciousness thus defined can appear in a great variety of forms and that class consciousness is only one among many possible manifestations of consciousness. It has nevertheless had particular historical importance as the form which accompanied the change from pre-industrial to industrial systems of work. It is the union of two principles: a worker's consciousness based on the job, the right to work and on expenditure of effort; and the consciousness of industrial society, this being the recognition of a fundamental antagonism.

Since these two principles are contradictory, group consciousness and recognition of the social order need to be distinguished in the course of sociological analysis as elements in a complex whole.

At a more detailed level, both Durand[28] and Vidal[29] have adopted Touraine's conceptual framework in studies of workers' consciousness and its relation to trade union activity. The three elements in union activity conceived as a system of action are: the definition of the opposition as the managing class, owners, state, for example; the context of union claims; and the principle of legitimation which provides the context for the operation of the other two claims. These elements can be defined more abstractly as identity, opposition and totality respectively. Union consciousness or ideology in this view is one of the possible expressions of workers' consciousness. If it is regarded as a relation between the working class and its chosen means of action, the evolution of trade unionism and types of consciousness becomes explicable not just as strategy or tactics within a given industrial and economic structure but as the constitution of a sphere of action defined by the relation between the three principles of orientation.

From a similar starting point we will examine the social consciousness of three groups of workers as a relation between the principles of identity, opposition and totality. In this perspective, the ruptures, breaks and surprise assertions which are so frequently suppressed in interpretations of interview material will be taken into account as indicators of the process of formation of images and as evidence that images are complex constructions and not simple reflections.

Touraine's categories have been examined and their use illustrated in the familiar context of industrial working-class communities. Of course there is no necessity for this since the categories are not tied to an *a priori* classification of work and community situations. Indeed, they provide one means to escape from the strangely blinkered view which associates images of society almost exclusively with white, middle-aged males of the manual working class. This interest in the industrial worker still dominated Touraine's earlier studies including *La conscience ouvrière* but they embody a method which can be generalised to other contexts and movements.

The image of society is then the basic material from which the project is constructed. As such it provides evidence directly or indirectly not only of the recognition of social norms and values but also of demands made upon them — the relation between this recognition and these demands being the source of new values and historical action. Touraine's definition of the image of society (which corresponds to the definition of the project, differing only in that it has reference to the individual's own understanding) states this quite clearly: 'the image which each person forms of society is thus a combination of recognition of an existing social organisation and of demands which are an indication of another possible mode of social organisation'.[30] With few exceptions, studies of images have concentrated on the first element — that of recognition or identity — and as a result have rarely gone beyond partial description and closed typologies. Their 'images of society' are constructs of the sociological observer not the subject. If the images of society which people use do in fact happen to represent the functional requirements of a social system, this in itself is neither adequate description nor explanation. There are numerous ways in which demands can be made upon society according to the nature of social organisation and the situation of the individual as well as claims according to the principle of totality. Any investigation which excludes these possibilities by concerning itself exclusively with isolated attitudes on the one hand or a purely abstract interpretation of consciousness on the other is in danger of turning the worker, the clerk or the capitalist into an unintelligible mosaic or a figure of myth.

Notes

1. A. Touraine, *La conscience ouvrière* (Paris, 1966), p.124.
2. The main sources used in this section are *Sociologie de l'action* (Paris, 1965), and *Production de la société* (Paris, 1973). Touraine's earlier publications, mainly in the sociology of work, are important in giving substance to his theory. See especially *Ouvriers d'origine agricole* (with O. Ragazzi) (Paris, 1961); *Workers Attitudes to Technical Change* (OECD, 1965); *La conscience ouvrière* (Paris, 1966). The lack of translations into English is hardly remedied by the publication of two theoretical articles by Touraine and a critique by J.-D. Reynaud and P. Bourdieu in A. Giddens (ed.), *Positivism and Sociology* (London, 1974). For those with some grasp of the theoretical position, *The Post-Industrial Society* (London, 1974) is a collection of Touraine's essays which help to exemplify the method, despite the inappropriate title.
3. See W. Ackermann and S. Moscovici, 'La Sociologie existentielle d'Alain Touraine: Note critique', *S. du Travail*, 8 (1966), pp.205 ff.
4. See, for example, Touraine's own studies of the May movement and Chile under Allende. A. Touraine, *The May Movement* (New York, 1971) and *Vie et Mort du Chili populaire* (Paris, 1973).
5. *Sociologie de l'action*, p.9.
6. Ibid, p.9.
7. The very generality of this notion poses a considerable problem of

distinguishing between 'labour' and 'action', as Reynaud and Bourdieu have
pointed out. See J.-D. Reynaud and P. Bourdieu, 'Is a sociology of action
possible?', in A. Giddens (ed.), *Positivism and Sociology*, p.108.
    8. *Sociologie de l'action*, p.56.
    9. Ibid, p.51.
    10. This expression may be unfamiliar to the English reader but it has a
precise meaning in French existential philosophy and sociology. Action, like
consciousness, must have an object. Since this is not directly given through
experience, action involves the apprehension of the object (things, social relations,
the 'world') as a 'totality'.
    11. *Sociologie de l'action*, p.121.
    12. *Production de la société*, p.27.
    13. Ibid, p.531.
    14. Ibid, p.35.
    15. The confusion engendered by the use of the word 'subject', with its
personal and voluntaristic connotations has led Touraine to substitute the terms
'historical action' and 'system of historical action', which are less likely to
mislead once the fundamental idea of historicity has been understood. (Cf.
Production de la société, pp.38 ff.)
    16. *Production de la société*, pp.163-4.
    17. Here our exposition is deliberately restricted to industrial societies.
Touraine claims that the theme of class relations is also relevant, though less
central, to the analysis of agrarian societies or 'post-industrial' societies, for
example. Cf. *Production de la société*, pp.180 ff.
    18. *Sociologie de l'action*, pp.282-3. The fullest account of the notion of
workers' consciousness, its relation to industrial work and to class consciousness
is to be found in *La conscience ouvrière*, especially Chapter V and Conclusion.
    19. *La conscience ouvrière*, p.305.
    20. *Sociologie de l'action*, p.229.
    21. *Ouvriers d'origine agricole*.
    22. *Sociologie de l'action*, p.148.
    23. Ibid, p.245.
    24. *Production de la société*, p.532.
    25. See for example, Reynaud and Bourdieu, 'Is a sociology of action
possible?', pp.111-12, and Ackermann and Moscovici, 'La Sociologie existentielle
d'Alain Touraine', p.209.
    26. *La conscience ouvrière*, p.314.
    27. Ibid, p.318.
    28. C. Durand, *Conscience ouvrière et action syndicale* (Paris, 1971).
    29. D. Vidal, *Essai sur l'ideologie* (Paris, 1971).
    30. *La conscience ouvrière*, p.114.

3 IMPROVISATION ON A THEME: THE PROBLEM OF METHOD

Attempts to demonstrate empirically that images of society exist have frequently had an ad hoc quality. More often than not, image of society data has been collected in the context of extensive surveys almost as an afterthought and even purpose-built designs have rarely made good use of the variety of techniques developed for the study of attitudes and opinions. Extended interviewing has not always brought the benefits of a more intuitive approach. These general weaknesses, we suggest, derive from the ambiguities of theory rather than from any inherent difficulties of collecting data and making inferences from it. That there are difficulties is obvious. The image of society is a sociological abstraction, a way of understanding complex and sometimes contradictory attitudes and behaviour and the data derive from a sphere of action, with all that this entails in terms of change, creativity and control.

The Samples

The theoretical issues presented in the two previous chapters leave the empirical investigator with a problem: how to reconcile frameworks of interpretation which lay unequal stress on various elements of 'experience' (the work situation or social circumstances of the worker) and his capacity to respond creatively to these situations? We have argued that images of society are best regarded as an 'original given mode by which we orientate ourselves to reality' to use Dreitzel's phrase.[1] They are not to be viewed simply as the product of a set of external conditions nor approached subjectively as though a person's representation of a situation or the meaning attributed to it were self-explanatory.

Having stated that awareness of society has the characteristics of a dynamic relationship, it must be acknowledged that the most direct evidence for states of consciousness will still be the ideas, thoughts and feelings expressed by individuals. However, the proposition that social consciousness is a social fact and evidenced by concrete statements should not lead to a methodology which conceives of this consciousness or image of society as a 'thing' which will be revealed automatically by a search within the individual. The concrete statements or elements of

48

discourse are the clues in a search for rules and regularities which represent an underlying structure. So, in the study of social consciousness, the statement 'if you come from a decent social background you get on better' can be interpreted simply as statement about opportunities as though its meaning were unambiguous, or as the surface expression of a structure which makes statements about 'getting on' possible. In normal discourse about opportunities among the skilled workers studied there are statements (about God's imminent intervention in the historical process, for instance, which was predicted by one person in the sample of fitters) which are anomalous in terms of this structure. These statements could be chalked up as evidence of a range of 'attitudes' or they could be dismissed as meaninglesss eccentricities. However, because such statements are felt to be 'breaking the rules' or upsetting the regularities, even if they are partly comprehensible, we believe they are valuable for demonstrating the normative structures of thinking and discourse which are used with a minimum of reflection.

These preliminary remarks are needed to counter the impression that could arise from our procedure of studying three distinct occupational groups (fitters, steel melters and clerical superintendents), at least one of which has been the object of 'community' studies.[2] The intention is not to identify a constellation of attitudes and orientations and interpret them as a function of social 'milieux'. Rather, the choice of three contrasting occupational groups has been made for a number of other reasons both theoretical and practical. In the first place, work is the central life activity for the vast majority of people and — regardless of the occupation — the primary sphere of 'labour' or the creation of values. The structure of work institutions and the variety of material and non-material inputs permits a range of constructions to be placed upon the process of labour. This variety is acknowledged in the chosen samples which maximise differences in production processes, social relations and physical conditions of work whilst maintaining comparability at the level of income and the length of time spent in training. Secondly, in order to judge the range of images, the samples were chosen with a view to minimising within-group variation. In practice this involved the selection of individuals at a single level within the institution concerned. Any differences which are found thereafter in terms of age, education and social background are taken into account in the analysis. A third consideration in the choice of samples was the legacy of the empirical studies discussed in Chapter 1, together with related studies of the changing class structure of industrial societies.

We gathered the empirical data for the study from three locations in Central Scotland between October 1972 and January 1974. The interview schedule was piloted and the first main sample was drawn from the workers at a single petro-chemical plant at Grangemouth, a town beside the Firth of Forth in an area dominated by modern petroleum refining and chemical industries. Those interviewed (a total of 34) were drawn by random sample from all the fitters employed in maintenance work at the plant. This group was suitable in two major respects for the purposes of the study: they were all manual workers with a high level of skill (i.e. certified craftsmen having served 4 or 5 year apprenticeships) and their basic earnings and terms of employment at the time of the study were among the most favourable in manual occupations in Scotland, directly comparable in fact with those of many clerical workers. Their average earnings were 15-20 per cent above the current average for manual workers in Scotland.

The location of the second group was the head office of a life assurance company in the heart of Edinburgh's central business district. The relative heterogeneity of clerical occupations and their career structures entailed greater sampling problems, but a group of 21 was selected according to the income criterion; each person fell into a single grouping of the salary scale (i.e. the top two grades) which was identical with the average earnings of the Grangemouth sample. Most of the sample, or more precisely, the 19 who were actually interviewed, were therefore clerical workers holding senior positions in a variety of departments within the organisation.[3]

In contrast to office employees, who have been relatively neglected in sociological research – perhaps because of an erroneous image held by sociologists – steelworkers have been the subject of a number of studies. It was in a sizeable, though relatively old steelworks in the west of Scotland that workers in the third group were interviewed, a total of 19. Again, the search for comparability led to that traditionally well-favoured group the melters, and the first hands in particular. At the time of the study, the weekly earnings of the first hand melters in the sample were £51.66, averaged over a period of 13 weeks immediately prior to the study compared with an average of £41.14 for manual workers in Scotland as a whole. This figure was exceeded by several of the other workers.

The Interview as Improvisation

The structure of the interview was primarily designed to initiate reflection and discussion on personal experience. A fundamental difference between studies of attitudes and opinions (towards political parties, war, minority groups or capital punishment, for example) and the study of social consciousness is not simply that the former focus on a single variable or that they are thought of as socially conditioned responses to the immediate stimulus of experience. Important as these differences are, they derive from the fact that in attitude studies, responses are modelled in terms of space. Whether this space is defined as an interval or an ordinal scale, multi-dimensional or hierarchical, does little to alter the method of collecting data, which is intent on 'filling' the space. This generally precludes any elaboration of responses or at least reduces the importance of such elaboration. The technique is to present the respondent with a question which must be answered within the terms of the study if it is to be of any use. It is an attempt to minimise the problems and ambiguities which arise from the dynamic nature of language and the contextual properties of speech.

Alternative to this procedure of basing the question on the respondent himself, the encounter can be made on the basis of the question of the enquiry. Instead of recording an object's behaviour in response to a stimulus, the respondent can be involved as a participant in the solution of a problem which is common to both himself and the interviewer. In this way the subject of the enquiry is incorporated centrally in the interview. Although the information acquired in this way is rarely measurable in any strict sense, it has a richness which corresponds to the respondent's capacity to relate to the subject of discussion far more closely than in other methods. And it is this relationship which is as important in the study of images of society as the response to any specific question which can be asked of the individual. In practical terms this technique means that the interviewer imposes the minimum of guidance and direction in order that the subject's definition of the situation should have full expression. This allows for an evaluation of the relative significance of aspects of the situation and their affective implications. In this way the interview becomes an improvisation on a theme provided by the interviewer — an improvisation which is of interest not only for its content but for its form as well. As with music of course, the improvisation has to take place within a very tight structure if it is to make sense. As far as possible, the shape of the interview corresponds with aspects of the personal experience of the interviewee. Thus the arguments presented, the choice of words and their relationships in phrases, the omissions, illogicalities and qualifications are an articulation of linguistic processes which are no less socially relevant than the arguments themselves. All the interviews were recorded in order to capture as far as possible the wealth of information in extemporised discussion.

The form of the interview can be regarded as a series of spirals (see Appendix I for the interview schedule). It is an attempt to gather material on a number of themes which have some direct bearing on the respondent's experience of society, particularly within the sphere of employment, the labour process and work, as being the central life activity of those interviewed. The schedule falls into two main parts, the first of which refers directly to aspects of the work and market situation: job history or experience of the labour market; the work task; the work organisation and social relations at work; the company; and the union. The second part directs the discussion away from work to social life outside work, non-work projects and eventually to as much discussion of society in its economic, political and social aspects as the respondent is prepared to provide or is capable of improvising.

Within each theme there is a movement from specific questions concerned with actual behaviour to more general questions. This return to specifics has two advantages: it helps the respondent to maintain some points of contact with his own experience, giving him a certain amount of leverage on the more general questions and greater confidence that he is capable of answering at least some of the questions to his and the interviewer's satisfaction. Secondly, it provides the minimum amount of information about actual behaviour that is necessary for the interviewer to understand more general statements and to assess their relationship to experience. Regarded as a whole, the interview is therefore far from being non-directed; it provides a structure of themes which on theoretical grounds are assumed to be significant in the creation of values and in the formation of social consciousness. But within each section, and in relation to each theme, the objectives and procedures of non-directedness are followed as far as time and circumstances permit. In practice, the 'horizons' of the respondents' experience and consciousness more often than not impose their own limits on the replies to open questions so that further probing brings about quite rapidly diminishing returns.

The Analysis of Content

We have already implied that the method used by Popitz *et al.* in their study of images of society is one of the most appropriate methods to have been tried so far. This is partly because it was developed for the purpose and was not simply an adjunct to or modification of traditional

survey techniques. The reproduction of some of the extended
discussions in the study is itself significant, implying as it does that
certain elements of the material are lost or deformed if the interview
is not treated as a whole. The authors assume that the interview is more
than the sum of discrete replies to each question. They also convey
with admirable clarity the quality of the responses and not least the
often highly articulate and comprehensive accounts of matters of close
concern to those interviewed. But perhaps the most important
contribution of this study is to the analysis of content as an expression
of the 'social Topic'. This requires some explanation and is best clarified
by quoting from Popitz himself. In his view there is a profusion of
aspects and perspectives in workers' discussions of their work and life
situations but the themes of the responses are neither random nor
unlimited, despite the vast range of possibilities. In fact he states that

> the workers' conceptions show a great deal of similarity, which even
> amounts to a similarity of wording. This has nothing to do with the
> interviews or the methods of transcription. A comparison of the
> protocols of the different interviewers shows that the stereotyped
> ideas, the frequent use of comparable expressions and even of certain
> figures of speech go right back to the respondents. . .It points to a
> general stock of conceptions, viewpoints and beliefs which are
> relatively enduring in outline, which are available to the workers as
> a whole and on which they can draw in their replies.[4]

The general stock of arguments can be likened to stratified deposits
which have gradually accumulated throughout the history of ideas.
According to Popitz, some of these concepts cannot be reduced to
great world views or movements of ideas such as marxism, bourgeois
liberalism, romantic individualism or nationalism. Instead, they have
flourished independently in a particular social environment — in this
case the environment of the manual working class.

> The fact of such a stock and the concomitant stereotypical ideas
> and representations is not surprising as long as one does not think
> it is limited to the work situation. This is certainly not the case. To
> overhear a conversation in a pub is to notice that here too individual
> statements are far from being dominant, that the commonplace and
> the catchphrase take over as soon as the conversation switches to
> general issues. General ways of thinking on general problems are
> usually dressed up in stereotyped cliches; they occur, to use a

philological term, in the form of Topoi. These Topoi, however, are
not arbitrary in the sense that any Topos is equally available for use.
On the contrary, the different social groups — to some extent at
least — make use of very different Topoi. At crucial points the white
collar workers in a large enterprise employ a different Topic from
that of the manual workers in the same establishment — to say
nothing of a social group as far removed from the workers as the
petty bourgeois small shopkeeper, for instance. Each topic, i.e. the
total stock of available Topoi, has its social location in which, as we
shall see, it proves to be meaningful. This is the sense in which we
use the term *social Topic*: whole catalogues of Topoi can be drawn up
for each social group which are specific to these groups. The
individual arguments and statements about technical progress and
the world 50 years from now, which we have collected and portrayed
above are, among other things, Topoi of this sort. The coding of the
interview material, which is taken as a basis for our classification and
presentation, amounts essentially to the construction of a catalogue
of Topoi.[5]

Popitz's use of the social Topic seems to imply a high degree of
cohesiveness in the values of the group. However, it is unnecessary and
perhaps unhelpful to assume that a group or community will always
be highly integrated in this way. It remains to be seen how far the
notion can be applied in de-structured social contexts. Popitz claims
that the majority of workers make a selection of Topoi 'which help to
clarify. . .in terms of their relation to a basic attitude, to a basic
determination to see and appropriate things in a certain way'. This
propensity to adopt certain Topoi and make use of them in a
consistent manner (though not necessarily in precisely the same
manner in any one group) points to the relatively enduring frameworks
of interpretation which give individual Topoi a powerful role in the
clarification and explanation of personal experience. According to
Popitz, these frameworks of interpretation are best conceived as
images — 'the Topoi of the worker's understanding of himself and
society are articulated in the framework of these different images of
society'.[6]

A close look at any particular Topos such as unemployment or
technical progress immediately reveals the problem of unity in diversity
which is at the heart of the difficulties of method and interpretation.
Mention has already been made of Popitz' contribution to the debate
about the relation between experience and attitudes or social

consciousness. At least part of this debate can be regarded as a conflict between a school of thought which emphasises personal experiences as the major determinant of attitudes and a school of thought which rejects this emphasis and argues instead that social consciousness is formed in the common experience of the social group and is represented in jointly held forms of thought and expression. The latter view is expressed by Geertz in his account of ideology as a 'cultural system'. He argues that cultural symbol-systems

> are extrinsic sources of information in terms of which human life can be patterned — extrapersonal mechanisms for the perception, understanding, judgement and manipulation of the world. Culture patterns — religious, philosophical, aesthetic, scientific, ideological — are 'programs'; they provide a template or blueprint for the organisation of social and psychological processes, much as genetic systems provide such a template for the organisation of organic processes.[7]

Such templates are necessary because the complexities of human experience often combine to create situations in which received traditions or formal rules for thinking and acting are incapable of providing precedents.

Popitz recognises this, and taking unemployment as a theme, he shows that, although the actual and possible range of personal experiences of unemployment is very great, this alone does not account for the diffuseness of the Topos and even less for its use by those with no direct experience of unemployment. On the contrary, the Topos not only provides an explanation of individual or collective experience, it 'enables and facilitates the worker's orientation towards current social and historical reality'. Moreover, since this reality is so complex and abstract 'the Topoi are probably the only means of orientation towards, and making sense of, reality which are available to the worker'.[8] It is undoubtedly true that personal experience would be incomprehensible without some means of structuring the experience both synchronically and diachronically. If the means for synchronic structuring are provided by the Topoi common to the social group in question, then the second or diachronic form of structuring requires frameworks which allow these experiences to be placed within the movement of society as a whole. The technique used by Popitz to describe these frameworks is the traditional one of constructing a typology.

A typological approach can be regarded as an attempt to define certain attributes of social reality as though they could be immobilised and divided up for the purposes of analysis. Several features of the six-fold typology of workers' images of society which Popitz constructs show that this is not an entirely appropriate technique when applied to a problem which is essentially a problem of social action rather than one of social structure or function. In the first place, the typology is far from exhaustive: one quarter of the respondents were found either to have no image of society or else were unclassifiable.[9] In view of the theoretical argument concerning the need for a structured and structuring social consciousness this result cannot be lightly dismissed. It is not just a blurring at the edge of the picture nor is it a result of workers' inability to express themselves. Following as it does the comparatively sensitive and flexible analysis of the worker's understanding of himself and society in terms of Topoi, it displays a difficulty in the typological method rather than a flaw in the assumptions about social consciousness. A second, and related, criticism is that the typological approach allows for little, if any, movement. It fails to show the changing pattern of the available interpretations of society and the strength of adherence to them. Of course the typology presented does not claim to be closed or to exhaust the range of social imagery. But it does place the investigator in the position of having to choose, in a more or less arbitrary way, a point somewhere between the extremes of saying that there are as many images as there are individuals — which is to deny the sociological relevance of images — or that there is scarcely any differentiation. The value of a typology is essentially heuristic. For this reason it should be regarded as a stage in the analysis and not as the object or culmination of the analysis.

An alternative to the typological approach, and the one adopted here, is to look for the underlying rules used in the structuring (and also the re-telling) of social experience. The notion of 'generative processes' which is familiar to students of language and grammar has relevance in this context. Using the word 'generative' in a mathematical sense, a set of rules that recursively define an infinite set of objects may be said to 'generate' this set. With regard to language, therefore, the grammar can be said to constitute the rules for the generation of the sentences of language. The grammar is a system of rules which allows the elements of the language to be combined in an acceptable way and which also provides a structural description of the resulting sentences. By analogy, there are generative rules by which the extreme complexity of social reality can be reduced to acceptable forms in human thought.

Just as the generative rules in grammar are the property that express the creativity of language – the capacity that native speakers of a language have to produce and understand an infinitely large number of sentences, some of which may be completely new in the sense that they have never been uttered before – the rules which people employ consciously or with only partial understanding to grasp their social experience express the creativity of social consciousness and social action. It may be, of course, that a single person or social group makes use of more than one set of rules or that these rules vary through space and time like dialects. Our task is to identify the rules and hence the sources of variation in social consciousness.

Traditional techniques of content analysis share the limitations of all approaches which regard language and discourse as something which can be broken down and manipulated, as something which can be immobilised, at least for operational purposes. To break down a text into units, to count and categorise them – any form of selection in fact – ignores a major part of the process of verbal communication. These techniques subject discourse to operations in which a large part of the information is lost or deformed. It is for this reason that we regard the materials of our study as a partial actualisation of largely unconscious processes; as a dynamic social potential and not simply as a set of specific messages.

Notes

1. H.P. Dreitzel, 'Selbstbild und Gesellschaftsbild', *Arch. europ. sociol.*, III (1962), p.183.
2. The study of occupational communities assumes that personal identity or self-image is tied to occupational roles. It seeks evidence of this in self-accounts, i.e. in the attitudes, beliefs and opinions that people hold about themselves. See for example, G. Salaman, *Community and Occupation* (Cambridge University Press, 1974), especially Chapter 2. Mining and shipbuilding are most frequently cited as examples. A classic study in this tradition is C.R. Walker's, *Steeltown* (New York, 1950).
3. The response rate for this sample compares closely with the rate for the other two samples. Practical difficulties rather than personal reluctance prevented a 100 per cent response.
4. H. Popitz, H.-P. Bahrdt, E.A. Jueres and H. Kesting, *Das Gesellschaftsbild des Arbeiters* (Tübingen, 1957), p.82. The term Topic is derived from Aristotle's *Organon* writings where it is usually translated as 'commonplace' and this passage is inspired by his system of rhetoric. According to one commentator, in the enthymematic system which is central to Aristotle's understanding of rhetorical discourse, 'an audience is assumed, and this audience is further assumed to share a stockpile of attitudes, of expectations, of scruples and conventions and truisms and commonplaces' and the linguistic management of an audience's stockpile of

attitudes and values is taken to be the key to the art of persuasion. 'The rhetor is conceived of as building his arguments upon various of these common beliefs, employing them as premises that sanction his conclusions'. E. Black, *Rhetorical Criticism: a study in method* (Macmillan, New York, 1965), pp.125-6.

5. H. Popitz *et al., Das Gesellschaftsbild*, pp.82-4.

6. Ibid., p.87. |

7. C. Geertz, 'Ideology as a Cultural System', in D.E. Apter (ed.), *Ideology and Discontent* (New York, 1964), p.62.

8. H. Popitz *et al., Das Gesellschaftsbild*, p.86.

9. Ibid, p.233. Popitz acknowledges this to be a product of his method, which was 'intended to produce a selective effect which is predetermined'; that is, the workers involved were not unclassifiable because they were unable to formulate views on their personal experiences — views which are potentially classifiable — but because they were unable to bring these views to bear on questions which go beyond the realm of immediate experience.

4 PATHS IN THE OCCUPATIONAL STRUCTURE

Work is formative of social consciousness: that is, work as an active confrontation with the world of things and the world of people rather than work as a necessity, the means of survival. In this active sense, an understanding of work is a prerequisite for understanding how workers integrate themselves in thought and reality to developing and changing circumstances. This approach does not simply regard the wor situation (or indeed the broader social context) as an environment in which attitudes are 'shaped' but as an environment which presents both an 'intermediary' and a 'barrier' between the worker and his work The worker is regarded as an active subject who appropriates meanings from an environment which has this character of both medium and message. The significance of work as a central life activity is then twofold: it provides possibilities and at the same time sets limits to what is possible for the worker. In describing the forms of social consciousness among the three groups of workers we will be describing the process of reconciling these two aspects.

The occupational context of the workers can be studied through individual biographies as well as through the description of work situations or the state of the labour market. 'Career' is another way of describing it. The term 'career' is usually reserved for occupations — especially the professions — with a structured set of positions filled in a standard sequence according to competence, seniority and other less public criteria. We will use it here in the more general sense which Goffman has employed. In his view there are certain 'changes over time which are basic and common to the members of a social category' (even though these changes occur independently to each of the members) and these changes are significant not just for structures — official position within an organisation, for example — but also for the individual's identity and self image.[1] It follows that commitment to a job involves commitment to a particular personal and social identity, which is itself an active component in the person's career.

We will describe in turn the dimensions and active components of the typical 'career' of the maintenance craftsman, the steel melter and the clerical superintendent. The data for this includes descriptive statistics of job histories, occupational mobility and methods of finding work together with data from introspective (and necessarily

retrospective) accounts of aspirations and perceived limits to
advancement.

The Craftsman's Career

The typical trajectory of a craftsman's career is easier to define than
for most other occupational careers because there is a relatively formal
and institutionalised process of socialisation into the skilled trades —
the apprenticeship. Apprenticeships are served for 4 (formerly 5) years
from the ages of fifteen or sixteen and the training given is a
combination of practical, on-the-job instruction and more theoretical
teaching either in the form of college courses or classes organised within
the firm. An apprenticeship scheme was in operation in the plant
studied but this does not mean that all, or even the majority of workers
received their training within the plant. In fact in the sample studied,
slightly more than one third had received their training with the
company; others had been apprenticed in a whole range of industries
and firms, in production as well as in maintenance.

The experience of apprenticeship, which provides access and
initiation to an adult role of high status among the working class is
undoubtedly of key formative importance. Since a detailed study of
the impact of this form of occupational socialisation would not be
possible here, even if the information were available, we will simply
attempt to describe some of the special features of the apprenticeship
system as they apply to engineering and to the plant in question.[2]
Differences of procedure have grown up in response to pressures from
craft unions to maintain their exclusiveness, from changes in technology
and from employers' demands for cheap labour.[3] However, the
differences between firms in terms of conditions, attitudes towards
apprenticeship training and the content of this training are not as
important as might appear at first sight. This is because, technically
speaking, the skilled trades in engineering initially only assume an
elementary theoretical understanding together with training in a number
of basic transferable skills; and also because the nature of the work,
which has certain 'craft' characteristics, is not firm- or industry-specific.
In fact, work in a skilled manual occupation involves a continuous
learning process which can be carried through to the limits of a worker's
own capacities either by working at new or increasingly complex tasks
within a single firm or by moving to an enterprise with a higher grade
of work. For example, the career of one of the fitters interviewed was
from basic foundry maintenance work to installation of compressors in
his present job and then (prospectively) to work with hospital

machinery. The end of the apprenticeship is therefore in no sense the end of 'training', or at least it need not be. Training is a continuous process for as long as technical change or mobility within or outside the firm permits. This is not to say that where such possibilities do exist they will actually be exploited. For example, the fitters in this study did not take up all the opportunities for pursuing higher education courses in engineering created by the firm's sponsorship scheme.

The craftsman's career typically consists of only a single step between the position of apprentice and that of foreman. According to Ashton, the movement can be regarded in many firms as a very short career ladder which

> consists of between two and four steps, although the majority of the positions are located on the second step. Most of the entrants into this type move from the position of apprentice to that of skilled worker, where they remain. A minority move to the next step, that of the chargehand's position, and of these fewer reach the ceiling of this career, that of the foreman's position.[4]

In the plant studied, formal differentiation is even less than suggested by Ashton's description. There is no chargehand status and no distinction with respect to salary or status among those with special responsibility for apprentices. The ratio of foremen to craftsmen is in the order of 1 : 10. The craftsmen can thus be seen in broad terms as a homogeneous occupational group whose identity depends above all on their monopoly of skill, such that the active cognitive component in group identity is directed towards external rather than internal differentiation. This has important consequences for social consciousness and behaviour on a broader scale which make it possible to describe this group in terms of 'craft consciousness' and 'craft solidarity'.

It would be naive to assume that the lack of formal differentiation is the end of the story. The continuous process which is the craftsman's career in the sense in which we are using the term is differentiated in a number of more subtle ways. It is helpful to think of these as a number of key points which represent a transition from one career stage to the next, stages which may or may not correspond to stages in the life cycle. We will discuss them in turn under the following heads: into work; consolidation; getting on; and mobility versus security.

Into Work

The 'career' has its origins in institutionalised experience long before entry into employment. It is widely accepted that socialisation, or the learning of new social roles in childhood and adolescence is a key to the process of entry into employment. The young person does not at first encounter the employment situation as a skilled dealer in a complex market; nor does he participate as a purely passive commodity. Instead, he approaches the occupational structures with certain values, preferences and motives which are the outcome of his experience of three main agencies of socialisation: the family, the school and the peer group. The possible roles open to a young person are restricted by this experience which includes identification with and imitation of parents, teachers and other adults, the learning of occupational stereotypes, and even prior role rehearsal. At all events, according to Liversidge, these pre-work experiences lead children to a 'startlingly accurate appraisal of life chances. . .and a shrewd appreciation of the social and economic implications of their placing within the educational system. . .Having accepted the role they are to play in life, they rarely venture out of it, even in fantasy'.[5] Similarly, Roberts criticises the commonsense assumption that young people exercise personal choice and are responsible for the jobs they have entered. He concludes that 'the typical pattern. . .seems not for jobs to be entered upon the basis of ambition, but for ambitions to be adapted to the occupations that young people find themselves able to enter'.[6] Thus, 'ambition' can be seen as a retrospective concept, as much a way of structuring one's biography and making sense of the past as a way of orientating oneself to the future.

It is apparent from the data on father's occupation and length of schooling that the large majority of fitters were the sons of fathers in the skilled trades or partly skilled manual work. A closer look at the list of jobs reveals that not only a large majority were skilled working class (craftsmen and foremen) but also that some of those in less skilled jobs were working either within the same form or in closely related industries as process workers or labourers. To be precise, 32 per cent of the fitters had fathers who were employed in three major petrochemical plants in the locality and others had more distant relatives in the same plants. This in itself does not show that parental influence was decisive but it appears to be one important element in a general configuration of circumstances. It favours the production of a self image which takes its bearings from the distinction between 'dead-end'

jobs and those which allow for the development of skills and for
personal involvement, within a specific industrial context at least. In
fact this distinction is a recurring motif in craftsmen's self descriptions.
The only group which does not regularly refer to this difference based
on transferable skills is the older fitters who entered employment
before the war. At the time market constraints were so severe as to
rule out any occupational 'choice', including the choice between
working and not working. One fitter referred to this time as 'the dark
days'. However, among the remainder of the sample, the early,
pre-employment experiences come to expression in a number of ways
which complement each other to form the following interpretation or
image of the state of affairs leading up to an apprenticeship.

If the sample is divided into two main groups consisting of those
with fathers in the skilled trades on the one hand and the remainder
on the other, two themes emerge which appear to reflect slightly
different emphases in socialisation in the respective groups. In both
cases there are references to parental and school influences in their
accounts of becoming apprenticed, but the rationale of these accounts
differs. Those with fathers in the skilled trades refer most frequently to
personal attitudes and the nature of the work, together with 'aptitude'
which is the link between them. This is expressed in the response of one
recently qualified fitter, the son of a 'commissioning engineer' who was
formerly employed in the same plant.

Q. Can you tell me why you came to this firm?
A. I applied to various firms along the Boness Road and [this firm]
   gave me an interview, the first interview I had. And they just
   sent back an acceptance!
Q. Did you know much about the firm because your father was here?
A. Yes, I knew quite a bit about it. I knew what I was coming to.
Q. Did it matter to you which firm you joined?
A. No, not at all, as long as it was actually engineering I was doing. . .
   I've always been interested in machinery and how it functions,
   so it was just natural.

Another stressed the influence of school as well as home, saying that
the 'technical career' is something 'instilled into you' as part of
specialisation in technical subjects at school. There is no evidence of
a strong peer group influence to counter this trend. However, in
contrast to this group who tend to speak of ambitions or aspirations
in quite specific terms ('I didn't actually want to be an electrician –

I wanted to be a fitter', or 'I wanted to be a fitter, working with my hands, with moving parts of machinery') the fitters with fathers in less skilled occupations give an account of their entry into the trade in more general terms, citing a greater variety of reasons and creating the impression of a largely random process following an initial decision about the relative merits of apprenticeship as opposed to less skilled but, in the short term, more remunerative employment. Thus, the son of a miner was advised by his father 'never to go into the pits'. Instead, he recalls that for his parents 'it was the recognised thing that you tried to get a boy or girl into an apprenticeship or a similar kind of job. . . My father felt he was doing better by sending me into an apprenticeship'. Similarly, the son of a general labourer indicated that his parents wanted him 'to become a tradesman of some description' but that his starting with the firm and entering his present trade was neither very predictable nor associated with any clear ideas on his part: becoming a fitter 'was the only opportunity open at the time. . .I had to take the nearest apprenticeship going. . .I just came down on the chance of getting a job'. These two varieties of description appear with sufficient regularity in the respective groups to indicate that social background — or, more precisely, the consequences for socialisation of different locations within the social structure — has a noticeable effect upon the image of occupations which is brought into play on becoming an apprentice. For the first group, it is meaningful to speak of assuming an occupational role with the benefit of prior anticipatory socialisation; for the sceond group, the occupation — initially conceived abstractly in terms of 'apprenticeship' rather than concretely in terms of a specific trade — is defined negatively as distinct from less desirable occupations in a less skilled category. These contrasting conceptions are likely to be reflected in contrasting expectations and aspirations, as are all differences of self-image, including those which are used to make sense of personal experience in the occupational world. Commitment, and consequently certain expressions of 'satisfaction', are indirectly related to these expectations, so it is to the early stages of the craftsman's career that we now turn. This career may be within a single firm or may span several firms.

Consolidation

It has been proposed that entry into employment is simply one stage in a developmental process whereby occupational ambitions, preferences and actual choice are brought from the realm of fantasy through an exploratory phase into the realm of reality.[7] The end result of this process is said to be a substantial degree of congruence between expectations of the career and the career as pursued in fact. This view has been criticised on the grounds that occupations are not usually chosen, as is generally assumed, but that ambitions or preferences are adjusted to the occupations that young people find themselves able to enter.[8] However, what is important for our present purposes is the correct emphasis on the fact that commitment and adjustment to an occupational role are not to be taken for granted but are part of continuing process in which a person's current commitments conform to the image which he uses to interpret his career. As we have seen, this image need not necessarily be shared by every member of a group; different accounts implying different images may be given even though they refer to the same set of circumstances. But the image notion helps in interpreting variations in commitment, since the image is a more or less conscious expression at the individual level of a person's understanding of his relationship to the world about him. This understanding is not just a passive awareness of favourable or unfavourable circumstances but is a non-neutral stance which actively intends one course of action in a complex network of possibilities. The image therefore is not a complete framed 'picture'; rather, it contains the elements of alternative forms. It is an act of imagination.

Since all the craftsmen in this study began their apprenticeships at the usual age of 15 or 16, we can for the moment bracket the possibility that commitment varies only in relation to stages in the life cycle and not in relation to length of membership of the occupational group. Also, the career in the craft occupations is not an ordered step-like sequence of jobs so it can be inferred that changes of job or industry must conform to some logic of advancement which is external to the work institution. For evidence of this we refer to responses about employment history and particularly to the rationale of ensuing discussion of the subject. A substantial minority of the sample received their training at the plant and have remained there ever since. This relatively static picture is typical of the fitters in general, because of the remainder, only 18 per cent had two or more previous jobs and any moves they made between industries or firms were entirely horizontal. Of course this is not surprising in itself but it provides the necessary background to the more important question of the direction of these movements and the reasons given for them. In reply to the open-ended questions 'Can you explain why you changed jobs and moved here?' or 'Can you explain why you came here and not to any other company?', there emerged a pattern of responses which reveals an interest in both intrinsic and extrinsic rewards. The pattern also discloses an important underlying mechanism for occupational placement. In order of frequency, the reasons given for moving were (allowing for more than one response per person): pecuniary (mentioned by 38 per cent of the sample); transfer arranged by management or union following redundancy (29 per cent); intrinsic factors such as hours and conditions of work (23 per cent); security (21 per cent); and personal reasons, such as the influence of a friend or relative (11 per cent). In only one case did prospects of 'promotion' figure prominently. To the extent that the career ceiling is low and more or less fixed, this is to be expected. The emphasis on monetary rewards is also to be expected in view of their relative immediacy and visibility compared with less tangible intrinsic rewards. However, less predictable is the stress on the role of work organisations in finding jobs for their members. This implies a degree of confidence in the ability of institutions — and not only the trade union — to modify the often harsh reality of the world of employment. For one younger worker it was a fact of life, something to be accepted. He admitted that he knew 'absolutely nothing about the firm before coming here; the iron works closed down and the union found us a job in here, so I just took it'. Another, older, craftsman under threat of redundancy or transfer to a less responsible job due to reorganisation explained that he was free either to accept these consequences or to seek an alternative. An interpretation of the self image of the younger worker is that it had not consolidated sufficiently to provide a means of assessing alternatives; the image, and the attitude of 'taking what comes' is an open one, which shows a readiness to explore the possibilities as they present themselves. The older worker on the other hand had reached a boundary, a turning-point in his projected 'career'. This caused him to make an active decision to seek new employment. He had reached the limit of his commitment which by then had a particular form. Any assessment of horizontal mobility by craftsmen therefore needs to take account of two things: workers' self images and the differentiation which exists in the occupational sphere.

A closer look at the priority given to financial rewards from work reveals that they, like occupational ambition generally, are a means of adjusting to and explaining a fait accompli. Within the prevailing market circumstances they do not provide an overriding motive for job mobility. One good indicator of the salience of financial rewards is willingness to work shifts, since shift work on a permanent basis is largely a matter of choice in the industry under consideration. All of the sample had experienced shift work at one time or another but only 18 per cent were currently working permanent shifts. Even among this group money was hardly a dominant consideration. Only in two cases was the additional money earned through shift work clearly a prime motive. It was still not so important as to exclude other considerations, for these workers also mentioned the advantages of relative freedom from supervision on shifts. For the others shift work was not a question of choice but merely a first position within the firm, a stepping stone to permanent day work in the short or the long term. In these circumstances, the cash nexus does not so much provide a motive as a rationale which helps the worker to reconcile himself with his present situation. For example:

> I hate shifts. Sometimes they've got their benefits, but to me, I just don't like shifts. I'm working them because I've got to — plus the money's quite good, the extra money. In this day and age you need the money.

Therefore, in the great majority of cases, shift work is accepted as a necessary burden or even as a welcome change on a temporary basis but it is not highly valued for its additional financial rewards. Paradoxically, the strong negative argument used by nearly all the permanent day workers — the unacceptable intrusion of shift work into the routine of leisure and non-work activities — was turned around by the shift workers to justify their own, albeit temporary, position. This is a warning that attitudes or judgements which are superficially similar may be used in completely contrasting ways and that they must be interpreted within a broader context of meaning. In this case the context is that of an occupational group in which shift workers are understood as a minority, which is a very different context from the occupational community of the steelworkers, as we shall see below.

The movements of craftsmen are for the most part horizontal within a formally undifferentiated occupation but that they are never simply the means of adaptation to market or any other circumstances. If the process of consolidation is often described by participants in retrospect as an opening or closing of possibilities provided by institutional frameworks, this already implies both a sense of identity with the industrial organisation (as a means to working out a career) as well as opposition (in that the organisation may cease to hold out these possibilities). These two aspects are the subject of the following two sections in which we look at the craftsmen's notions of advancement or 'getting on' and the possibility of further career moves, which involve considerations of relative security.

Getting On

We have argued that research into images of society has hitherto attempted to reduce their complexity by artificially halting their 'flow' and treating them in a static way. This neglect of time in self and social consciousness has had serious consequences, for it involves an assumption which is only partly valid: that past experience is the key to the interpretation of images of society. In fact, the future and the possibilities which it contains, together with perceived means for realising these possibilities, is integral to any developed conception of the self and society. There is evidence for this at two levels: in the general stock of concepts available for judging actual and potential progress in the world of work, and in orientations to the future based directly or indirectly on these concepts.

Deciding what constitutes the general stock of relevant concepts is a difficult, if not impossible task. However, one of the aims of a pilot study among the fitters was to identify a short list of terms which signified these concepts and which also formed part of the fitter's active vocabulary. The open-ended interview schedule which was used in the main study allowed enough room for discussion and interpretation of questions for the danger of different understandings to be minimised. In some cases, including the question concerned with general interpretations of personal advancement and achievement (Q.32) the interviewee was invited to respond to a number of pre-selected items derived from the pilot study. To ensure that answers were in fact related to similar concepts, those interviewed were invited to say what they understood by the terms they had been invited to consider. The list of terms included both aspects of personal character (ambition, hard work, intelligence) and ascribed characteristics (social background, education, luck).

At a first glance, the answers reveal a pattern of moderate to strong emphasis on personal effort and drive together with the good fortune of having useful personal contacts. The frequency with which the items were selected as being 'important for a person to get on' (in the occupational world, that is) is shown in Table 1. In an occupation in which minor educational differences are not transformed into obvious income or status differentials, it is not surprising that effort and influence on a personal level are given high priority and figure prominently in craftsmen's interpretation of their own experience. For

Table 1: Assessment of Factors Relevant to Personal Advancement:
  Craftsmen

	Percentage who regard this factor as important
Hard work	65
Knowing the right people	56
Education	50
Ambition	47
Intelligence	47
Character	40
Luck	26
Social background	15
n = 34	

the most part, any links between life outside work and occupational
advancement are regarded as irrelevant or purely coincidental. Hence
the fitters generally deny that 'luck' or 'social background' are involved
at all. This stress on intrinsic qualities of application and motivation
together with a measure of ability is part of an orientation to work
which can still be described in terms of 'craft consciousness' or a
particularly strong identification with a particular range of skilled tasks.
However, it is indicative of the changing circumstances of the craft
worker and his increasingly ambiguous position within highly complex
technical systems that education (theoretical knowledge and formal
education as opposed to understanding gained through experience) is
highly valued but is regarded for the most part as a means of
advancement in technical, professional occupations and not within the
craft occupations. This may be the reason why many of the craftsmen
wished to equate intelligence with education and account for their
own experience in terms of their innate capacity, leaving education as
an equivalent factor in other occupations. This pattern of response
does not vary according to age. On matters of education this need not
be surprising because most workers have recent experience of the
educational world if not as participants then as parents. A small
minority of workers (9 per cent) pointed out that education *should*
be the key to where you work and how far you go, but that this is not
necessarily the case; they recognised and could cite cases of intelligent
people hindered by lack of education and highly qualified people
unable to get jobs.

The importance of 'knowing the right people' (i.e. being well placed to benefit from personal contacts, family reputation or acquaintances made outside work) was recognised by a surprisingly large number (56 per cent) of the craftsmen. It was regarded as being of importance both within their present work context as well as in other occupations, but nearly all of those who mentioned this denied that they themselves had advanced by this means. It was explained by one fitter in the following terms:

Q. Did knowing the right people apply in your own case?
A. No, just in general. An instance in here is becoming a foreman. You must have ambition to become a foreman, plus a reasonable amount of education to know about the job, plus you must know the right people to become a foreman. . .
Q. Did the fact that your father was employed here make any difference?
A. I don't really think so. . .my father was a general labourer here but it didn't make a difference to me. It's really merit: you've got a test, and if you impress a person, that's it.

The fact that the apparently fortuitous or non-achieved attribute of 'knowing the right people' is highly placed on the list is not therefore inconsistent with the important achieved attributes. In fact it could be described as the result of deliberate cultivation of personal contacts.

This consideration of some of the generalised concepts which are used for interpreting career paths (and other concepts could be added, such as the notion of 'merit' occurring in the above quotation) now needs to be made more concrete. Many of the ambiguities of the above responses derive from the fact that they were not the principal means for interpreting personal careers but were rationalisations of more generalised career patterns. In terms of the fitters' own careers, therefore, enquiry was made into their self assessment insofar as it included a future horizon and possibilities.

The main vertical career step available to the craftsmen is the step from craftsman to foreman. The fitters were asked whether they had hopes of promotion to the position of foreman and were invited to discuss their stated attitude, including the theoretical limits to advancement in their occupation. Briefly, the results indicate that the large majority of fitters did not anticipate an appreciably different future for themselves. Altogether, 85 per cent either did not expect to be made up to foreman, did not wish to be, or did not know. Only

15 per cent predicted this as a likely move in the future. It is safe to
conclude that the career as an unfolding of new possibilities for work
and control leading eventually to the position of senior area foreman
is not a preoccupation of the fitters, nor is it a key to their actual
conduct, except in a very few cases. The attitudes imply an
understanding of work which is not especially open to the future but
one which shows a fairly subtle appreciation of the meaning of
promotion and the conflict prone role of the foreman. Some of the
following remarks would not be out of place in a sociological text
illustrating the conflict inherent in the role of foreman.[9]

> Well, actually I had the chance [to become a foreman] but I just
> didn't fancy it. My own idea is that you're caught in between two
> sides of people and you're shunted a bit.

> If you're a foreman you're a dog's dinner for the people above
> you — they can tell you what to do. And you're not really friendly
> with the people underneath you. (You are friendly, but there's not
> the same feeling, you're not 'one of the boys'). . .I don't know if
> I would take the job.

> I don't particularly want to [become a foreman]. I always look at
> foremen as a sort of chopping block. I've done a deputy foreman's
> job. . .Well, as a deputy it wasn't that I couldn't handle the job —
> some of the things they ask you to do, they're just out of order
> but you have to go and ask the men to do it.

The understanding of the social consequences of promotion in these
and many other replies shows that although the future is seen as
holding out definite possibilities for most craftsmen, few actually take
the step either through applying for or being offered a position and
accepting. Of course those who are prepared to take the step are
usually no less aware of the consequences than the others, including
the adoption of a new reference group; they simply have a more
sanguine view of the intrinsic, financial and status rewards. An
interesting point can be made concerning financial rewards, however.
Some respondents were invited to estimate the additional earnings of
foremen and they were invariably conservative in their estimate which
varied from as little as £2 to £3 per week to £7 to £8 per week (little
more in fact than could be earned by doing permanent shift work).
At the time of the study, the foremen in the plant were actually among
the highest paid (nationally) within this industry. It is well known

(largely due to Runciman's studies of 'relative deprivation') that popular estimates of the earnings of other occupational groups tend both to be extremely inaccurate and consistently underestimate the extent of actual differentials. The ignorance of the fitters is not therefore out of the ordinary but neither should it be seen as the reason for the craftsmen's lack of career consciousness. Rather, it can itself be interpreted as a function of the characteristic consciousness of this group, regardless of whether the craft as a social entity or as work is the main referent. Both are part of the 'craft consciousness' of the fitters but, according to which aspect is emphasised, they can lead to different orientation to the future. On the one hand, if the emphasis is on the group for reference, the foreman's role may be conceived as a fundamentally new social relation beset with problems, and if work is stressed, as a position enabling the exercise of new, higher and more varied skills not qualitatively different from those of the craft itself. The relative importance of these two aspects in any assessment of the future cannot be understood within the framework of the occupation itself. Like other forms of social consciousness, craft consciousness is not just an image of an occupation or even a normative orientation. Its object is the world of work as a whole and the relation of the craft to other occupations. It therefore allows for different interpretations of the foreman's role and contrasts in behaviour, within a single mode of consciousness.

Mobility Versus Security

The theme of mobility and security which dominates horizontal movement is complementary to the theme of vertical movement within the plant. Few of the sample of fitters were contemplating a move at the time of study. On the basis of replies to the question: 'have you considered moving to another job since coming here?' within the general context of discussion of comparative earnings in other local plants, only 9 per cent said that they had actively explored the labour market in any way. Of the remainder, 61 per cent claimed not to have thought seriously about this, considering a future move to be unlikely and 30 per cent said it was out of the question for reasons of age or otherwise. Among craftsmen with transferable skills in a relatively favourable market position, this result may be considered surprising. In fact, that very flexibility means that factors extrinsic to work assume unusual importance.

One of the most important extrinsic rewards from work is of course the money earned. As we have already seen in the case of shift work, readiness to accept inconvenience or simply change in work cannot be linked directly with monetary incentives. Income, or rather additional income, must be interpreted in the broader context of the meaning which the craftsman attributes to his work as a whole. The other possible extrinsic rewards which enter the picture are relations at work with other craftsmen and with the firm in general and the relation of the craftsman to his work.

When faced with a more specific question about their 'projects' for the future the craftsman's replies reflect the general lack of incentive to move which we have just noted. Only 6 per cent claimed to have any current plan for a move (whether or not they had actually reached the stage of application or interviews). Twelve per cent said that they did have plans which they had now abandoned and the remaining 82 per cent appeared never to have had a definable project which would have taken them outside the plant or the firm. This cannot simply be attributed to lack of opportunities or even a tradition of immobility within the occupation. Being employed in a large international corporation there were good prospects of working overseas in the short or long term for a substantially increased income. And the Scottish tradition of emigration provided many of those interviewed with examples of successful mobility within their own family or circle of acquaintances.

For the large majority of craftsmen their image of the future can be regarded as being directed towards the preservation of their existing relations within and outside the firm, a direction which is based to a large extent on an assessment of the economic position of the firm within a national or even international context. Hence all but a few of the fitters judged their position as an employee to be secure and likely to remain so by virtue of the fact that petroleum products and by-products are central to the smooth running of almost every aspect of life in modern society. As one craftsman expressed it: 'oil is the hub of industry'. They regarded the industry and their employment within it as relatively privileged within the industrial context as a whole. Conditions were frequently mentioned as being particularly good including the fact that maintenance work is generally less arduous and tedious than production work. Wages, although regarded as approximately equivalent to those in corresponding types of work, did not figure prominently in their assessments except in the 'fringe' aspects of provision for sickness and retirement, which were highly regarded.

Although previous mobility between firms was higher among the craftsmen than in the other two samples, and this is generally to be expected given the nature of both craft and maintenance work in modern industries, there are still many constraints upon movement when this is interpreted as a search for security and predictability in a relatively hostile market for labour. Most of the craftsmen had reached the point (and this point does not appear to coincide with a particular age or stage in the occupational 'career') at which alternatives were defined negatively in relation to their present position, reflecting a commitment which is stable and unlikely to be altered by minor changes in external, or for that matter, internal, circumstances.

Careers in the Melting Shop

Unlike the engineering craftsman who acquires skills in a variety of work situations, the skills of the steel melter are highly specific to a production process and even to a type of furnace. They are learned over a long period of time in subordinate positions in the melting shop and through gradual introduction to a collective stock of experience. In the steelworks where the study was carried out, the steel furnaces were of the open hearth type, operated continuously on a three-shift basis by teams of melters under the direction of a first hand who is responsible for its satisfactory operation. Modern instrumentation has not entirely removed the need to judge the appearance of the furnace and recognise the condition of the charge. Thus the first hand is the one with the longest experience and, in theory at least, the one with the greatest skill in judging the requirements of the process. The extent to which this is actually the case can be assessed by looking at the same 'career' stages as were described among the group of craftsmen.

Into Work

The notion that occupational socialisation occurs before actual entry into the world of work through agencies such as the family, school and peer group, receives as much support in the group of steelworkers as it did among the fitters. There is an equally close correspondence between father's occupation and the present position of the first hand melter as there was in the previous group. In only one case was the father's occupation − that of policeman − in sharp contrast to the labouring or semi-skilled jobs in the main local industries of iron, steel, coal mining, which were the general rule. And if the presence of members of the same family in a firm is indicative of an occupational 'tradition' and 'community', then the steelworkers score highly, as 47 per cent of them had close relations who worked, or had previously worked at the plant.

In view of the high average age (58) of the steelworkers and the time elapsed since entering employment, any account of this event should be regarded as an interpretation in the light of present conditions rather than as an accurate description of the state of mind at the time. For nearly all the steelworkers the first few years of work, after leaving school at 14, were spent in a variety of jobs in the shop and distributive trades. This transition period almost certainly benefited hard-pressed families in the interwar depression period but these jobs were in no sense an entry into work capable of providing an independent future. Accounts of the search for work at the age of 16 or later are overwhelmingly dominated by the theme of lack of choice and the harsh conditions of the labour market in the 1930s. It is not possible to divide the sample according to expectations as was the case with the craftsmen, on the basis of a view of the job or trade. The homogeneous social background reinforced by the market condition for labour left little room for alternatives. The only significant difference in this world of basic industries and basic existence was between being in work and being out of work. Although it is impossible to discover under which circumstances, if any, it was possible to escape to another environment, it is significant that none of the steelworkers confessed to having occupational aspirations outside their actual sphere of work. Occasionally negative feelings were expressed with regard to mining as an alternative: 'at that time [1930] steel was the only place with any prospect of a job, but the mines, and I didn't want to go in the mines.' One worker stated that he had 'gone idle' for two and a half years in preference to working in a mine, claiming that mining 'had ruined his father'.

Under these circumstances, it is hardly surprising that the family in the world of work is often seen doing the work of a direct agent as well as being a prior socialising agent. More than one fifth of the steelworkers stated that a member of their family had been instrumental in getting them a job at the steelworks, usually by 'speaking for them' to a foreman. The influence of the family is also felt in the supply and processing of information about jobs in local industries, although in the last resort, as several workers described, the search involved 'trying everywhere . . .it was the depression years, you just went out and looked for a job wherever you got it'. In an area which has known continuously high rates of unemployment even since the war, such experiences have remained alive and still inform descriptions of the world of work. The iron and steel industry still dominates the local market for jobs yet the future of these jobs is in doubt. The situation

has, of course, changed since the workers interviewed began work, not
least because of the possibility of travelling to work over much longer
distances and as a result of the establishment of a handful of new
industries. But it has not changed enough to invalidate the
steelworker's description which compares past hardship with present
difficulties and the inevitability of their own entry into the only
available sphere of employment with the continued lack of
occupational choice.

Consolidation

Market conditions for labour, however difficult, are not adequate to
explain the very long service of most of the steelworkers and their
correspondingly simple occupational histories. For this we must refer
to conditions internal to the plant. The melting shop particularly in an
open hearth works of the old type provides an occupational microcosm
which, once entered, can provide the worker with a lifetime's career —
a source of commitment and integrated experience to provide a
developing social and personal identity.

In contrast to the formally undifferentiated occupational world of
the craftsmen and their relative independence of work organisation,
the steel melter even as a fourth hand becomes part of a team which
demands a high level of commitment. The rewards of steelmaking both
financial and psychological are embodied in the occupational and
professional pride of the first hand who, as one worker put it 'was really
an idol, he was a big man in those days, a really big man'. These rewards
were available to anyone prepared to endure the logic of the seniority
system and learn the skills of eye and hand required to operate a
furnace. However, these skills are highly specific to a particular process,
even to types of furnace, and they therefore tie the experienced worker
with an increasingly firm bond. Many comments testify that the
furnace (which is attributed with a 'feminine' temperament and usually
referred to as 'she') is capable of provoking a wide range of human
feelings but they nearly all represent a form of attachment. The
dependence of the steel melter on the furnace includes dependence on
fellow-workers, for here is a socio-technical system in which relatively
relaxed periods of caretaking alternate with periods of intense and
closely co-ordinated activity in physically difficult and hazardous
conditions. Such dependence of course carries its own rewards in terms
of recognition and solidarity. Moreover, this is reinforced by the
homogeneity of the community and the fact that work in the melting
shop is invariably shift work. For the steel melter, therefore, his job *is*

his furnace, his team and his plant; so much so that a move within the plant (to the soaking pit for example) is no less an upheaval than moving to a different company or works.

Getting On

Since all the first hand steel melters were at their peak of their careers and within sight of retiring age, the key to their occupational self image lies in their past, rather than in future aspirations. This past can be regarded as an experience once defined by alternatives which had a future aspect. Whether or not these alternatives represented genuine possibilities for change has little relevance; their existence in consciousness is essential to defining and making sense of an occupational career. Clues to this are found in replies to those questions which elicited generalised interpretations as well as information on careers in the melting shop.

The melters were virtually unanimous in the view that they had no further to go, that they had reached the top. In theory, a first hand can become an assistant sample passer and a sample passer. (This is a supervisory position carrying responsibility for the tapping of a furnace but not for its routine functioning.) In the past, sample passers were regarded as an aristocracy among steelworkers, earning up to ten times the wage of a labourer. These differentials were reinforced by patterns of dress and behaviour untypical of steelworkers in general. As one sample passer explained, 'when there was a death in the melting shop, sample passers would turn out in frock coats' and they were not averse to displaying other symbols of status. Small differences of dress remain, but other signs of privilege have all but disappeared, leaving the sample passer in the position of the aristocrat déclassé. The end of the promotion line for the large majority of melters is the position of responsibility for the furnace; advancement into supervisory positions occurs in the remainder of cases and presupposes technical aptitude and willingness to assume a different kind of responsibility. Such an offer of promotion was turned down in one case among the melters interviewed. He can be regarded as a spokesman for most of the others when he said: 'I've reached the top of the tree — you're not a melter until you're a first hand.'

Progress to the top is made strictly according to seniority. There is no formal recognition of differences of skill and experience among melters, although these may emerge in performance figures and be reflected in personal relationships. Hence the only threat to steady progress in the line of promotion is from factors which are extrinsic to performance in the work task: redundancy, closure of the plant and accidents (one of the workers interviewed had been obliged to become a stocktaker at a much lower income following an accident). In contrast to the craftsmen, therefore, the occupational image of the steelworkers can be said to be a single mode of consciousness which combines awareness of the work task with an awareness of the furnace team as a social entity. It is a mode which relies very little, if at all, on comparison with other occupations. The reason why such a lengthy wait — up to thirty years — to become a first hand melter is endured, according to one worker is

> because the top man on a furnace is the one that's earning money. Therefore the man at the bottom of the tree is quite prepared to accept because one day he might be a first hand, because he's in the line of promotion. That's the reason why we accept these things and why the steelworker is contented — everything is in the line of promotion. . .his big day will come.

Whether or not this emphasis on income differentials is general, the plans and projects found among the craftsmen which implied reference to the wider sphere of employment were absent from the group of steelworkers and, it can be assumed, would have been absent even at an earlier stage in their career. In fact, only two of the melters claimed to have considered moving to a different job since entering the steel industry and only then at a very early stage, prior to promotion.

As far as general assessment of the factors relevant to 'getting on' at work are concerned, Table 2 shows that the steelworkers as a group are both more consistent in their judgements (i.e. a high proportion agree on the importance of certain factors) and appeal to a smaller range of factors than did the craftsmen. Within the limitations of the method which uses preselected items, Table 2 shows a predictable lack of emphasis on both education and ascribed rather than achieved characteristics — predictable in view of the strict application of the seniority principle in promotion and the intuitive understanding which is a large part of the steelmaker's skill. To an even greater extent than the craftsmen, the steelworkers emphasised intrinsic, personal qualities combining aptitude with motivation and application. There is little of the ambiguity with regard to formal qualifications and experience which was found among the craftsmen. For the majority of the steelworkers, education was lacking and was not missed, nor did it constitute a threat in the line of promotion. Its importance was recognised in other occupations and increasingly in steelmaking with more subtle instrumentation and manufacture of special steels. However, nearly all the first hands thought intelligence rather than education to be the necessary quality in their own sphere of work. It was to be seen, for example, in the second, third or fourth hand who learned the job in advance to be ready for promotion when it came.

Although 'ambition' was regarded by 72 per cent of the steelworkers as being necessary to 'getting on' at work, nearly the same proportion (67 per cent) denied being ambitious themselves or at least claimed that their ambition had been stunted by age. This may reflect the generally low morale of workers in a plant scheduled for closure but it is probably also indicative of the decline in the relative income and status of the first hand in recent years and even disappointment at reaching the 'top' only to find the perspective downwards rather shortened.

> When I came in here, my great aim was to come up into the melting shop and become a firsthand — not for any great love of the job, because I didn't even know what furnaces were like at that time, but it was the money that was the attraction. But since then, the money has deteriorated to a terrific [extent] . . .it used to be top wages that were paid to first hands, but not now.

Differentials have in fact been narrowed to the extent that unskilled workers in the 'cutting out squad' (labourers who remove the linings

Table 2: Assessment of Factors Relevant to Personal Advancement: Steelworkers

	Percentage who regard this factor as important
Intelligence	90
Ambition	72
Character	56
Hard work	44
Education	22
Knowing the right people	11
Social background	6
Luck	—
n = 18	

of old furnaces) can, with bonuses, earn as much as a first hand melter.

The close similarity between responses is almost certainly to be accounted for by the shared and highly integrated experience of a lifetime in the melting shop. The horizons of this experience are narrower and less varied than those of the craftsmen or the clerical workers and only in recent years have they been threatened by fundamental changes in wage differentials and the impending closure of the plant, which to a steelworker in a promotion line means a loss of seniority if he moves to another works.

Mobility Versus Security

The tight vertical structuring of the steel melter's career makes the question of horizontal movement largely irrelevant. Security and upward mobility are not in conflict. It is possible that this lack of horizontal mobility and any need to project an alternative future accounts for the almost complete absence of plans for retirement. Nearly all the first hands looked forward to their imminent retirement with apprehension as though it were a void. Only one expressed any pleasure at the prospect and only he and one other intended to look for alternative part-time or full time employment. This may be taken as evidence that for nearly all the workers in this sample, their work permeated their non-work activities, their values and their interests to such an extent that the prospect of retirement was almost literally 'unthinkable'. The lack of separation between work and non-work is often said to be the chief distinguishing feature of 'occupational communities', so that this high degree of fusion is sometimes held to be directly responsible for a distinctive image of society. In Chapter 6 we will give fuller consideration to the question of whether the steelworkers can actually be said to have an occupationally-based social consciousness.

Clerical Careers

Of the three samples, the clerical workers fit most closely into the conventional 'career' pattern of a structured set of positions filled according to performance and other criteria. In the insurance company concerned, the positions and grades are structured according to their relative value by a job evaluation procedure regarded by the management, as 'the most scientific method yet developed for this purpose'. However, as with the other two samples, there are stages which are common to each clerical worker regardless of his official position within the organisation. This official structure establishes the dimensions of the clerical career but its active component is to be found in the plans, hopes and fears which are associated with experiences common to each member of the group. For convenience and to allow comparisons to be made, we will discuss this experience under the headings used in the two previous sections. It is not, however, intended to deny the possibility that progress in the formal structure of the organisation may be more of a salient feature for the clerical workers than for the other groups studied. Or it may be that certain non-work experiences are just as central. According to Pahl, for instance, 'it is the tension between the conflicting value systems of home and work, or family and "career", which provides the dialectic of social reality for the middle class'.[10] For the moment we regard this as a hypothesis awaiting further confirmation.

Into Work

The notion that young people exercise a significant degree of choice in the jobs they enter receives little support from the experience of the clerical workers, even those in the younger age group. The distinct occupational stereotypes based on work tasks which provided a means of orientation for both the craftsmen and the steelworkers were lacking among the third sample. 'Office work' is not perceived to offer choices after the fashion of manual work in the mining and steel industries, for example. This contributes to an explanation of the fact that a third of the clerical workers attributed great importance to the influence of a Youth Employment Officer or school careers master in finding their first job. Of course, the direct intervention of a specialised institution does not reduce the importance of the other agencies of socialisation. The family continues to exert a decisive influence on expectations, while education cultivates and often reinforces these expectations. But the advice of specialists is one of the few ways to penetrate the subtleties of work in the large bureaucracies, which at least some of the sample felt destined for. The second most common method of entry into the first job was through advertisements in the press. More than a quarter explained that they had used this method and regarded their employment by one company rather than another as 'accidental' in view of their own lack of knowledge or preference. In the few cases where there existed an image of the occupation about to be entered, it can be accounted for either by direct parental influence (21 per cent of the sample had fathers in clerical jobs in either the Civil Service or in insurance) or by the image of the organisation itself as opposed to the nature of the work involved. One worker who described his entry to the insurance company as 'purely accidental' explained it as follows:

> I'd completed my studies as far as I could go at the High School. . .
> so I left and (as I thought) was destined for a Civil Service career.
> At that time my Civil Service appointment wouldn't be through
> until the start of the following year, so I took employment here.
> I settled in here quite well and decided not to pursue the Civil
> Service idea at all. [Why the Civil Service?] Largely that it seemed
> a reasonably sound form of employment and one in which you
> could advance by your own efforts without the benefits of a
> university education.

Above all, clerical occupations were regarded as 'very stable', 'safe'
and 'secure'. Significantly, none of the sample referred to intrinsic
features of the job in the way that craftsmen had referred to their
interest in machinery and natural aptitude for the work. Nor is it
possible to differentiate the clerical sample in the way that was possible
with the craftsmen, according to father's occupation. In contrast to the
steelworkers, for whom the job is no more and no less than the physical
task and the institutional means to carry it out, there are strong
indications that the job for the clerical worker is his career (in the
conventional sense) and that making a career is his lifetime's work.
Whether or not his view was held by each of the sample on entry into
the world of work, experience of the occupation up to the time of the
study had at least strongly encouraged this orientation.

Consolidation

Mobility within a single bureaucratic hierarchy has traditionally been
the mode of advancement of clerical workers. With increased
mechanisation and division of labour according to formal educational
qualifications, this is becoming less true — a fact which is reflected in
the previous horizontal mobility of younger workers in the sample.
A comparison of occupational histories shows that of the 58 per cent
who had been employed elsewhere previously (excluding National
Service) most had held jobs in insurance. Their move to the present
company can be seen as a form of adjustment to expectations of a
career, as several of the responses show.

> The [other company] was becoming a rat-race. The chances of
> promotion were nil.

I was with a small branch of the insurance company and although
I quite liked the work, I was still a junior clerk after four years,
stamping mail, etc. . . . .There didn't seem to be too much opportunity.

Taking into account the problems of a retrospective account of
behaviour and intention, there is nevertheless a strong contrast between
the emerging sense of purpose and concept of the career which these
responses display and the earlier responses which reveal 'nebulous ideas',
'no particular inclination' and anything but sights firmly set on a career
path in insurance. As was the case with the craftsmen, the growth of
commitment entails both a sense of identity with the organisation
which provides the career framework (and which provides work for the
craftsman) and a sense of opposition to the extent that it slows down
or prevents advancement. The gradual consolidation of commitment
for the clerical worker is a process in which both aspects of his
relationship to the organisation are enhanced.

A closer study of the reasons for moving to the present company
shows that a desire for security and a concern for 'opportunities' were
by far the most important considerations for the majority of the sample.
Allowing for more than one response per person, the reasons given
were: security (mentioned by 53 per cent); opportunities or prospects
of advancement (31 per cent); external reasons — for example, fears of
redundancy following a take-over (26 per cent); pecuniary (21 per
cent); and personal advice or encouragement from friends and relatives
(21 per cent). Comparing these results with the craftsmen's stated
reasons for moving, the most significant difference is the relative
importance of financial rewards and security in the two groups. It is
also interesting to note the relative importance of formal and informal
methods of finding employment. Whereas 29 per cent of the craftsmen
acknowledged the direct help of a union or management in finding their
present job (usually a transfer arranged in the event of redundancy)
none of the clerical workers had any such experience, although 21 per
cent of them were helped in some way by friends and acquaintances.
This experience of being an individual agent helps to account for the
stress on 'security', which is regarded as a state of personal safety
sheltered from the impersonal forces of business and bureaucratic
organisation. Dependence, which is the condition of all those who work
for a wage, can thus involve different combinations of personal and
impersonal elements. A consideration of these is necessary if we are to
understand the meaning of 'security' and the importance it has in the
career plans of the clerical workers.

Getting On

The concern for security cannot be regarded as a response to past experience of insecurity or even to a future threat. None of the clerical workers had been made redundant or had been unemployed and only one felt that there was even a slight possibility of this happening in the future. For most of them the prospect was so remote as to be right at the horizon of their occupational thinking. The following response is typical.

> I have never given serious thought to it. It would be a bit ironic if I were [made redundant]. It's not a thing that would happen to me in the foreseeable future. I haven't given it a great deal of thought.

Clearly the notion of security is not bound up with difficult experiences in the labour market nor with collective fears of such difficulties, which was the case with the steelworkers who intended at all costs to remain where they were. It is likely that security for the clerical workers means the sense of certainty which comes from well-founded confidence, if not in a brilliant future of boundless opportunities then at least in a position free from anxiety and apprehension. Whereas for the steelworkers, as we have seen, security literally means protection from the dangers of redundancy and unemployment.

The clerical workers' desire for security is not therefore incompatible with mobility plans. It appears in fact that plans to change jobs are more likely than not to be made from a position of security. Sixty-eight per cent of the sample had actively considered moving in search of a different job (i.e. had reached the stage of making an application, or of going for interviews) and several had turned down offers of alternative employment. These projects varied from plans to move to other local companies, to plans to start an independent broking business and applications to emigrate. Although there is no way of comparing those projects with the plans of workers who actually moved, there is one feature which indicates that plans are not always to be interpreted at their face value as the expression of a genuine desire to move. Some were expressions of the earlier stage of career consolidation. Other, usually current, plans appeared to be a means for workers to define their current situation in the broader occupational sphere and to reconcile themselves with it. Thus one worker who described his plans to move (which led to two recent interviews) as being prompted by 'frustration', was not prepared to bring an end to this by moving, even though he saw opportunities. Another, aged 35, claimed to look regularly in the press, but as if to dispel thoughts of moving.

> I wouldn't say I'm happy here, but this is probably where I'll end up. I don't see me changing — I don't think I've got much to offer anyone else; that's why I'll stay. Now I still look, but not seriously.

Unlike the steelworkers, whose well-defined world of the melting shop tended to define the main elements of non-work life, the dull certainty of the clerical career does not appear to be a defining characteristic of life outside work. Details of unrealised aspiration and ambitions show that they are often at least partly fulfilled in leisure activities. Nearly one third of the sample spoke of occupations with a high physical and active component such as flying, seagoing and professional sports. Nearly all of the remainder said that they had once hoped for occupations with a high degree of autonomy in business, teaching or the professions. Although very few of the sample defined their present situation *in terms* of these unrealised ambitions or aspirations, they took the form of a plausible alternative self-image used sometimes to highlight and sometimes to soften the image of a routine and monotonous existence.

Responses to the preselected items regarded as being most important for 'getting on' in a clerical job in insurance have a more diffuse pattern than was the case with the steelworkers. Moreover they reflect priorities which differ from both of the other samples. The possibility that the same items may be understood in different ways means that these results cannot be taken as more than an indication of trends in thinking but there is reason to believe that the items reflect standard concepts in judging career progress. Luck, for example, was defined by nearly all of those interviewed as a question of 'being in the right place at the right time'. Similarly, other concepts were readily defined by cliches such as 'having a face that fits' or 'it's not what you know, it's who you know'. The most striking feature of the results presented in Table 3 is the high priority give to 'luck'. Ambition and intelligence were emphasised by a large majority of the steelworkers and nearly half of the craftsmen. But the fact that these qualities were also emphasised by the clerical workers is tempered by the finding that 53 per cent of the sample (including many of those who gave priority to ambition and intelligence) regarded luck as one of the most important factors in personal advancement. Only a quarter

Table 3: Assessment of Factors Relevant to Personal Advancement: Clerical Workers

	Percentage who regard this factor as important
Ambition	58
Intelligence	58
Luck	53
Hard work	47
Education	42
Character	37
Knowing the right people	21
Social background	5
n = 19	

of the craftsmen thought of luck in this way and none of the steelworkers. It reflects the inherent ambiguity of the clerical worker's career and the possibility of interpreting it in either of two ways: as an equal competition with the best man winning or as an obstacle course with arbitrary handicaps. The obstacles, or the influence of luck on a career is seen as impersonal rather than personal, as the effect of organisational changes or, more simply, the death or departure of colleagues in the line of promotion. This explains the low prominence given to the other extrinsic factors ('knowing the right people' and 'social background') which are regarded either as irrelevant or pernicious.

The relation between intelligence and education in the assessments of the clerical workers is no less interesting than in the other two samples. Like the steelworkers, but unlike the craftsmen, they regarded intelligence (which includes notions such as commonsense and an ability to learn quickly) as more important than education. In fact, many of the sample were furthering their education in preparing for professional examination and interpreted education as the formal qualifications obtained at school. There is therefore a deliberate emphasis on intrinsic, personal attributes and ability combined with application which is a feature of the other two samples. However, in place of the stress on personal influence ('knowing the right people') which was found among the craftsmen, the clerical workers chose to emphasise the impersonal and arbitrary features of their career.

The application of these general concepts is to be seen in

interpretations of the future possibilities and limits of advancement. Nearly all the clerical workers had reached positions of supervisory responsibility and were nearing the end of the clerical grades. Since most of them had reached this stage long before the end of their careers — usually between the ages of 30 and 40 — it is perhaps surprising that none expressed any confidence in future promotion prospects. In theory, and to a large extent in practice in the past, some clerical workers could expect to reach the position of a junior official of the company. With the increasing professionalisation of management and with the introduction of actuaries and actuarial trainees into junior management positions, these opportunities have now been dramatically curtailed. Hence the general pessimism and even hostility towards the 'change in management attitudes', the introduction of 'outsiders' and the actuarial 'closed shop'. In view of this change, the two remaining ways to get ahead in the company are regarded as that of the actuary and that of the salesman in a branch office. Reasons of age and education prevented any of the sample from seriously contemplating these as alternatives.

Mobility Versus Security

With the effective curtailment of career prospects to one or two grades in the clerical system, the sense of pessimism and frustration which is to be found in many of the replies is hardly surprising. On the other hand, there is an equally strong sense of resignation which is expressed in such terms as

> I've made use of opportunities insofar as they did exist.

> I've had moments when I really thought I was going places and then a couple of years later you found you weren't really going that far! From now on I can't see a new position being created.

> If I'd been astute enough I should have got out years ago and bettered myself. But it's pointless saying that, because I haven't. . . When I joined, I became part of [the company] — whether it was right or wrong is irrelevant.

The final remark provides the clue to the problem of reconciling an apparently high level of dissatisfaction with a failure to initiate mobility plans. Not only is there a negative feeling that a move endangers a secure position but there exists a positive pull which the worker described as 'being part of the company'. And far from being an isolated sentiment, this can be regarded as one of many feelings of 'attachment' to the organisation. Sometimes seen in terms of 'teamwork' or 'family feeling', sometimes experienced as individual fate bound up with the fortunes of the company, this attachment evokes a sense of loyalty and allegiance even among the disaffected. It is this sense of being 'for the company' which is one of the distinguishing marks of the occupational and social consciousness of this group. It is not a 'career consciousness' in the conventional sense, since the career paths of many of the clerical workers were truncated and, at best, unpredicatable. Nor is it a consciousness of unequivocal loyalty to the employing organisation. It is a unique combination of the principles of identity and opposition in a principle of totality which we will label 'collusive' consciousness.[11] A full description of this, and the image of society to which it is intimately linked, will be the subject of Chapter 7.

The essentially descriptive account of this chapter has prepared the way for the analysis of 'occupational consciousness' in its various guises. We have identified the major occupational constraints on each group of workers and have indicated their potential for personal advancement. These descriptions immediately suggest certain themes: the 'craft consciousness' of the fitters, for example, or what we have called the 'collusive consciousness' of the workers in the insurance company. However, this is only the beginning of the analysis of images of society. There are at least two further problems to be solved. Firstly, changes in the occupational sphere, including the long-term evolution of work processes, have to be assessed to find out whether the occupational basis of social consciousness is being undermined or transformed. And secondly, the possibility that similar experiences of work and community may generate very different images of society has to be taken into account. These are the main concerns of the chapters which follow.

Notes

1. E. Goffman, *Asylums* (Harmondsworth, 1968), p.119.
2. There are few specific studies in this area, but relevant material may be found in G. Williams, *Recruitment to Skilled Trades* (London, 1957); M.P. Carter, *Home, School and Work* (London, 1962); E. Tonkinson *et al.*, *Commercial Apprenticeships* (University of London Press, 1962).
3. See E.T. Keil, C. Riddell, B.S.R. Green, 'Youth and Work: Problems and Perspectives', *Sociol. Rev.*, 14 (1966), p.130.
4. D.N. Ashton, 'The Transition from School to Work', *Sociol. Rev.*, 21 (1973), p.103.

5. W. Liversidge, 'Life Chances', in W.M. Williams (ed.), *Occupational Choice* (University of Keele, 1974), p.74.

6. K. Roberts, 'The Entry into Employment', in W.M. Williams (ed.), *Occupational Choice*, p.147.

7. See for example E. Ginzberg *et al., Occupational Choice: an Approach to a General Theory* (New York, 1951).

8. Cf. K. Roberts, in W.M. Williams, *Occupational Choice*.

9. See for instance, M. Dalton, 'The Role of Supervision', in A. Kornhauser, R. Dubin, A.M. Ross (eds), *Industrial Conflict* (New York, 1954), pp.176 ff.

10. J.M. and R.E. Pahl, *Managers and their Wives* (Harmondsworth, 1971), p.107.

11. 'Collusion' may be defined as a secret understanding which usually contains an element of deception. R.D. Laing's use of the term, admittedly in a different context, gives some idea of what is meant here. 'Collusion has resonances of playing at and deception. It is a "game" played by two or more people whereby they deceive themselves. . .each plays the other's game, although he may not necessarily be fully aware of doing so. An essential feature of this game is not admitting that it is a game. . .A slave may collude with his master in being a slave to save his life, even to the point of carrying out orders that are self-destructive.' R.D. Laing, *Self and Others* (Harmondsworth, 1971), p.108.

5 CRAFT CONSCIOUSNESS: THE MAINTENANCE FITTERS

If there is such a thing as social consciousness which is occupationally based, it is reasonable to suppose that it will be found especially among workers who can relate to a set of work tasks in an intrinsically meaningful way. The maintenance craftsmen, and skilled workers in general, fall into this category.

The term 'craft consciousness' is therefore chosen here to designate the theme which, more than any other, helps to make sense of the statements, images and Topoi of the maintenance workers. The use of an apparently simple term like this has its dangers. For example, it may be equated with 'commonsense' or everyday understandings of craft and craftsmanship. Alternatively, it can become a category with a static content (e.g. a specified range of attitudes, convictions and feelings about something) instead of a means of analysing and explaining these continually changing phenomena. Thus it might be used, for instance, to describe and differentiate between occupational groups in terms of whether or not they display 'craft' characteristics. But it is potentially a much more dynamic tool, especially if it used to designate a relationship, a particular form of *Leistungsbewusstsein* or consciousness of achievement in work.

The sense of 'having a trade' or 'being a tradesman' is so central to the maintenance worker's self-description that it provides an immediate starting point. However, in focusing on the 'craft' aspects of maintenance work we do not intend to exclude other aspects which might be equally relevant, including the erosion of skills and the dynamics of growth and decline in the labour market. As we shall see, these are important. Craft consciousness is not an expression of the craftsman's oneness with the world and his work. Nor is it the opposite. During the study there was a general absence of overt conflict between the fitters and other workers and between the fitters and management. Expressions of conflict in terms of absenteeism, high rates of labour turnover and restrictive practices were at a very low level. However, the interests of employers and employees in a capitalist society must always be opposed in certain ways in the long term, so this apparent lack of conflict is no less a problem to be explained than strikes or lockouts, had they occurred.

Craft Occupations

The term 'craft' (or trade) is widely used to denote a range of
occupations which can be distinguished from other kinds of manual
work by a number of special features. The most important of these is
usually considered to be skill level as measured by manual dexterity
and the exercise of judgement — abilities which are acquired during
an extended learning process such as the apprenticeship. The exercise
of skills is possible because the division of labour is not highly
differentiated; workers either construct the total product from raw
materials or make substantial contributions to it. In the craft
occupations this knowledge and these skills are used in a variety of
work situations or at least in a complex job with a range of integrated
component tasks, even if the task is repeated. By virtue of his
specialised knowledge, which means that the instructions he receives
are for a completed product, the craftsman in theory has power to
control the amount of work done. Even if there is not complete
autonomy, control tends to be in the shape of norms of professional
competence so that it is more internal than external. By the same
token he is free to choose his own work methods. Supervision is
therefore at a minimum. Another feature is that whatever the scale or
sophistication of the machinery and technology he is concerned with,
the craftsman is in a position to control, and he usually operates with
manually-controlled work implements.

According to surveys of attitudes and adjustment to work there is
evidence that occupations with the above features are conducive to
high degree of involvement and self-esteem and are relatively low on
'alienation'.[1] However, it is by no means certain or self-evident that
the crafts are seen in this fashion by craftsmen themselves.
'Craftsmanship' as popularly understood may not be directly related
to the craft occupations or the skilled trades. Bensman and Lilienfeld
for example apply the term to a certain kind of technique or method
in any occupation. According to this rather romantic conception the
technique pertaining to each occupation 'induces' or 'creates' a special
consciousness or occupational perspective.

> There is an autonomy in the development of craft technique,
> attitudes towards materials and media, and the development of skill
> and virtuosity, which are indigenous to an occupation. They give it
> distinct and peculiar characteristics of its own. They create a sense
> of pride, loyalties, and attitudes of virtuosity and craftsmanship

which isolate occupations from each other regardless of the similarities of their relationship to the market or to the ownership of capital.[2]

It is not surprising that these authors only examine a range of non-manual, mainly professional, intellectual and artistic occupations. Few hourly-paid employees in the modern trades would recognise themselves in this account.

There are of course many lines of division within the craft occupations. Of these, perhaps the most important is the division between maintenance and production work, which has to be kept in mind in the following account. In traditional craft jobs the division of labour is based on specialisation with respect to a total product or a large section of that product, which means that the relevant skills are in many cases not transferable to other industries or occupations. The traditional manufacture of boots and shoes would be a case in point. And in the steel industry, the melter's trade may be directly threatened by quite specific technical and economic changes. On the other hand, maintenance craftsmen are much more likely to possess skills which are not tied to specific products and processes. Even if they are industry-specific (skilled trades in ship-repairing, for example) they are potentially applicable in any branch of engineering. Maintenance is very likely to be associated with a high degree of involvement because maintenance craftsmen — especially in process production plants — are required to understand not only the theoretical basis of their own activities, but also have a general understanding of the production processes. They consequently have considerable perception of how their work is related to the work of others because work tasks are dispersed throughout a plant and they frequently require co-operation between different crafts. It is not surprising, therefore, to hear the following sentiments being expressed:

The satisfaction in the craft side is when you've done a big job and it's run up, finished — everything completed and it's running well. Somebody turns round to you and says: 'that's fine, it's going well.' That's the craft satisfaction. . .The oil industry is interesting in the sense that there's quite a bit to it (compare mining: all you see is coal coming off the face, up, and going away in a truck). But here you can see more, throughout the plant you can see oil coming in (mucky black stuff) and at the other end you get stuff that's clear, like water. And so it's a wider aspect in here. . .there's so many things that can be done with oil.

It may be for these reasons, as Mallet suggested in his study of the Caltex refinery maintenance workers, that their conditions of working are closer to those of the earlier artisan occupations than other modern craft occupations:

> The maintenance services, recruited from highly skilled workers in the metal, engineering and electrical industries, enjoy. . .full and complete responsibility within the limits of their function. Their conditions of work are closer to those of former artisans than to those they experienced in the engineering industries from whence they came.[3]

Factors internal to the work situation combine with the craftsman's relatively advantageous position in the labour market (possession of a scarce commodity — skill) to produce the high levels of 'satisfaction' which a number of investigators have claimed to observe, at least when the skilled trades are compared with industrial work which is characterised by fragmentation, lack of responsibility and mechanical pacing.[4]

The craftsman's position in the broader context of economic and technical change also merits attention. It is clear that the knowledge and skills acquired through a long period of training are likely to put the craftsman in a strong market position, provided that the demand for these skills does not diminish or disappear. In traditional craft types of production (shoe manufacture, cooperage, etc.) this is a very real danger because mechanisation can remove a large proportion of the necessary knowledge and skills. In these occupations the skills are job-specific and are not interchangeable. This was recognised as long ago as 1920 by Goodrich, who argued that craft control was a survival from an earlier technology and would not survive the process of technical change.[5] More recently Braverman has described the degradation of skills from a similar perspective.[6]

In our view, these arguments are correct in describing the general process of mechanisation and automation as leading to the displacement, de-skilling and de-humanisation of the labour force. However, they do not accurately describe the fate of the categories of skilled maintenance worker depicted here. Some crafts have been more resistant to change than might have been anticipated. In maintenance work especially, the skills in metalworking, electrical, joinery and other trades are not

specific to a particular task, nor indeed to a particular industry. For
example, to be apprenticed as a fitter in a foundry does not preclude
the use of the skills acquired there in a power station or an oil refinery;
the basic knowledge and skills are transferable, and a craftsman is
expected to understand and adapt to technical changes in much the
same way as a professional is trained to apply a body of knowledge
and techniques to a whole range of situations.

In the chemical and petroleum refining industries there is one
feature which disturbs the maintenance worker's apparently favourable
position. Increasingly, the technology is being developed in such a way
that maintenance during the normal functioning of a plant is minimal
and nearly all maintenance is carried out during the shut-downs which
occur at regular and predictable intervals.[7] This obviously has
considerable repercussions on manning patterns.[8] For instance, the
numbers employed in scheduled and breakdown maintenance can be
drastically reduced and the peak demand for labour can be met by
using contractors, a practice which appears to be more widespread in
Germany and other European countries than in Britain.[9] This freedom
to use contract labour is considered by management to be important in
preventing breakdown or damage to plant but, like other attempts by
management to achieve 'flexibility', it can represent a threat to job
security.

Differences between crafts should not be allowed to obscure the
more fundamental cleavage within the manual working class which
helps to account for differences in social consciousness. Some of the
consequences of this division between the skilled and the unskilled for
the history of the working class and its alleged accommodation to
capitalist society have been investigated by historians and sociologists.[10]
There is a conceptual difficulty here, however, because 'skills' can be
measured on a continuous scale. What justification can there be for
identifying a special category or 'aristocratic' group? 'Labour
aristocracy' has a long history of use as a term to distinguish groups of
skilled workers from unskilled workers, and its use by Hobsbawm
suggests that there are some parallel features between such groups in
the nineteenth century and their present-day counterparts. Hobsbawm
points out that the level and regularity of worker's earnings are by far
the most important factors by which skilled manual workers can be
distinguished from the rest of the working class and that the history
of the labour aristocracy under nineteenth-century capitalism (and
subsequently under monopoly capitalism) can be interpreted in terms
of their efforts to protect and consolidate their relatively privileged

position.[11] The political consequences of this are not immediately obvious: a tendency towards either conservatism or radicalism might be an equally appropriate response. But it is the broad changes in the work and market contexts − for instance the shift in the centre of gravity of the labour aristocracy from traditional crafts to the metal industries, and the growth in the number of semi-skilled operatives with relatively high and stable earnings − which must provide an explanation of the paradox which has been observed in the area of industrial conflict. At times, the labour aristocracy has been in the vanguard of labour movements, while at other times it has adopted a reactionary stance more typical of non-manual working groups.

These tensions can still be identified to some extent in the union to which all the maintenance fitters in this study belong − the Amalgamated Engineering Union. The AEU retains important internal features of craft unionism; but in other respects it is more like an industrial union for the engineering and allied trades and in still others it appears as an occupational union of mechanics and metal workers in general. Historically, the reasons for its expansion have been to provide a means to control the changing wage differentials which were beginning to appear in the metalworking industries − changes which threatened the standards of the skilled workers. The present diverse composition of membership − wide range of skills, work, industries − helps to account for the rather disturbed history of factional disputes within the AEU.

The Maintenance Fitters

In most respects, the work performed by the sample of fitters can be shown to include the characteristics of 'craft' occupations as defined above. The fitters make up the bulk of the maintenance work force in the plant (although electricians, instrument artificers, welders, etc. are also represented) − all qualified craftsmen who have served their time in an apprenticeship for at least four years. They carry out a wide variety of work tasks and although the allocation of jobs is made to a certain extent on the basis of differences in skill and experience, all craftsmen are expected to be capable of completing most of the tasks in routine maintenance without close supervision. Job differentiation has chiefly to do with the different processes and services which occur in a petro-chemical process plant. Work is organised by sections, such as the cracking plants basic to the refining of crude oils, plants producing by-products, the power station, vehicle and engine repair. A substantial number of fitters work in the central maintenance workshop where jobs requiring the use of lathes, drills and other heavy machine tools are carried out.

It should be noted that changes in continuous process technology over the last 10 to 20 years — especially the integration of process units, reduction in storage capacity and compaction of supporting services — has led to a downgrading of some of the skills required in fitting. The most obvious change is the increase in the amount of work which is simply replacement as opposed to repair. On the other hand, innovations have included the installation of new compressors and other machinery which requires the learning of new (and sometimes more advanced) skills.

In all the sections of the plant, tasks are carried out with a maximum of autonomy and a minimum of supervision. For the most simple jobs such as the replacement of valves, or pipework, there is virtually no supervision — the job is allocated, and because the relevant piece of machinery is likely to be isolated from the other centres of activity, the worker only sees his supervisor on completion of the job, or in the event of unforeseen technical problems. In other situations, where complex machinery like a compressor or centrifuge is under repair, there is much closer and more frequent interaction between the craftsmen, foremen and engineering staff, but it is of the consultative kind.

The role of the maintenance workers is quite different from that of the process worker, the other main group within the plant itself. (There are less skilled members of the labour force, but the ratio of mates to fitters is approximately 1:3.) The highest grades of process personnel are paid less than the maintenance workers for a job which, despite Blauner's finding that continuous process production systems are less likely to produce 'alienation' of workers than large-scale mechanised production systems, is characterised by a limited range of tasks which demand relatively few skills and which need only a short period of training. Although it was not possible to observe contacts between maintenance and process workers, occasional spontaneous references were made in interviews to the frictions between the two groups — usually arising from incompatible demands to both keep up production and carry out essential maintenance work.

Contacts with staff are generally limited to brief encounters with engineers, the frequency of these contacts again depending on the nature of the work in hand. Informal contacts are also minimal. Staff and workers' canteens are adjacent but separate and the offices have a separate access apart from the rest of the site.

With these features of the work situation in mind, we can now turn to the situation as perceived by the workers themselves. Both the workers' own description of their work and answers to more specific questions designed to evoke self-images and conceptions of the firm form the basis for the following analysis of 'craftsmanship'. Despite the lack of overt differentiation within the group of fitters, it became clear from the responses that neither skills nor work tasks were evenly distributed. In other words, most workers acknowledged the fact that some fitters were more skilled than others and that, without any formal distinctions being made, they were entitled to a large share of the more complex and demanding tasks. Allocation of tasks (the responsibility of the labour co-ordinator and foremen) according to criteria of skill and interests was recognised as being legitimate. However, the introduction of the grading of craftsmen — which is not an unusual practice in the engineering industries — was rejected, as was a scheme to introduce a pay differential for craftsmen involved in on-the-job training of apprentices. This indicates a certain level of group consciousness at the plant level, but there is little indication that the group of craftsmen in the refinery see themselves as part of a wider reference group of craftsmen with common interests in other firms and industries.

'The Good Craftsman'

As a general question to conclude the section on 'the work task' in the interview schedule, and to elicit the respondent's own definition of the craftsman, the following form was used, with minor variations: 'What would you say it takes to be a good craftsman?'

A number of themes, some of which recur quite frequently, appear in the replies. Listed in order of frequency, they are as follows:

1.	Commonsense; intelligence; a bit of education.	8
2.	Conscientiousness; pride in work; discipline; hard work.	8
3.	Interest in the job; dedication.	6
4.	Experience.	3
5.	Clear thinking; steady nerves.	3
6.	Patience; even temperament.	3
7.	Natural ability.	1
8.	Technical skill; knowing how to use the tools.	1
9.	Don't know.	6

(Of the 30 cases for which data is available, a possible maximum of two themes is recorded).

Many of the replies, and especially those in categories 1 and 2, were given without hesitation and included words and phrases which had not been used before, which suggests that certain common assumptions or ideals (i.e. Topics) have been received and incorporated into the definition which workers have. Some typical responses in the first category run as follows:

> Commonsense: think about the job you've got — you've got to plan it — just stand back and look at it, then away you go. I'd say commonsense to start with; reasonable intelligence. . .You've got to have a wee bit of intelligence as regards the type of work you're doing — commonsense comes an awful lot into it. And taking a pride in your work, too. . .leaving a job tidy.

The second most frequent theme was that of interest in the job:

> A man who is dedicated to his work, who takes care what he's doing is really wanting to make a good job of it, instead of just hashing about. . .If you really take an interest in it; if you've got pride in a job.

In the majority of cases, therefore, the meaning of 'craftsman' was more a question of undefined personality attributes than work-specific experience and skills. The latter may simply be assumed, so that the result is determined by the form of the question. But whether or not this is so, the cliches of 'commonsense' and application are clearly of some importance; their source (possibly in the socialisation process of apprenticeship) and relation to actual industrial behaviour needs to be elaborated.

These responses, which reveal something of the 'pride in work' aspect of the craft ideal among the majority of those interviewed, should be set alongside other responses (sometimes from the same individuals) which indicate a much lower degree of involvement in work, something verging on an 'instrumental' attitude. One fitter saw it as a fundamental division in the maintenance workforce: '50 per cent are here for the money, because it's a job and only a job; and 50 per cent love their job — they're in love with their job and wouldn't say anything against it. . .It prevents a lot of strikes; there's half that like their job and are quite content with their wages.' He described his own attitude as — 'willing to work anywhere as long as I get my money.' There is no evidence that this division has anything to do with age

differences. It implies instead that even craft work can have a variety
of meanings, which may be either complementary or contradictory.
The replies to the question on perceptions of the enterprise help to
show how this is possible, as craftsmen relate themselves and each
other to the structures of authority in the firm.

We chose to introduce this subject in the form of a question which
has frequently been put to workers in attitude and perception studies.
This is not because the question is inherently satisfactory or even
particularly coherent. On the contrary, it was an opportunity to use it
to demonstrate the problems involved and to test the rather hasty
conclusions drawn by other workers in this area. The question (Q.23)
presents the respondent with two contrasting images of the firm: one
in which 'teamwork' prevails because it is to everybody's advantage and
another which regards teamwork as impossible because employers and
employees are really on opposite sides. The respondent is then asked to
say which he agrees with most, and why. Normally, only two choices
are offered or construed from the replies. The two views are taken to
express in a very simplified form two of the main emphases in
sociological theory — consensus and conflict respectively. Previous
studies which have used the question in this form have generally
assumed that expressions of agreement with one view or the other can
be taken as evidence to validate either of the two theories.[12] One of
the few investigators to cast serious doubt on the use of this question
is Ramsay, who argues that the unitary view of the firm has far fewer
adherents than is suggested by the usual interpretation of the question
and responses.[13] However, the way in which the 'unitary' or consensus
view is taken up by the workers is important because it colours the
whole picture of the industrial firm in conventional thinking. Fox has
called this the 'unitary ideology' and he characterises it in the following
terms:

> A unitary system has one source of authority and one focus of
> loyalty, which is why it suggests the team analogy. What pattern of
> behaviour do we expect from members of a successful and healthily-
> functioning team? We expect them to strive jointly towards a
> common objective, each pulling his weight to the best of his ability.
> Each accepts his place and his function gladly, following the
> leadership of the one so appointed. . .[14]

Fox maintains that this represents a vision of what industry ought to
be like which is 'widespread amongst employers, top managers and

substantial sections of outside public opinion'. The alternative,
dichotomous view of industrial firms likewise receives support both in
terms of social theory and conventional (especially 'proletarian') ideas.
Responses to this question therefore pose numerous problems of
interpretation: do they express an ideal, or what people actually
perceive to be the case? Are the responses simply the 'acceptable'
answer to what is a very general question, or are they based on personal
experience? Does the question maximise the range of possible responses
on the image of the firm? The answer to this last question is clearly 'no',
although we followed up the response to this question by asking for
reasons and examples where possible. Ramsay warns against too facile
interpretations and suggests that while employees may accept the
rather vague notion of co-operation contained in the first part of the
question, they tend to qualify this general approval with illustrations
from their own concrete experiences in the employing company. Thus
'we need to distinguish between acceptance of a consensus ideology
expressed through generalised statements, and its more frequent
rejection in the concrete circumstances of an actor's own experience'.[15]
With this in mind, it is clear that any straightforward attempt to count
the number of responses which express agreement, disagreement or
lack of opinion on the question would fail to do justice to the
complexity and predictable ambiguity of the replies. Instead, we will
discuss the findings in terms of four main categories or themes which
recur in a large number of the responses: dichotomy; interests in work
(i.e. the 'craft' aspect); economic interests; and the nature of authority.

Although the question itself presents the possibility of there being
two sides within industry, nothing more than this is implied and an
alternative is simultaneously presented. So it is interesting to note that
phrases which denote a dichotomy were used quite spontaneously by
virtually all (30 out of 33 cases) of the respondents, *whether or not*
they expressed agreement with the second view of the firm as consisting
of opposite sides. The dichotomy was referred to in a number of ways,
including 'workers/management', 'us/them', 'men/company',
'union/company', which tends to correspond with Popitz' finding that
some kind of dichotomous image was held by a large majority of the
workers studied, although the dichotomy was capable of being given a
variety of meanings even within a single plant.[16] Similarly, in the case
of the maintenance workers, the recurrence of dichotomous concepts
does not in itself explain anything, unless it is assumed that they simply
'reflect' a social structure. It was pointed out earlier that 'social
consciousness' is not to be understood in this crude sense, but rather as

a process of signification. Consequently, the meaning of the 'two sides' metaphor has to be inferred from its use in context, i.e. in explaining the opportunities and obstacles presented by social relationships in industry.

These relationships are complex but they are organised around two major axes which can be termed the 'cash nexus' (as expressed in the market dependence of labour on capital) and authority structures or control over the work process.[17] Replies to the question on the perception of the firm can be classed around these two axes, which for reasons of simplicity we will call 'economic interests' and 'interests in work'. If these categories are further divided according to whether or not they are evaluated as essentially harmonious or conflicting, each of the responses can be allocated to one of the cells of a 2 X 2 table. The allocation of responses is not without its problems. It is not always possible, for example, to distinguish between a response which represents an 'ideal' view and one which represents an actual situation or experience. It was made clear in the interview that the latter was the main point of the question, but nevertheless more than half the respondents endorsed the 'teamwork' view as an ideal, though much less frequently as a reality. Taking the view of the firm as it is actually perceived, the responses are distributed as shown in Table 4.[18] A clear majority expressed views which can be interpreted as pointing out the contrast between the two aspects of involvement in the firm: on the one hand a common interest in the work itself, the need to co-operate in production and maintain harmony in work relationships, and on the other hand the basic opposition of interests in terms of the extrinsic rewards of work — the basic antagonisms expressed in union negotiations in particular. Several replies show this very clearly. For example:

I suppose. . .you have to work as a team — everybody working together. But when it comes to money. . .it's always one against the other when it comes to wage rises.
I think there's harmony in the firm as far as both sides are concerned — as regards work. . .The worker always wants money and the other side always bats the worker down, moneywise.

The next most frequent kind of response indicated that antagonisms extended as a matter of course to relations at work — whether this had to do with 'bad communications' between men and management, the exercise of authority without legitimation, conflicting demands of

Table 4: Perceptions of the Firm

| | | Economic Interests | |
		Harmony	Conflict
Interests in work	Conflict	6%	21%
	Harmony	18%	44%
n = 33			

production and maintenance or disputes between trades. For example, one fitter attributed lack of harmony at work to the impersonal authority structure:

> . . .'they' are telling us what to do. A lot of the time we're taken just as a number (No.416 will go to. . .etc.). . .that's why it's 'them and us'.

It is almost certainly significant that the third group, who saw an essentially harmonious situation in both respects, consisted — with only two exceptions — of men within a few years of retirement. Typically they had been with the firm for most of their working lives and they looked back with some nostalgia to a time when the plant was smaller and there were more frequent personal contacts between workers and managers. They felt that this state of affairs had not been altogether superseded, despite trends towards impersonal administration and an influx of more youthful and, in their view, more 'militant' workers. Some still felt that they were on first name terms with certain members of the senior management.

Two individuals gave responses which fall into the final, rather anomalous, category. They regard the sphere of work rather than the market relationship as the site of endemic conflict. This is attributed to the presence of the trade union. Conflict at work is institutionalised because 'if you've got a union in any place you'll always get disagreements'. These workers were of the opinion that there is no essential clash of interests between workers and management but that the conflicts which do arise are the result of unions working in their own interests rather than in the interests of the workers they claim to represent.

The fact that nearly three quarters of those interviewed perceived their work as a sphere of unified interests, and that many were concerned about keeping it from the sphere of institutionalised conflict, should be seen in the light of the 'craft ideal' mentioned earlier. Since many of the craftsmen saw themselves as possessing at least some of the features of this model, it should be possible to establish some connection between the different kinds of response. The following suggests itself as a plausible hypothesis: the more the worker sees himself in terms of the 'ideal of craftsmanship', the more he will tend to answer the question on the nature of the firm in terms of the possibilities or barriers it presents to the exercise of his skills, and the more he will distinguish between this aspect of work and the aspect concerned with extrinsic rewards (whether or not he perceives a necessary conflict in the latter realm). There is some evidence in the above responses that this is the case and there are various reasons why this should be so, including the following: as a general rule, 'pride in work', and hence personal satisfaction and self-esteem for the self-styled craftsman, is incompatible with 'restrictive' practices, withdrawal and mild forms of sabotage which are expressions of conflict in other work situations. With a highly integrated technology and increasing interdependence of work tasks, it is likely that skilled workers will have a sense of personal involvement and responsibility conducive to close co-operation; the closer the approximation to the craft ideal of 'autonomy', the greater the freedom from conflicts arising from the structure of authority.

However, the demands of technological integration are not easy to reconcile with the traditional autonomy of the craftsman, which problem introduces the fourth main theme: the nature of authority. There are elements in the process of work allocation and supervision which depart considerably from the craft ideal, namely the bureaucratisation of the administration of work. Stinchcombe's contribution to the understanding of administrative methods which are adapted to particular kinds of production is relevant here.[19] Although neither of his examples (the construction industry and mass production in manufacturing) are analogous to maintenance fitting, the general argument is applicable, namely that craft administration is a functional equivalent of bureaucratic administration in that it substitutes 'professional training of manual workers for detailed centralised planning of work'. Stinchcombe maintains that the key factors that encourage the bureaucratisation of administration are the stability of work flow and income and the long-term economic stability of the enterprise. The work situation in the petro-chemical plant fulfils the latter requirement but clearly not the former on account of the intrinsic nature of maintenance work. This helps to explain why certain features of the system of administrative communication (a system of job classification in terms of priority, 1-3; standardised written communication; a stable structure of authority by areas) come under some strain during emergencies, large-scale maintenance work (on shut-downs) and to some extent even in the daily fluctuations in maintenance requirements.

Some of the interviews produced evidence of tensions of this kind, but only indirectly, in reply to other questions. It is therefore impossible to apply a systematic analysis. However, responses such as the following show that the problem may merit further attention. It may be symptomatic that despite relatively infrequent contact with foremen, the following remark could be made − 'management are often just trying to justify their existence. . .there are too many foremen.' One fitter stressed that the 'conflict' view was more true because 'in here. . .you can get conflicting instructions from an area engineer, a senior foreman and a foreman, and you can't keep them all happy'. But such responses are not frequent, which suggests that there is not a strong clash of interests between the two modes of administration. This can be partly accounted for by the fact that all supervisory and management personnel are themselves either former tradesmen or technically qualified; their professional competence is (or is seen to be) essentially technical, rather than managerial.

Union Involvement

The 'two sides' metaphor of employees and employers with its 'us and them' terminology occurs with almost the same frequency in the discussion of trade unions, and the engineering union in particular, as in discussion of labour-management relations. Previous researchers appear to have overlooked this finding, which can hardly be unique to the present sample. We have no means of judging the overall scope and frequency of the metaphor but it stands as a warning against placing too great an emphasis on any one apparent dichotomy in workers' thinking. As the simplest form of differentiation, the two-fold division is likely to be the basis of many crude descriptions and classifications. It is therefore important to consider the evaluative as well as the cognitive aspects of these patterns.

The questions and answers on union involvement which reveal this lack of personal identification with the union have to be seen against a relatively peaceful background of industrial relations within the plant. Industrial relations within many firms and industries elsewhere could not be said to enjoy the same degree of harmony for this was the period of concerted activity by the labour movement against the Industrial Relations Act. As we shall see, this situation was to change, but not immediately. At the time of the study, as far as most of the workers were concerned, to be 'union-minded' was to watch with approval the regular negotiations by full-time union officials at the national level and to co-operate constructively in working the flexibility agreement. Any 'issues' which the workers did choose to discuss in this context were internal to the plant and many workers expressed the hope they would remain so. They expected the union to work in their interests without making more than minimal demands on membership and participation.

Recently before the interviews were conducted a small change had occurred in this state of accommodation. The workers had made a move to exclude union officials and negotiate at the plant level through the shop stewards. The result was a deadlock, at which point the union was asked to return. The offer then standing was soon accepted by the union, without consultation with the members. The fact that this occurred, and that the workers accepted it without taking any further action is a good illustration of the union's rather ambiguous place within their social consciousness: an 'established' reality supposedly acting in their interests but scarcely subject to their control.

If the term 'union-mindedness' is taken in the sense implied by the respondents who used it (i.e. acceptance that a union is a necessary institution to protect workers' interests or to counter management interests and recognition that it demands a minimum loyalty in terms of membership and payment of dues) the number of those interviewed who could be said to subscribe to this view is nearly three quarters of the total. At the same time they acknowledged that they were 'not active' trade union members. Less than 10 per cent of the sample attended union meetings regularly and there were none whose interest in the union could be said to extend beyond the plant in common cause with workers in other firms or members of the same trade. Among the remainder the view expressed most frequently was 'I'm only in the union because I have to be'. This was often accompanied by expressions of fatalistic acceptance of superior management expertise and prerogative. For example:

The unions strike me as being a big fat person trying to keep up with a dancer — the management can dance round them all the time — they just can't seem to hit management at all. They get tied up in knots with red tape. All they've got is a strike, and nobody wants a strike, really. It's no good for either side.

This overwhelmingly passive view of the trade union is perhaps not altogether unexpected among a group of skilled workers with above average earnings in one of the leading industrial corporations, removed from the struggles of less favoured groups. However, the interview replies contain some interesting details which guard against any facile interpretation of this group as privatised or lacking in collective consciousness. The details of language and expression show that the static, almost dismissive approach could easily be transformed into a more dynamic and critical involvement in social relations at the plant. In the history of the labour movement there are lessons to be learnt which might well be applied here. In the early decades of this century there emerged a highly class-conscious labour movement with explicitly revolutionary intentions. Instead of being based among the most deprived sections of the working class its main vehicle was the 'labour aristocracy', the skilled trades. However, the craft consciousness which was potentially a subversive force was at the same time the key to the failure of the movement because of the reluctance of its members to abandon their sense of craft exclusiveness.[20] To the extent that a craft consciousness persists among the maintenance workers this potentiality for action and reaction still exists. It can be detected in several features of the interview discourse.

Firstly, there is a fundamental inconsistency in the description of trade union functions on the one hand and some of the general criticisms which are levelled at trade unions on the other. When asked what the main functions of a trade union ought to be, what priorities it should have, the fitters were almost unanimous in saying that the union should be responsible for preserving and improving wages and conditions of work (i.e. *their* wages and *their* conditions). The responses were so automatic that they unmistakably fall into the class of a 'social Topic'. They have the character of a stereotype and there is a similarity of wording which points to an enduring image of trade union activity. In the following examples, note the appeals to 'fairness' and the rhetoric of struggle. The union's main tasks, according to these workers, are:

Fighting for better wages and conditions
To get the best possible conditions and the best wages for its members
Trying to get a fair deal for fellow workers

To fight for conditions and better wages
Getting workers' rights. . .fair do's in the work
To protect the working class and ensure that everything possible
is being done as regards wages, conditions, etc.
Fighting for wage increases for the men
To keep working men as a body. . .to fight for a better standard
of living

The use of conflict terminology (fighting, defending, striving, etc.)
should not be taken literally to indicate antagonism. This language
evolved at a time when these terms were more relevant and their present
use is anachronistic in the context of what most of the workers see as
a consistently high, almost guaranteed, income. In any case, nearly all
the above examples were qualified in one way or another to neutralise
these expressions. For example, the second statement above was
followed by 'within reason' and another later invoked the idea of a
'fair deal for management' as well as a 'fair deal for the workers'. Also,
there are further examples which appear to contradict rather than
qualify the description of union functions.

They should concentrate on asking for decent rises if firms can give
decent rises. No asking for the sky
The union should keep the men happy — but keep wages in hand

All of these replies indicate a distancing of the trade union member
from the object of the discussion; so also do the replies which express
the view that trade unions are too large, top-heavy, self-interested and
divided by factional disputes. The patterned responses draw on a shared
vocabulary based outside personal experience. They are not even
exclusively tied to the collective experience of this particular group of
workers. Neither does the vocabulary appear to express the
consciousness of belonging to the manual working class as distinct from
non-manual workers and employers. The occasional references to the
'working class', 'fellow workers' or 'working men as a body' cannot
disguise the fact that these terms do not appeal to any concrete current
experiences of solidarity between groups of workers. There is instead a
strong impression of standard responses being produced to order — in
this case at the instigation of the interviewer but they could just as
easily have been advanced as an opinion in conversation. On the topic
of trade unions (but not in most other areas of discussion) the labels
and phrases seem to float free from the circumstances of everyday life.

The more detached and stereotyped they become, the more contradictory a person's opinions and perspectives are likely to be. This can be seen in the criticisms of the union movement volunteered by many of the maintenance workers.

The language of these criticisms is the language of 'crisis'; not the crisis of capitalism, however, but the threatened breakdown of an ordered society. At the time of the study, the first of these perspectives was not even hinted at by any in the sample.[21] The sense of change in the industrial and political climate was put down to other causes. In the context of quite specific questions about the union and union membership in the plant, and without prompting, nearly half the workers in the sample began to voice complaints about the unions in general. This alone is significant because it reveals a sense of hostility or grievance not based in the work sphere itself but elsewhere. And, what may be even more important, these externally mediated perspectives are appealed to *a priori* in judging the meaning and quality of group experiences at work. This must cast doubt on the assertion that the work situation and work relationships create or give rise to occupational and social perspectives.

The most common complaint was that, nationally speaking, unions had grown too big and powerful. This contrasts sharply with the other general feeling that the unions had in practice become almost superfluous in the present work context. But on occasions the two views occur almost in the same breath.

> You've got to be in the union but apart from that I think they're a waste of time. [What is the union's job, then?] Before it was to get good working conditions, money and a bit of security for the boys but we've got this and I think they outlived their usefulness. They're getting too big, too strong.

The only way in which the final phrase can be reconciled with what went before is by inferring a change of reference — from the firm and industrial relations at the plant level — to the state (the political sphere). This juxtaposition is not an accident of the interview method because general comments on the trade unions in society were not solicited. Instead, it is a manifestation of conflicting views of the same object which have been triggered by a single question. The two views arise from distinct sources: the collective experience of the group of workers and the highly mediated images of trade union activity deriving from 'public' sources, especially the mass media. Discussion of trade unions can produce both kinds of response.

The fitters, nearly all of whom were regular viewers of television and readers of the *Daily Record* or the *Daily Express* were quite fluent in their use of the arguments and frameworks of interpretation which dominate these media sources. Thus, one stated the consensus view that

> the unions should be trying to help with the economics of the country. . .I think the unions are overstepping themselves. The wages they're going for to my mind in some cases are preposterous — some of the rises. After a £5-6 rise they're back in a few months for another rise. I think the unions have overstepped themselves.

Another put forward the even stronger view that

> there are too many unions in this country. I think this is where the downfall of the country starts. . .I've no doubt about it, the unions have got too much say in this country. And I think the unions are losing power to certain members of their union. They've been hijacked.

These are the statements of workers who claim the right and argue for the necessity to press for better wages and conditions through the union. If 'cognitive dissonance' is to be avoided, there has to be some way of reconciling these two partly opposing interpretations. The most readily available rationale is in the form of a conspiracy theory, and its logical outcome is a call for order and stricter control. In its strongest form it leads to the following proposal.

> If the unions did their job it would be okay but they have too much power. They shouldn't be able to hold the country to ransom. . . The country is going from bad to worse because of too many strikes. They don't do any good — the two sides should negotiate. I think we need a strong man to get rid of the militants.

There is no evidence that these views emerge from the work and community situation as a 'reflection' or description of everyday experiences of social relationships. The same themes of militancy, social responsibility and lack of relevance are sometimes discussed, but in completely different terms. For instance, a former shop steward complained of the 'big fellas sitting down there in London getting all the perks' and another worker complained of 'a lot of politics going on at the top of the union'. In these references to the way in which the union impinges on their experience there is no hint of the conspiracy explanation. The same is true at the plant level where 'militancy' is criticised rather than invoked as a threat.

> If [the shop stewards] are very militant, communist types, they're always putting forward the suggestion that the firm is trying to get something for nothing and we'll need to watch this move and that move. Most union officials I'd say are very reasonable and if they're like that I think it's quite a good effect.

We conclude that apparent inconsistencies of perspective are most likely to arise when matters of personal experience are at the same time matters of public debate and opinion. In this case it is likely that opinions and views about trade unions are neither governed by personal whim (as, say, in preferences for ice cream flavours and most other choices in the sphere of personal consumption) nor are they derived directly from 'official', institutional, or media sources. They will almost certainly contain elements of both, giving an impression of inconsistency and even randomness. We can therefore predict that matters of discussion which are farthest removed from individual and group experiences will be most vulnerable to mediation by ready-made accounts and interpretations. We will expand on this theme in the light of evidence from the most far-ranging questions about society and politics.

Meanwhile, our analysis once again faces the fundamental problem of whether there is a characteristic social consciousness among the maintenance craftsmen. Other observers have found similar evidence of 'inchoateness' and inconsistency in workers' socio-political perspectives, especially when participant or biographical methods rather than standardised survey techniques have been used.[22] The question is whether the apparent lack of coherence makes sense in terms of an explanation which uses occupational experience as a datum, and whether this explanation can allow for the way in which workers respond to their environment differently from one month or year to the next.

The problem is illustrated by the more recent history of the Grangemouth labour force. The background is the deepening economic recession and the establishing of the social contract between the TUC and the Labour government. From the point of view of this study, one

of the most significant events which occurred during this period was a
strike in the chemical complex adjacent to the plant used for this study.
Maintenance work and conditions are almost identical in the two plants.
The strike, which was over a pension scheme and other fringe benefits,
lasted a week. It suggests that within a fairly short space of time the
attitudes towards the unions and strike activity which we have outlined
above can be transformed into the kind of attitudes and actions which
were once so widely disdained.[23]

No firm conclusions are possible wihout the evidence of a
longitudinal study but the framework we have adopted does not lead
us automatically to suspect any change — rational or irrational — in
the social consciousness of the group of workers. If social attitudes
were merely a reflection, the decision to strike would have to be seen
as a fundamental reversal of opinion brought about by a change in the
environment. However, there is an explanation which holds to the
assumption that the basic parameters of social consciousness are
relatively static because they are based in collective experiences of
work and social relations. The environment (of economic and social
circumstances, with its subtle changes of skill, power, income and
status) is then not a source of change in social consciousness but its
precondition. It is the object of the relationship which we have
defined consciousness as being.

Therefore, in some measure a shared social consciousness will be
independent of changes which may occur in the work environment.
For example, the degradation of skills may not lead to an immediate
proletarianisation or decline in craft consciousness. The opposite may
occur. Strikes may be evidence of heightened craft awareness rather
than indicators of absorption to a proletarian movement. The
components of craft consciousness in its 'ideal' from, as we have
defined it, include intrinsic gratification in work and a sense of status
which derives from consistently high and regular earnings. Both of
these features were deliberately included in the sample. Each aspect
represents a particular relation of consciousness but it is their
combination which is of special interest here. We noted earlier the
ambiguity of orientations to work, which included elements of craft
and instrumental attitudes. This may be taken as recognition by the
worker that work is the source of its own rewards and the condition
of other possibilities; that it contains a double imperative to create
and control.

While craftsmen are by no means unique in recognising work after
this fashion they may well be distinctive in giving both elements almost

equal emphasis. The professional attitude is more likely to stress work itself as a possibility and unskilled workers are more likely to perceive work as an obstacle. There is a similar ambivalence in attitudes towards status: a strong sense of the value of particular kinds of work together with a general denial of the relevance of social distinctions. These attitudes are not altogether unusual but the central idea of craft consciousness helps to explain the particular way in which they are combined. Among the several possible grounds for defining social distinctions as invidious, the craftsman's are that these distinctions make no sense in terms of the criteria of skill and income by which they define themselves. Further analysis of answers to questions about the social structure will show whether craft consciousness can be said to involve a particular 'class image' of society.

Identity, Opposition and the System of Historical Action

One of the most important lessons in the history of research into workers' consciousness is that few workers are 'class conscious' in the sense that they can clearly re-present society as a complete stratified, hierarchical or otherwise structured system. After all, even social scientists rarely demand or achieve such coherence and clarity in their own descriptions and theories. Yet workers can be expected to relate to society as a totality because social life would be impossible without concepts like 'country', 'nation', 'the economy' and 'government'. These and other concepts are necessary to cope with the experience of being an object of social change and social processes, however inaccurate they may be as descriptions. Further ideas such as 'class', 'working people' and 'Party' may be equally necessary for the individual to experience society as a subject.

The interviews were designed to provide conversational material in which these concepts were applied at the most general level but within the context of specific questions about social relations in the community, voting behaviour and so on. For each interview there is a discourse of approximately 500 words within which we have attempted to identify the three components used by Touraine in his analysis of 'historicity', the way social actors participate in systems of historical action. It will be remembered that these are firstly, the *principle of identity* or unity which is the consciousness of self and the rationale for making claims upon society; secondly, the *principle of opposition* which defines the adversary; and thirdly the *principle of totality* which refers to the whole of society and is a definition of the sphere of social conflict. These are analytical principles which do not necessarily relate

Craft Consciousness: The Maintenance Fitters

in a one-to-one fashion with workers' own interpretations. Indeed, within a single group of workers it is unlikely that there will be equal evidence of each of these principles.

The responses provide a way of testing Touraine's claim that the most significant change in consciousness with progressive industrialisation has been increasingly direct reference to the principle of totality, i.e. to economic and social progress as the basis for evaluating social processes. According to Touraine the fitters are employed in an occupation and industry in which this tendency is most highly developed and relatively independent of occupational experience which is the basis of the identity principle.

The discussion of 'getting on' reported earlier can be interpreted as an expression of the criteria which the maintenance workers use for making 'claims' upon the rest of society — that is to say, the principle of identity. In the same context, any sense of grievance can be taken as an indicator of the principle of opposition. The weight given to each aspect may be an important characteristic of consciousness, although no firm conclusions can be drawn from the existing data. The questions about craftsmen's career progress were framed in such a way that there was more emphasis on the legitimate means of advancement than on possible obstacles to advancement. However, there are two general features of the replies which lead us to anticipate that the tensions between what are regarded as legitimate claims to status or other rewards and any failure to realise them will be resolved in a particular way. Firstly, since 'getting on' was ascribed to personal effort and drive to gain knowledge and skills together with a measure of good fortune in personal contacts (and not to luck or social background) we can predict that the image of society will tend to legitimise expert knowledge and education as a basis for social differentiation. Secondly, it was established that judgements about 'getting on' were made within a restricted horizon of experience. Not only was there a general lack of incentive to career mobility among the fitters but the position of foreman was regarded as the normal limit to advancement. This is an important restriction upon the claim to social recognition.

On the basis that action within the social system depends on the successful articulation of the principles of identity, opposition and totality, we would expect the fitter's view of society as a whole to include the following features. Firstly, there will be recognition of differences of skill and status based on work. Secondly, because knowledge and skills are regarded as legitimate criteria of social differentiation, there will be hostility to other claims to status (based on birth, wealth, etc.). Thirdly, there will be acceptance of differences of life-style based on income, provided that these are related to the possession of expertise.

Analysis of the replies only partly confirms the above predictions. There is certainly widespread resistance to forms of social differentiation which are not based on achieved knowledge and skills but there is much less certainty that these distinctions are withering away. In fact there is considerable confusion about the basis of social differentiation. What is quite clear is that the entire sample, without exception, recognised social classes and could discuss without difficulty the existence of social divisions. Class is still a meaningful category of social description although not necessarily the most salient one. When asked in the context of the questions about careers what they thought about class, 46 per cent of the sample indicated without prompting that they thought it referred to a conventional three-fold division between upper, middle and lower groups. These were variously described as the 'upper, middle and lower classes'; the 'idle rich, management and the working class'; the 'very rich, the middle class and us'; the 'upper class, white collar workers and those who get their hands dirty'. Of the remainder, 8 per cent described a two-fold division and 46 per cent gave no details – just the implication that there are a variety of groups who assert their values or claim superiority over others. This group usually claimed that class divisions were declining in importance, though not always without self-contradiction.

Q. Do you think social class is important today?
A. Class? No, not nowadays.
Q. Do you think classes still exist?
A. Oh yes, there's snobs going about [refers to an area engineer]. He thinks he's superior, not that that worries me.
Q. What do people mean when they call someone 'working class'?
A. If you go to an ordinary·school I suppose you're working class. They work for the money they've got – not landowners, just ordinary people. You can't have class nowadays. The children are getting equal opportunities – like you and I.

This and other statements may appear to be inconsistent almost to the point of incoherence but they are not random selections of attitudes. They are expressions of an active process of negotiation between competing definitions. The use of a phrase like 'equal

opportunity' is a measure of the success with which public definitions
and vocabulary can infuse the speech of craftsmen who are generally
more at home with concepts based in personal attributes. Thus

> You need real backbone to resist a bad social background.

> If a boy's got intelligence and ambition, [social background] won't
> matter. You see it often — people from the Gorbals, etc. have gone
> down south and made successes of themselves.

> [Class depends on] what kind of confidence you've got. If you
> class yourself as upper class, if you act that way, you can just look
> down on other folk. Business owners. . .they think themselves
> above you.

It is not our intention here to create another typology of workers'
images of society based on this evidence. The sources are too
fragmentary and the interview context too artificial to make this a
satisfactory procedure. Also, such an exercise would immobilise what
is essentially a dynamic process.

We can, however, list the rationales which were used by the
craftsmen in the course of their discussion of class and society. None
of these rationales provides even a crude 'social theory'. For example,
of those who were asked to judge whether 'class' distinctions were on
the decline, more claimed that they were static than claimed they were
diminishing but none could explain why. But this is not to say that
categories or themes were unavailable for grasping the topic; the
craftsmen did make use of a number of themes derived from
occupational and other sources. The most important of these is the
theme of personal character attributes discussed above. In certain
typologies (based on the work of Goldthorpe *et al.*) this emphasis on
individual rather than collective attributes might be interpreted as
evidence of a 'privatised' image, particularly as it is frequently
associated with statements about money as the basis of differences in
life-style. Leaving aside the problem of how *social* consciousness can
be *privatised*, the source of these approaches to social differentiation
is most likely to be based in the occupation which already stresses
these attributes, and not elsewhere.

Money figures as the next most important theme. The worker who
gave the example of 'the boy from the Gorbals' continued as follows:

> [Classes] still exist. You used to have upper class, middle class and

working class. You've only got two now. The working class is more middle class — we're all coming into a sort of par there — and you've got them that's really got it. They've a different life altogether. You used to have the chappie that was on the floor and the men that were above them, like section engineers. They were miles apart in money but now they've both got the same, really. Money makes the difference. Money makes classes.

Again, this can hardly be said to be a 'pecuniary' model of society. It has very little to do with the calculative exchange of labour power for extra pay and is actually quite consistent with the high value placed by the skilled worker on work itself. The choice of reference group above rather than below is a feature which implies a sense of security and satisfaction and it contrasts strongly with the sense of threat experienced by many in the clerical sample. The rather limited horizons of discourse are also characteristic of the sample as a whole. As might be expected, nearly all examples and illustratons were drawn from everyday experiences and encounters with other workers, management and businessmen. The narrowness of this field is important because these relationships provide only very limited material for the manufacture of social images and explanations and they make the workers all the more vulnerable to the ready-made images which come from 'external' sources. These are the sources of the remaining themes in the discussion of class and social change. The use of 'equal opportunity' in an earlier quotation is a clear example of a theme deriving from political, educational or media institutions which manufacture ideology at the national level.

Other examples refer to political and economic institutions as the medium of change in society. This is not out of a sense of party loyalty. Although nearly half the sample voted for Labour at the previous general election (the remainder were divided equally between Conservative and SNP), the majority of these and the majority of the sample as a whole disagreed with the statement that 'Labour is still the party of the working people'. It can therefore be assumed that political allegiances are neither the result of unshakable traditionally-held beliefs nor indeed are they a matter of great significance to most of the craftsmen. This is confirmed by the finding that few could point to any differences in Conservative and Labour policies and ideologies. Equally significant is the discovery that social policies (towards unemployment, economic growth, industrial relations, etc.) are regarded with scepticism and even pessimism.

If Touraine is correct in arguing that the tendency of workers' consciousness is to confront reality less and less as 'natural' and 'given' and increasingly to approach society as a system of social action, these results must be regarded as an important qualification. The limits of social change, if they are defined at all, are marked in the interviews by a special feature of discourse — the rhetorical question. Such questions do not pose a problem for argument and eventual solution as do most questions. Instead, they define a boundary between what is questionable and what is beyond question. Thus, in a statement about the limits of inequality and prospects for change, there is a boundary-defining question:

> I think we'll always have this situation in this country. I can't see it ever changing. To change in this country would mean a revolution, wouldn't it? I don't think we'll ever see that here. I think we'll always have the rich and the poor.

In another reply to the same question asking whether there will always be inequality of wealth and income there is a similar statement which also has the effect of placing the issue outside the realm of discussion. 'That would bring communism, to change it as much as all that.' The most unexpected feature of these replies (some referred to Russia as an 'alternative') is not so much the presence of these references but the complete absence of any other references to more plausible and less drastic alternatives within the western industrial world. The examples of the USA, Germany or Sweden which could have been used to indicate possible paths of development were ignored. Even a question about 'life in 5 years' time' failed noticeably to elicit responses which showed any confidence in industrial society's ability to solve its own problems.

In Touraine's terminology, society is conceived by the craftsmen more as an aggregate of social groups than as a system of action. That is to say, within an industry in which the principle of totality might be expected to be most fully expressed, we find an essentially traditional reliance on identity of group interests, occupational autonomy and a vision of society based on work as a system of production rather than as a system of control.

Notes

1. See for example, R. Blauner, *Alienation and Freedom* (Chicago, 1964);
J.M. Shepard, *Automation and Alienation* (Cambridge, Mass., 1971).
'Alienation' is understood by these authors to refer to the four components
discussed by Seeman: powerlessness, meaninglessness, normlessness and
self-estrangement. See M. Seeman, 'On the Meaning of Alienation', *Am. Sociol.
Rev.*, 24, 6 (1959).

2. J. Bensman and R. Lilienfeld, *Craft and Consciousness: Occupational
Technique and the Development of World Images* (New York, 1973), p.3.

3. S. Mallet, *La Nouvelle Classe Ouvrière*, p.113.

4. These investigators include Blauner, Touraine and Shepard.

5. C.L. Goodrich, *The Frontier of Control: A Study in British Workshop
Politics* (London, 1920/1975), quoted in T. Nichols and P. Armstrong,
Workers Divided (London, 1976), p.50.

6. H. Braverman, *Labour and Monopoly Capital* (New York, 1974),
especially pp.220 ff.

7. These are bound by statutory requirements. For example, the maximum
interval between inspections of waste heat steam-raising pressure vessels is
14 months after construction with subsequent intervals of 26 months.

8. See for example L.C. Hunter, G.L. Reid, D. Boddy, *Labour Problems
of Technical Change* (London, 1970), pp.271 ff.

9. See NEDO, *Manpower in the Chemical Industry* (HMSO, London, 1967)
and NEDO, *Chemicals Manpower in Europe* (HMSO, London, 1973).

10. See especially E.J. Hobsbawm, *Labouring Men* (London, 1964) and
R. Gray, 'The Labour Aristocracy in the Victorian Class Structure', in
F. Parkin (ed.), *The Social Analysis of Class Structure* (London, 1974).

11. E.J. Hobsbawm, *Labouring Men*, pp.272 ff.

12. Cf. A. Willener in G.K. Zollschan and W. Hirsch (eds), *Explorations in
Social Change* (London, 1964); J.H. Goldthorpe, D. Lockwood *et al., The
Affluent Worker in the Class Structure* (Cambridge, 1969); D. Wedderburn and
R. Crompton, *Workers' Attitudes and Technology* (Cambridge, 1972);
G.K. Ingham, *Size of Industrial Organization and Worker Behaviour* (Cambridge,
1970); J. Cousins and R. Brown, 'Patterns of Paradox', in M. Bulmer, *Working-
Class Images.*

13. H. Ramsay, Research Note 'Firms and Football Teams', in *Brit.J.Ind.
Rels.*, vol.XIII, no.3 (1975).

14. A. Fox, *Industrial Sociology and Industrial Relations*, Research Paper 3,
Royal Commission on Trade Unions and Employers Associations (HMSO,
London, 1966), p.3.

15. H. Ramsay, 'Firms and Football Teams', p.397.

16. H. Popitz *et al., Das Gesellschaftsbild*, especially ch.5.

17. According to Westergaard and Resler 'only a single strand, the "cash
nexus", ties the worker to his work, his boss and supervisors, society at large
in its present form. Stability of the order hangs by one thread: the market
dependence of labour on capital', *Class in a Capitalist Society* (London, 1975),
p.401. This overstates the Marxist case. The firm is not only a set of market
relationships but a social system which makes demands on its members far
beyond those of the market. However 'false' a consciousness this may lead to,
these claims should not be underestimated. They are usually backed up by strong
claims to traditional authority (by paternalist managements) or technical
rational authority (by firms such as the one in the present discussion).

18. We have sometimes used other statements made in the interview if the
replies to this question were too ambiguous or too fragmentary to be sorted

in this way. Only three responses were unclassifiable.

19. A.L. Stinchcombe, 'Bureaucratic and Craft Administration of Production', *Admin. Sci. Quarterly*, vol.4 (September 1959).

20. Ref. J. Hinton, *The First Shop Stewards Movement* (London, 1973).

21. T. Nichols and P. Armstrong, in *Workers Divided* state that workers at Chemco did not begin to realise the implications of the end of the post-war expansion until well into 1973, when 'uncertainty about their own job prospects began to take hold' (p.32). There may be a special reason why the response did not occur sooner among Scottish workers in the oil and chemical industries, namely the commercial exploitation of the North Sea oil fields.

22. See especially T. Nichols and P. Armstrong, *Workers Divided*.

23. The fitters themselves were on strike for three weeks in the summer of 1977 over a closed shop issue.

6 PROLETARIAN CONSCIOUSNESS: THE STEELWORKERS

Having already drawn attention to the contrasting age profile and occupational history of the melter's sample we can proceed to an analysis of the special features of the steel melter's job which provide the materials for the construction of a characteristic social consciousness. Within the range of the skilled manual occupations, the contrast between the work of the craftsmen and that of the steelworkers could hardly be greater. This alone is a ground for suspecting differences of social consciousness between the two groups regardless of variation in market circumstances or community traditions. Just as we used the term 'craft' to designate the formative aspects of the fitter's consciousness, so we will use the term 'proletarian' here to emphasise the steelworker's dependency on the occupational system of work, as opposed to a craft system or technical system.[1] Classically, 'proletariat' refers to a class of industrial workers whose rise is indissolubly linked with the development of the capitalist economic system and we have chosen the term for this reason. The steelworkers, in their relation to technology, work, capital and the labour movement are very strikingly dependent on an outdated and virtually obsolete phase of industrial development. Their social consciousness expresses this dependency but in a positive rather than negative way by investing great significance in occupational identity.

In previous usage, the term 'proletarian' has been applied especially to workers in the mining, docking and shipbuilding industries.[2] It is surprising that the steel industry is rarely included in this list because there are many parallel features. It is nevertheless true that 'the steelworker has remained a distant and largely unrecognised figure' in sociological literature.[3] It may be partly because observers of 'proletarian' communities have typically regarded them as conflict-prone that this has occurred, because the steel industry until the late 1960s and early 1970s had a record of comparatively stable industrial relations. Thus, it is argued, 'eclipsed by the aura of solidarity surrounding the miner, the docker, the engineer and the shipbuilder, and undistinguished by any folklore of deprivation or struggle, [the steelworker's] identity is indistinct and his position within the ranks of manual work obscure'.[4] As we shall see, this is not entirely correct but it does help to explain the relative lack of comparative sociological data upon which we can draw in our analysis.

Existing studies have concentrated upon two main aspects of the work and consciousness of the steelworker, neither of which delineates the exact area of our concern. Studies concerned with attitudes and adjustment of work have selected technology and specific technological changes as the major variable. This is too narrow a preoccupation from our point of view, which sees consciousness as something more than a response. The second focus of interest has been the 'occupational community' of the steelworker.[5] Exclusive attention to this aspect fails to do justice to labour itself as both creative of meaning and as a response to historical necessity. Therefore, our initial task is to describe the special features of the labour process which sets the sample of melters apart from others in the same plant, the same industry and the working class in general.

Steel Melter – Top Trade or Dead End?

The open hearth method of steelmaking certainly has many of the characteristics of harsh conditions, teamwork and relative freedom from technical and supervision constraints which are usually said to characterise the 'traditional' occupations and they go with a special occupational pride. In the words of Patrick McGeown, who operated the open-hearth process in a plant not far from the one studied here and who has written vividly and at length about his experience:

> The whole district and for miles beyond it was a hotbed of steelworks, iron puddling works and coal mines. It was a place given over to the worship of strength and durability. Indeed it needed strength to look at it and durability to live in it. The steel furnacemen, the iron puddlers and the coal miners were mostly men of few words, which they repeated eternally about steelmaking, iron puddling and coal mining. They were so proud of their occupations that they never shut up.[6]

The steelmaking process of which he writes is almost exactly 100 years old and it has not changed radically in that time. Although furnaces are no longer charged by hand and instrumentation has been developed to meet the closer specifications of modern steelmaking, the work is still hot, heavy and dirty and greater precision has not eliminated the moments of uncertainty. This means that a measure of personal judgement is still necessary, if only because the furnaceman should be able to judge from the appearance of the furnace whether the instruments are showing any appreciable inaccuracy.

The steel furnace is operated by a team which is highly stratified, unlike the craft or maintenance side of the labour force. In steel melting, as in ironmaking and steel rolling, there are three main groups which are arranged strictly in order of seniority. The first hands are the top workers in the production teams and they have responsibility for the work in their section. The second grade (e.g. second hand melters) are partly skilled assistants who will one day occupy the senior positions. Finally, there are labourers who may or may not regard themselves as being in line for promotion to the second and first hand positions.

All accounts of steelmaking place great importance on the cohesion of the furnace team. McGeown supplies a personal example:

> I knew some good fellows among the melters, in fact, I knew many, for mine was a friendly trade and it bred good men and it still does. It was the most common thing for the furnace team to enjoy each other's company and when that was so the time went by on wheels.[7]

The point is made in a different way in the following advice from a recent manual of steelmaking which emphasises the teamwork in operating a steel furnace and underlines the first hand's (i.e. worker's) continuous responsibility for its satisfactory operation.

> A modern melter must be in control of a keen, co-ordinated and enthusiastic team. He must anticipate the requirements of his furnace in advance and see that these requirements are fulfilled. . . Instead of automation detracting from the need for skill [the steelmaker's], skill is enhanced by it, so that anyone who is sufficiently keen and enthusiastic to apply modern developments still has an extremely interesting, rewarding and, one hopes, not unprofitable occupation, which will allow him to exert to the full all the intelligence, keenness and organising ability which he possesses.[8]

In fact there is ample evidence here and in our own observation of the melting shop to show that steel melters have skills which conform in some ways to the 'craft' ideal described in the previous chapter. The first hand has specialised knowledge, the span of the work task is broad (a furnace cycle varies between 12 and 16 hours) the work is quite varied and there is freedom from close supervision. However, the crucial difference between the steel worker's job and the craft ideal is that whereas the craftsman's knowledge is geared for change, the melter's can only adjust to change very slowly, if at all, because it consists of rules of thumb, precedents, trial and error and is not a 'theoretical' system. The steel melter is dependent on technology in a particular shape and form tied to a single industry. Moreover, in the plant studied, obsolescence of the technology was more than a threat, it was a certainty. The British Steel Corporation's programme of rationalisation leaves no place for small plants using the open-hearth method. Only the oxygen process will be used for the production of ordinary steels although some open-hearth furnaces may remain for the production of special steels. Already at the time there were signs of low morale, indicated by low tonnages and slow turn-round times. Technological decline is bound to be reflected in the melter's attitudes towards work: their sense of 'being in a good trade' is tempered by these apprehensions about its future and their future within it.

The Meaning of Work — 'Breeding Good Men'

The majority of the melters, like the craftsmen in the previous sample, had a ready answer to the question about the qualities needed in their job — 'what does it take to be a good first hand?' With even greater regularity than the craftsmen, the melters refer to personal qualities; not, however, to 'commonsense' and 'intelligence' but to qualities especially appropriate to handling difficult materials and situations. Overwhelmingly, the references are to 'patience', 'temperament' and the ability to keep a level head. For example:

The most important thing in steelmaking is patience and temper, which are related. That's what I was always told and that's what I've found.

The most essential thing for a first hand is to have a steady head, to keep the head and not fly up.

In the first place you've got to have temperament, you've got to have patience.

Well, I would say patience — this is one of the things that helps.

What makes a good first hand is. . .a fellow that can make up his mind and act on it.

The first of these replies provides a clue to the origin and transference of these ideas. In place of the socialisation process of apprenticeship there is an even longer and more thorough process of accommodation to the role of first hand which typically lasts more than twenty years. Nothing is more effective in ensuring the continuity of occupational tradition, in language as well as in practice. Typically, this is the context within which the stratified deposits of conceptions, viewpoints and beliefs are most clearly to be seen in their 'Topical' form. Here they remain relatively undisturbed by the movements of the history of ideas and they are sheltered from continuous erosion by the media. Although there is a stress on personal qualities in the melter's responses (and this may be a function of the question which has to do with the particular, special worker rather than workers in general), there is a difference between the maintenance worker's and the melter's replies. We described the former's definition of the meaning of work as being non-work-specific. They rarely spoke of particular tasks or skills. This contrasts strongly with the melter's statements which nearly always referred to the personal qualities of patience and temperament in the context of particular applications to technical and human problems.

> Mark you, any man will always lose his grip at some time or other. It might be with general help or may be a little technical trouble, a 'difficult' charge. This tends to get below your skin at times.

> A good melter sees that these jobs are done effectively, not leaving anything shoddy. [For example] the Saturday night shift; you've got to show a wee bit of incentive yourself, so you're showing an example.

The themes of technical skill and social skill in these and other examples are highly work-specific. This is to be expected in view of the steel melter's deep dependency on a particular technological form and it will be a recurring theme in the interviews as a whole.

The meaning of work as a creative process is most emphatically expressed in the melters' accounts of their own activities around the furnace. There is less evidence that interest in work extends to interest in the social control of production, i.e. there is a less equal emphasis on the 'double exigency of creation and control' which Touraine identifies as the source of meaning and which appeared to have balanced emphasis among the craftsmen. The melters were unanimous in approving the technical changes which had occurred in their experience

in the melting shop but as often as not this approval was tempered with
a more negative view of changes in the social aspects of the work. The
two points of view are expressed in answer to the same question but as
a rule, no connection is made between the two types of change. This
can be seen in the following replies. Firstly, there is this typical
description of technical progress:

> The work is a lot easier than it used to be — all press button.

> When I started in here it was very heavy work. You had to pull
> chains to charge the furnaces to open the doors and it was all brick
> doors and jambs and if you worked there you got a roasting. There
> was no such thing as water-cooled doors or hydraulic — you had to
> pull them up and down.

> When we first came here it was the old type furnaces. . .the change
> to water-cooled was a big step in the right direction. There has been
> a big step, big increase in output, also new cranes. There've been
> quite a number of changes in the melting ship, also in the steel pit.

> Oh marvellous changes. They are for the better, although there was
> a lot of hard work with the hot metal practice at the start. We've
> seen the changeover from producer gas to coke oven and blast
> furnace gas — and using oil along with it. Water-cooled linings.
> Silica brick to magnesite brick, which enhances the life of the
> furnace. These were great advances to us. . .taking off the heavy
> sweat.

It is interesting to note the frequent use of the first person plurals,
'we' and 'us' in these and subsequent replies. They can be read as
further evidence of the similarity and homogeneity of the melters'
occupational experiences. However, assessments of the non-technical
aspects of work do not convey the same optimism. One of the workers
quoted above seemed to indicate a loss of morale when he spoke of a
time when teams were 'better'.

> There was more life in the men, it's more boys now. I think they're
> just coming and going now. When I started I was nearly 10 years on
> the boxes before I got started on a furnace.

Another referred to a lack of interest among less experienced workers:

> We have men coming onto the job that just aren't interested. We have

to try and make them interested [Why is this?] They want to get ahead quick and make money — that's the motivation of the present day.

In recent years we find that promotion is rapid, so much so that we've had young lads from the pool who've had to be stepped up as third or even second hands. . .Where you've got young lads coming on, you don't expect them to learn everything in one day or in one week. This is a job that — it doesn't matter how long you're in the job — every day you learn something different. No two charges work alike.

In none of the replies was there any spontaneous attempt to link the changing technology of the open-hearth furnace (and its impending obsolescence) with the problem of low morale and the increasing reluctance of younger workers to follow the traditional patterns of promotion. Equally significant is the melter's reluctance to make these connections even when prompted by questions such as 'do you think this has anything to do with the possible closure of the plant in the near future?'. It implies that the steel melter's perspective is so narrowly based on occupational experiences that these experiences can only be interpreted and explained according to the prevailing occupational criteria of evaluation and not according to criteria diffused more widely throughout the steel industry or throughout the working class. In these constricting terms, technical change is something which the worker relates to as an external object beyond his control. The dependency which this creates over a lifetime's employment in the same plant and the same shop means that the threatened termination of the relationship to work is almost impossible to contemplate. For the same reason, as we observed previously, the first hand melters found that the prospect of retirement was virtually unthinkable. This is because, at worst, the termination of the relationship between the melter and his work (which is embodied in 'his' furnace and 'his' team) will be the end of his identity as a worker and more — his identity as a person. The claims to recognition which the steelworker makes upon society are based in his role as a worker at the top of his trade of steelmaking and not principally as a wage-earner, supporter of a family or member of the working-class. The older and more established the melter is in his trade, the more this is likely to be the case. The present sample, with its very high average age, is therefore likely to embody the consciousness of occupational identity more fully than most groups; more fully even than the 'craft' workers in the previous sample, since in their case occupational identity incorporated a greater range and variety of meanings.

The work experience of the steel melter is synonymous with membership of a particularly cohesive work group. In the first instance the furnace 'team' is bound together by external ties: the exigencies of shift working, the need to remain by the furnace even during meal breaks and the need for co-ordinated effort. Meal breaks are taken on the job 'to suit the furnace'. But these ties eventually become indistinguishable from personal identification with the team and solidarity within the hierarchical group structure. The pattern of authority is perfectly clear within this structure and between it and the foremen or 'sample passers' who have the responsibility for tapping the furnace. There is none of the ambiguity that exists between the craftsman's expertise and, say, the engineer's theoretical knowledge, in the relationship between the melters and those who test their product in the laboratory. In fact there is rarely any direct contact at all. Authority in the melting shop is indisputably based in experience defined simply by the number of years spent on the job. The opinions of the team may be offered or given but, as one first hand put it, 'you're responsible for the whole process from tap to tap'.

The solidarity of the furnace teams, the unambiguous nature of authority and the melter's freedom from obvious external control led us to abandon the question based on contrasting images of the firm. In each interview the dominant tendency was to express relationships within the steelworks — and not only within the furnace team — according to the 'unitary' or cohesive image. In the few cases that the alternative of 'teamwork or two sides' was presented, the melters misinterpreted it — a sure indication of its lack of relevance, at least in the form supplied. The replies showed that harmony in work was taken for granted as the norm. The possibility of conflict either in work or in the broader context of employer-employee relationships was not even considered by any of the few workers who were asked the question. The unitary view, expressed in terms of 'common interest' and 'what benefits the organisation benefits each individual' called forth these reactions:

It's teamwork from top to bottom.

Everybody works here as a team, from the labourer right on t)ugh the first hand and to the staff. I've always found. . .comradeship was

between every man. The majority in the steel trade. . .if you know
a foreman or manager and they know you, they'll speak to you.

These replies, complete with anecdotes about personal encounters in
which the boundaries of status and position are transcended, ignore
completely the possible conflict of 'economic interests' between
groups of workers or between management and workers. This is
noteworthy, even after allowing for possible distortion caused by
perceiving work relationships from the summit of one's career (and the
likely tendency to overlook details which might contradict the
self-image of the 'successful first hand'). It reinforces the outline which
has been emerging of a group of workers whose relationship to work
hinges on performance of the job, on the *métier* as distinct from
emploi. Among these workers there is a highly developed occupational
consciousness – in the narrow sense of occupational, because not all
workers' consciousness involves the same close relationship to the
labour process and its products. It tends to obscure the market
dependency which workers in the more highly evolved technical
systems of assembly and automated work are likely to experience. But
this dependency is a reality in the steelworkers' lives, not least because
of the radical insecurity of their employment in a declining sector of
the industry. Most are able to come to terms with this because their
impending retirement provides a form of release, but the problems of
outdated technology are by no means new. Alternative methods of
steelmaking have been known and have been in use elsewhere for
most of the working lives of the first hands. We therefore looked for
signs of awareness of the evolution of industrial work, a sense of the
changing situation of the industrial worker which was not narrowly
based in the technical changes which had occurred in the melting shop
itself.[9]

Nationalisation and Rationalisation

There were two themes which we hoped would provide the evidence
by starting within the boundaries of the melter's own experience,
namely, nationalisation and rationalisation. Nearly all the first hands
had lived through the successive changes of ownership: nationalisation
in 1949, de-nationalisation in 1953 and re-nationalisation in 1967.
They had also recently become aware of the BSC's investment and
modernisation programme announced in 1973 which would involve a
large reduction in the steel industry's labour force over the next decade.
All were aware that their own plant would have no future under this

programme although no date had been set on its closure.

On the question of nationalisation, the majority of the sample were prepared to identify changes which had occurred and two-thirds gave these changes their approval albeit with some qualifications. Several cited improved wages and better conditions of employment as the most significant change but the most common observation was that management styles were different since nationalisation. However, opinions about recent managers and management styles were almost equally divided, doubtless because judgements were usually made according to subjective, personal criteria and not according to productivity or the plant's industrial relations record.

I think there's more co-operation with the management now. . .
I think the management work together more with the men.

Of course it's not up to me to comment on the managers as such, but the first manager we ever had I reckoned to be the best of all. . . For instance, for a long while you couldn't move about in the steel pit because of scrap — walking was dangerous — but while that manager was there, that whole pit side was completely clean.

Under private ownership if a manager showed his nose everybody jumped to attention, moved to their work or did what they didn't have to do. Now they don't interfere with the first hands in the normal run of affairs. . .Management at present just don't know their job. There's a lack of experience of open-hearth furnaces in management.

These comments reveal less about specific attitudes to nationalised management than about the place of management in general in the melter's consciousness. The replies give the strong impression that nationalisation and even rationalisation are not matters of fundamental interest except in one crucial respect. One of the first hands speaks for most of the others when he says:

We've still got to work, still do your job. If a man does his job he doesn't have to worry who is the top lad.

Another declined to give an opinion about nationalisation for much the same reason.

I don't know whether to answer that by saying that the people that

can give us work can create work. That's what we're looking for,
no matter. . .under nationalised or private industry. Whoever's
going to give me the work I would say right, that's it.

There is perhaps a naive faith in the view of work as a 'gift' rather than
as a right or even as a duty but it has some justification in the
experience of the steelworkers. The steel industry, with its high
capital-labour ratio has had a comparatively successful history of
assimilating technical changes without overt redundancies.[10] And in
an area of Scotland where rates of unemployment have been
consistently high and the signs of industrial decline all too obvious,
the steel melters have maintained an elite status earning relatively high
and steady incomes. However, these signs are not read by the steel
workers as indicating their aristocratic status among the working class,
regardless of how closely their circumstances may appear to correspond
in theory with the 'labour aristocracy'. Instead, they experience their
circumstances as a state of personal good fortune, deserved because
waited for, but not the reward of special intelligence, skills or effort.
The essentially passive wait for promotion in the seniority scale has
its counterpart in the neutral, almost complacent attitude towards
change in the industry. This conclusion receives some support from a
survey conducted in another steelworks in the same year as our own
study. Without drawing any general conclusions the authors noted that:

> Over the long-term prospects of the plant, three-quarters of the
> sample accepted that technological change was inevitable and could
> eliminate certain existing jobs. Despite such changes, however, job
> prospects were felt to be better than before steel nationalisation
> for those remaining in the industry. It is interesting that steel
> employees on the whole felt that their own jobs were secure in
> spite of being aware of future changes.[11]

Within the industry itself, such attitudes and confidence in the future
might be attributed to good propaganda and personnel management
but, in our view, the discovery of similarities of outlook within the
same industry in different plants and regions suggests that the
explanation is more deeply embedded. Workers in the steel industry
have a common experience of technical change which is essentially
positive. Their work has become lighter, cleaner and cooler without
fundamentally disrupting their traditional skills, and many new skills
have been successfully incorporated. In the light of this, it is

understandable that they should extrapolate and see their destiny in the same way, whether or not this is justified by the evidence of more recent circumstances, especially new steelmaking techniques. We are not asserting here that the melters have a particular image of technical progress *because* of a positive experience of technical change. There are examples which show that this is not necessarily the case, especially among our sample, for whom the open-hearth method of steelmaking is basically the same now as when most of them started work. We are putting forward the more complex hypothesis that until their predicament changes or unless they have direct access to the experiences of other groups of workers (through the labour movement, for instance) the melters will find it difficult to relate to technology except as a fact of life like the weather or sickness. The differences between this attitude and an image (which contains the openness and vitality of a metaphor and may have general applicability) is obvious from the flatness and finality of the following reply.

> The only thing now is that the BSC are building another big steelworks, so eventually we're going to close down and we're going to suffer. But there might be other, younger men, who might be re-employed somewhere else.

We took a special interest in the theme or 'topic' of technical progress, partly because this was salient in the replies of the sample of workers from a Ruhr steelworks interviewed by Popitz et al.[12] Attitudes to technology were one of the most important sources of data for constructing the typology of images of society. However, unlike Popitz, we found that replies on this subject were relatively barren. According to his typology, nearly all the first hand melters would have to be classified as having no image of society at all because their statements (especially but not only in this area) did not refer beyond their immediate experiences and there was a distinct reluctance to see their individual social position within a broader social context. In the interviews conducted by Popitz the conversation of those who were said to be without an 'image of society' was 'in no way colourless or boring' but 'as soon as it is extended beyond the limit of immediate experience. . .for all practical purposes it comes to an end'.[13] In our experience this is a good description of the majority of replies from the melters in our sample and not just a minority 20 per cent as in the German study. For this reason we cannot simply set aside the result, as Popitz does, or explain it away as an artifact of the interview method.

In our case it cannot be dismissed as a residual category. However, it would be premature to arrive at conclusions on the basis of the replies analysed so far. There are further questions about the role of the trade union and the labour movement as well as questions about class relationships which can be expected to provide further data and a fuller picture of links between personal or group experiences and the wider social context.

The Union — 'As Blue as a Melter's Glasses'?

All of the melters interviewed belonged to BISAKTA, the main production workers union in the steel industry, one of the six unions forming the TUC Steel Committee.[14] They are members of a Branch of about 250 workers. Attendance at Branch meetings is low although many workers blame the shift system for this. More than one third of the sample had previously worked for the union in one capacity or another, from collector to branch secretary. Their involvement in trade union activity is therefore somewhat greater than among the previous sample and is typical of the steel industry in being based closely on the work itself. Other unions in the works (for craftsmen, clerical workers and labourers) are also occupationally based and our finding confirms those of other observers who have drawn attention to the strong relationship between occupations and union attachment in the industry.[15] Like the previous sample, the melters had little or no direct experience of overt industrial conflict. Strikes had occurred in the plant but they were confined to other groups. The most obvious difference of any consequence between the two samples is that whereas the craftsmen are bound by agreements at the national level, the melters are able to negotiate locally. In practice, that means that within a nationally agreed framework there is negotiation over the proportion of wages based on the time rate and the bonus respectively. In an older plant, like the one studied, there is an effort to strengthen the time rate to make up for the static or declining tonnage bonus. This general framework, which is based on a strategy of co-operation with the employers provides a background which is rather different from the state of accommodation between management and unions which prevailed in the first sample. Given that this is not a new phenomenon but the continuation of a long tradition of conservative leadership in BISAKTA it helps to account for a number of variations between the replies of the melters and the maintenance craftsmen.

Firstly, the melters appear to have a much stronger sense of the union as being their union. For example, this can be seen in the frequent use of the possessive pronoun. None of them made the comment 'I'm only in the union because I have to be' or adopted the overwhelmingly passive attitude of the majority of craftsmen. Some melters criticised the union for being too 'political' or for not assisting the government; others either deplored militancy or blamed the union for not being aggressive enough. But these were often expressed as self-criticisms. Thus:

> Perhaps we've been dissatisfied at times with the wages but it never amounted to a strike because we always started negotiations through the management and at the end of the day we always got a settlement of some kind.

> Your trade union is only as strong as you make it.

Secondly, the union is regarded as an effective force in maintaining and increasing wages. Whereas the craftsmen repeatedly said that the union's main task was to improve the wages and conditions of its members but implied that they were not up to the task, the melters also attributed an important role to the union. This is true even when the comments are critical.

> I think it is quite possible to get more money. . .[the decline in wages] is the fault of the union because they've accepted certain things that have put the scale down instead of advancing it.

> I think we're quite capable enough of handling our own affairs.

> Well, as far as I'm concerned, the union has done more for the time men than the tonnage men. The tonnage men have never got a fair crack of the whip in here, never.

> [The decline in wages] is the fault of our union.

> Well, I think [the union's] doing a good job just now as far as we're concerned. I mean, we never gave them any cause to — we've never talked about strikes or anything like that.

As several of these comments indicate, one of the major topics in this part of the discussion was the level of earnings among the melters relative to other workers. This proved to be an important current issue as labourers (members of the General and Municipal Workers Union) and especially the furnace-demolishers or 'cutting out' squads had in the last five or six years practically closed the gap between their earnings and those of the melters. Moreover, they had achieved certain 'privileges' (e.g. bathing facilities and cooling-off time) which were not enjoyed by the melters. The differentials issue is a useful source of data about the melters' interpretation of their standing relative to other occupations and the closure of the traditional gap between their earnings and those of other production or maintenance workers.

The most striking aspect of the responses is the general lack of a sense of being threatened by the decline in differentials. Among a group of workers whose consciousness is based on a very narrow sense of occupational identity it is reasonable to suppose that the erosion of status and income will be resisted. However, this is not the case, and the results are more in keeping with our earlier finding that this occupational identity is based primarily on the *métier* and not on the cash nexus of the melter's position in the labour market. Therefore identity is not typically asserted at the expense of other workers. Instead, as often as not, there are expressions of sympathy and solidarity with other workers who have improved their earnings position.

> There are good trade union men for the labouring, 'cutting-out' squad on the hot jobs. Their wages are up on ours, and I'm all for that because they're entitled to it. We haven't had much rise over the years. We had to do away with other workers to give ourselves a rise.

> In the past there was such a difference in the wage scales in the steelworks. . .there used to be a vast difference between the lower paid man and the higher paid man. I think it's better the way it's worked around. I worked in the lower paid region, in both. You don't want to go back. You want to pull the other man up.

> In the likes of this job at one time in comparison with a labouring job there was a great discrepancy in the wages and you knew that if you started in the low job you would eventually work up to this. . .[Do you think it's a good thing that the low paid have come up?] Oh yes, I do. I don't mind them getting their few bob, y'know.

These remarks indicating solidarity are made always within the horizon of the melter's immediate experience — from a superior stance, looking down as it were. But this position of privilege is not defended according to the criteria of skill, theoretical knowledge or education which might be used to justify the higher earnings of a craftsman, although these criteria could be applied. In fact the superior position is hardly defended at all but is accepted 'naturally' as the reward of patience and application to the task. While these are thought to be deserving of a good wage, the melters did not deny that other qualities might deserve equal rewards. If these statements reveal a measure of 'solidarity' it is limited in the same way as other responses. So far these expressions of solidarity do not go beyond the confines of the plant or the industry.

Discussion of strikes and the steel industry's relatively strike-free record provides an opportunity of seeing whether the occupational identity of the melters involves an awareness of collectivity which extends to the manual working class as a whole. Strikes in other industries, including the contemporary miners' struggle, can be a pretext for sentiments of sympathy or antagonism. The steel melters' own direct experience of strikes is limited to one or two very short stoppages of a week or less in previous jobs in the steel industry or elsewhere. The melting shop itself had not been affected by a strike. After establishing these facts, a question was put to the melters about the relative 'peacefulness' of the steel industry compared with other basic local industries like mining and shipbuilding. They nearly all accepted it as a meaningful question but few of the replies can be said to contain any understanding of the difference between steel and other industries which explains it or refers to a mechanism such a 'militancy', low wages or bad conditions. There is hardly anything in the replies which suggests a rationale for strike action in any of these industries, let alone a common cause with workers in general. Instead there is a circularity of argument which combines and confuses interpersonal harmony with industrial harmony.

I've been in here 48 years and I can't remember a strike. . .There were strikes, but they were internal, confined maybe to tradesmen. But the steelworker himself, the man that's at the furnaces or at the machines, I've never known them to strike. . .Throughout the years, to my knowledge, there's always been a happy relationship between the men and the management, so this goes a big way towards the harmony of the steelworkers.

That's a hard question to answer. There have been no strikes, so they must be happy with a lot of things. . .I mean we've never been on strike and that, so we must be quite happy.

I've never been on strike in my life, in 43 years. It must be that everyone's satisfied. They must be satisfied, because there've never been any rumblings in the melting shop.

In a way which is now becoming familiar, these replies, which are typical of at least half of the sample, are occupationally centred. The differences between steel and other industries is explained in terms of the steelworker and not in terms of the miner or the shipbuilder, as it might have been. The only comparative references which are made refer to another recently-built steelworks in the vicinity which owes its 'bother' to a more militant and youthful labour force. It is as though the melters have no independent criteria outside their immediate occupational experience by which to judge this question — not even the collective experience of a working-class community.

Notably absent from the discussion are the 'official', 'institutional' and media interpretation of industrial relations which coloured many of the craftsmen's replies in a similar context. For example, none of the melters condemned the union for being 'too powerful', 'overstepping themselves' or 'holding the country to ransom' as did the craftsmen. In strong contrast with the inconsistencies we detected in the craftsmen's responses, there is a straightforwardness and simple clarity in those of the melters. They begin and end with personal, occupational experiences. This does not necessarily conflict with our prediction that matters furthest removed from personal and group experiences will be most susceptible to mediation by ready-made accounts and interpretations. According to this criterion, the steelworkers with their lack of strike experience should rely heavily on derivative and cliched vocabulary and arguments. In fact this is not the case because the melters do not step outside their own experience to answer the questions so artificially posed. Their reluctance to do so is an important finding. Quite simply, although their horizons are more bounded than the craftsmen's, their occupational and self identity is complete and sufficient. It is this fixed point from which all elaboration of replies takes place and because it is so stable (historically, physically and socially) there is much greater homogeneity and consistency in the melters' social consciousness than among the previous sample.

There were two replies which did attempt an explanation of the peaceful industrial relations record in the steel industry. Even these are one-sided, occupationally based interpretations of the benefits of hierarchy and differentials. Having 'something to look forward to, a goal to aim at' is regarded as a source of contentment and stability.

The steelman has always been a contented man. He's the most
contented worker, I would say, in Britain; because you'll never get
any grumbles, he's never gone out on strike. [What's the secret of
this?] As far as I know it's the variation in wages (first, second,
third hand melter) where the money comes in, and even down
to the bottom. . .

These statements embody a rudimentary social theory which is
not altogether different from the relationship between work and
attitudes which is assumed in certain factory studies. It is the
idea that the work situation or work relationships create or lead
to occupational and social perspectives. We have previously
dismissed the strict version of this assumption as being inadequate
to explain conflicting views of the same object. However,
from the results of our analysis so far, the sample of melters appears
to conform quite closely to a simple cause-effect model. Their
replies correlate closely in substance and in the form of their
expression with the typical concerns of the occupation and with
the horizon of occupational experience. Thus it seems that an
explanation of social consciousness can proceed without much
difficulty along these lines, but only so far. When these horizons are
deliberately crossed or removed then thinking has to draw on other
resources.

The questions on 'social background' and 'social class' and politics
can be regarded as a deliberate attempt to probe the limits of one of
the horizons of experience. They are a means of finding out which
reference groups are used in judging questions of personal status and
in arriving at political decisions.

Relating to Class

We observed in our analysis of replies to the question about 'getting on'
that there was general agreement about the most relevant contributory
factors and that these had virtually nothing to do with impersonal
social circumstances like 'knowing the right people', 'social background'
or 'luck'. We also noted that employment, despite some harsh early
experiences of being without work, was received unquestionably rather
than being either coveted or denigrated in particular forms as it was by
some of the fitters in the previous sample. These findings led us to
suspect that the melters would also have a relatively passive view of
social structure. Just as work was seen more as a sphere of action in
creation rather than social control, so we predicted society would be

taken for granted as a given sphere in which personal adaptation takes place and not as a sphere of social action (i.e. a sphere in which the direction or control of society is determined by the outcome of struggles between competing groups).

The influence of 'social background' was denied by all the workers in the sample – sometimes quite strenuously. Typically, a 'good' social background was taken to mean those qualities of emotional stability, friendliness and honesty which 'shouldn't have anything to do with work'. It 'shouldn't matter because you should take a person at their face value'. It may seem paradoxical that some of the very qualities of character which were used to define the 'good first hand melter' are being allocated to a private sphere deliberately removed from the sphere of work. However, because 'success' in the seniority system of the melting shop is self-legitimating it is not altogether surprising to find a stress on equality of personal worth. This is expressed in a variety of ways but often with reference to the differential in earnings among the melters. For example

> They're a good class of people in here. . .[Do you think it makes a difference how much you earn?] I couldn't speak for anybody else but it's never worried me none because I've come up the ladder there from 30 shillings up to what I've got now and it never bothers me now. I still go with my friends. . .[Does it allow you to lead a different way of life?] It's a poor man who can't better himself, but I don't know, some people overdo it, then go over the limit. But it's never bothered me none, anyway, speaking for myself. The men here have got cars but it doesn't change them much – maybe they don't drink so much now. But they're still your friends, they don't snub you – they can't snub me anyway, because they're just equal to me.

> It depends on a chap's make up. . .I believe money does make people different. Higher earnings, £3,000, £4,000 or £5,000 a year gives you a sense of security at your back, makes you immune from the fears of having to scrape by, meet bills and save for small luxuries – the fear of being absolutely without. And it can make a person socially class conscious. But if he had any character at all, he would enjoy these benefits but be the same bloke as he was in meeting old friends, etc.

> The first hand leads a better life because he spends more money, because he's got money to burn. I've gone out with first hands in the

works and they more or less try and treat you. But I will always
buy him a drink too because I'm not going to make him any better
than I am. He doesn't change in any way. They're not stuck up in
any way.

The reference group for these discussions is unmistakably limited to
the occupational group although the questions were not limiting in
this way. It is interesting to note that, unlike some of the craftsmen,
the melters never referred to staff or clerical workers even negatively
in this context. And one respondent quite explicitly rejected that
suggestion that money can put people in a different stratum.

I was fortunate [money] never made any difference to me but I've
seen it for years. [Because people look to another social group to
copy?] They may look, but they'll never penetrate it. They just
haven't got the know-how or anything or the adaptability to go in
there.

These replies generally confirm our prediction that melters would have
a predominantly passive view of social structure. In fact, nearly all the
statements conform to what Popitz called the 'static order' image of
society in which social relationships are not seen as developing and
changing, neither are they described in terms of power and
domination.[16] There is a fundamentally unquestioning relation to
'things as they are' and while we would not accept that as a full
description of the melter's social consciousness, it is true that
'constructing one's image of society in this way has something ultimate
about it and is both naive and exceedingly self-assured'.[17] From the
analysis of replies so far, it is not clear how far this goes, whether it
extends to social structure at the national level or whether it is a way
of describing social relationships in the community. One worker who
was asked to elaborate on the meaning of 'social class' was unable to
do so, beyond saying 'I haven't seen it in here' and 'where we stay
I don't see it existing'. He was prepared to accept and use the term
'middle class' but claimed never to have personally encountered the
middle class, despite having held several jobs before becoming a
steelworker. Such responses pose the problem of whether it is
meaningful to ask questions about class division at all if they are not
salient in a person's consciousness. In our view, it does make sense to
ask questions about social differentiation at the most general level for
two reasons: it gives a guide to the horizons of experience within a

social group and it is a particularly fruitful source of information about
the interaction of categories and themes derived from occupational
and other sources. One of our objects in the present context is to
establish (as we did with the craftsmen) whether the melters construct
images and explanations from the materials of their own experience or
whether they appropriate ready-made images from 'external' sources.

The first observation which can be made about this part of the
interview is that the melters found greater difficulty than the craftsmen
in discussing social differentiation according to a similar rather abstract
formulation. This is not to say that the melters failed to recognise
'class' as a meaningful category but only one quarter of them identified
three or more social classes compared with nearly half of the craftsmen
and their vocabulary was restricted almost entirely to 'upper', 'middle'
and 'working' class, without any of the variations used by the craftsmen.
The following reply is typical, the next rather more idiosyncratic.

> Oh yes, classes exist. There's been no change as far as I've seen —
> always the upper class, middle class and working class.

> Oh yes, classes definitely exist. To me there are three different
> classes of people and they classify themselves as social distinctions.
> Working class, because they stay in a nice home or stay in a nice flat.
> They're better than the lad that lives next door who can't get this
> good area to live. Middle class, where the whole house is working.
> Money is no object to them. Third class, in England at least —
> you've not an Englishman unless you stay below Bucks!

Few of the melters were able to elaborate on class differentiation in
terms of money, status or anything else with any fluency. This also
distinguishes them from the craftsmen, who laid hold of the problem
with these themes and categories, though not without confusion and
inconsistency. Moreover, there was an equal absence of those anecdotes
and examples from personal experience which the craftsmen used to
embellish their discussion. It is in keeping with the general outline of
'static order' which has been emerging that any dynamic understanding
of class divisions as 'withering away', converging or diverging is also
absent from the melters' discussion. Like employment, and the
occupational community, social divisions exist. However, they are
indefinite and indistinct, and because they are not experienced as
oppressive the worker is not provoked to strong approval or disapproval.
Neither the work situation nor the community milieu of the steelworker

provides significant experiences to upset this neutrality. On the contrary, there is evidence that 'traditional' patterns of association are dominant. We have already noted the close correspondence of occupation from generation to generation and the fact that nearly half the melters had close relations who worked in the same plant. Ties of kin and friendship at work are part of the closely textured pattern of sociability in the wider community which is based on pubs, clubs and churches within a very close geographical radius of the steelworks. One worker embodied these characteristics to the unusual extent of having, at one time or another, a father-in-law, two brothers-in-law and three sons working in the same plant. He described his kin and friends (most of them from work) as being 'like one big family'. Such sentiments are not unusual and it is more than likely that the influence of the community, which is hardly separable from occupation, will be even stronger than among the craftsmen.

In distinct contrast with the craftsmen, the melters had political allegiances which can be described as 'traditional' in that they tended to cast their vote out of a sense of loyalty, if not to a party as such, then to an idea. Very few had changed their vote in the last few general elections and only one predicted a switch at the next. Seventy-four per cent of the sample voted Labour at the last general election and 26 per cent Conservative. None voted for the Scottish National Party, which was favoured by some of the craftsmen. The replies clearly show how voters for both main parties ground their decisions.

I'm a Labour man. . .I've always been a Labour man all my days.

I've always voted Labour because I'm a working man.

I voted Labour of course. . .I suppose you more or less grow up to that, plus the fact that during my early days I'd quite a lot of unemployment and it was said that the Conservatives wanted 9 men to apply for 1 job so they could pick and choose and keep wages low. Labour has tried to give full employment. This early experience tends to throw you towards the left.

I'm not strict Conservative or strict Labour. I'd like to see a coalition — people in for their ability in business sense. . .A lot depends on your environment. My people were always strict Conservative. But that didn't mean I voted all the time for that. . . The working man wants decent living conditions, a decent wage, security. There's no saying what government's in — if he gets that, as far as he's concerned it's fine.

There is evidence, in many of the responses, of a lack of faith in parties and governments to 'deliver the goods' and a reluctance or inability to state differences between party policies and ideologies. But these expressions of disenchantment are not backed up by any discussion of social change and decline. For example, there was only one reference to crisis — 'the state this country is in at the moment we need a coalition, this is a crisis like wartime'. There are no references to 'alternatives', not even of the rhetorical 'but that would mean. . .' kind.

Taking these results with the previous findings they provide further evidence of a lack of reference to society as a totality and to its economic and social development. There is no aggregate of attitudes and perspectives which amounts to a view or image of society as a whole. This is a significantly different conclusion from that reached by other researchers into 'traditional' communities (especially Brown *et al.* and Bell and Newby). These authors note the range of variation, lack of homogeneity and the ambivalence of agricultural and shipbuilding workers' images of society. However, they cling to the expectation that workers will have and on occasion, will need to use a 'totalising' approach. Indeed, they perpetuate Lockwood's assumption that the solidarity of traditional occupational communities — if not destroyed by internal conflicts — is particularly conducive to the emergence of a class image of society. There is no evidence from our own study to justify this assumption. Not only is there not a strong class interpretation of society, there are few indications of a social consciousness which extends beyond the confines of the occupation, community and class. In our view this is one of the most important results of the analysis so far. The social consciousness of this group of steelworkers is strictly based on the principle of identity which means that their self-definitions are based in the *métier* and are not frustrated by its limitations (on skill, advancement, remuneration, etc.). It follows that we were unable to register any but the mildest expressions of opposition. If the principle of identity were extended to other workers in the steel industry and beyond them to other workers then there would be a chance of recognising the fundamental antagonism of industrial society between capital and labour. In this case the combination of these elements would be the basis of a social consciousness based on class. It is quite clear, however, that this developed form of 'proletarian' or class consciousness has not taken root among the steelworkers. It has been arrested at an earlier stage, which has not yet transcended the occupational characteristics of work, to identify the nature of work itself as something more than personal

destiny. There are numerous reasons why such a development should
be retarded, most of which have already been referred to. They include
the technology which makes such great demands of effort and
attention, the conservative attitudes of management and union, the
relative isolation of the steelworks and the community based upon it
and the slow speed of change in the system of work. This last point is
crucial: the generation of melters interviewed (unlike the craftsmen
and to a lesser extent the clerical workers) had not themselves
experienced the sudden change from an occupationally based system
of work to a technically based system and would never experience it
directly. We conclude from this that the conventional view that images
of society are likely to be well-formed among traditional occupational
communities should be rejected in favour of something like the
following: the more homogeneous, self-contained and stable the work
and community experience of a group of workers is, the more
prominent will be consciousness of identity; and conversely, the less
prominent will be consciousness of opposition and totality, i.e. the
more fragmentary and blurred the 'image of society'. This is compatible
with Touraine's understanding of workers' consciousness as long as a
slight modification is made to allow for the effects of 'community' as
well as 'work situation'. Community relationships are perhaps most
significant in providing reinforcement for occupational identity which
might otherwise be vulnerable to interpretations of self and society
which derive from the media, the market place and other external
sources.

Notes

1. The significance of these terms is that they refer to the dominant forms
of pre-industrial and industrial work. The place of each in the evolution of work
is described by A. Touraine in *La conscience ouvrière*, Part I.
2. Cf. D. Lockwood, 'Sources of variation in working class images of society' (1966).
3. P. Bowen, M. Shaw, R. Smith, 'The Steelworker and Work Control: a
sociological analysis and industrial relations case study', *British Journal of
Industrial Relations*, vol.XII, no.2 (July 1974), p.249. Studies which have
investigated aspects of labour in the steel industry include W.H. Scott *et al.*,
Technical Change in Industrial Relations (Liverpool University Press, 1956);
O. Banks, *The Attitudes of Steelworkers to Technical Change* (Liverpool
University Press, 1960); J.E.T. Eldridge, *Industrial Disputes* (Routledge and
Kegan Paul, 1968); J.K. Chadwick-Jones, *Automation and Behaviour* (Wiley,
1970); L.C. Hunter *et al.*, *Labour Problems of Technical Change*. Workers in
the steel industry were the subject of studies by both A. Willener, *Interpretation
de l'Organisation dans l'Industrie* (Mouton, Paris, 1967), and H. Popitz *et al.*,
Das Gesellschaftsbild des Arbeiters.

4. P Bowen *et al.,* 'The Steelworker', p.249.

5. E.g. C.R. Walker, *Steeltown* (Harper Bros., 1950).

6. P. McGeown, 'Steelman', in R. Fraser (ed.), *Work*, vol.2 (Penguin, Harmondsworth, 1969), p.57. See also his autobiography, *Heat the Furnace Seven Times More* (London, 1967).

7. McGeown, 'Steelman', p.64.

8. A. Jackson, *Modern Steelmaking for Steelmakers* (London, 1967).

9. Cf. A. Touraine, *La conscience ouvrière*, pp. 43 ff.

10. O. Banks, *Attitudes of Steelworkers*, describes how one such change was effected in a steel mill.

11. P. Bowen *et al.,* 'The Steelworker', p.256.

12. H. Popitz *et al., Das Gesellschaftsbild*, especially pp.232-47.

13. H. Popitz *et al.*, in T. Burns (ed.), *Industrial Man*, p.319.

14. BISAKTA, The British Iron, Steel and Kindred Trades Association. For details of the history of trade unionism in the steel industry refer to *Men of Steel*, by A. Pugh, Iron and Steel Trades Confederation (London, 1951).

15. E.g. P. Bowen *et al.,* 'The Steelworker'.

16. Popitz *et al.*, in T. Burns (ed.), *Industrial Man*, pp.281-7.

17. Ibid, p.284.

7 COLLUSIVE CONSCIOUSNESS: THE CLERICAL WORKERS

The 'curious neglect' of clerical workers as an object of sociological study which was noted by Lockwood in *The Blackcoated Worker* has scarcely been remedied.[1] In Britain, at least, there is no comparable recent study of clerical workers which takes such a broad perspective of their 'market', 'status' and 'work' situation and the transformations which have occurred in the size of the occupational group, its increasing internal differentiation, methods of organisation and applications of machinery. Some attention has been paid to the specific problems of white-collar unionisation and office automation but clerical workers' class or social consciousness has been largely ignored.[2] It is especially noteworthy that the study of social imagery in the British sociological tradition has been synonymous with the study of manual workers' images of society and not those among non-manual workers of the middle and working classes who are more significant numerically. The reasons for this, which may derive from a romantic pre-conception of the industrial worker as hero or ideological interpretations of the obsolescence of class, need not detain us here. In our view there is no good reason for limiting the study of social consciousness to one or even several groups in society. In fact, to do so is a positive hindrance to understanding because it excludes much relevant data. If the dynamics of social consciousness are to be fully understood, not only will adult male manual workers have to be studied but children, women and old people as well, from the whole range of occupations and social class.

The present task is more limited. Our third sample of clerical workers with incomes at the same level as the fitters and the steel melters was selected because of this similarity of income and also in order to maximise any possible contrasts arising from occupational circumstances. We have already described some features of the clerical 'career' and we have implied that there is a characteristic social consciousness among the clerical workers which is forged from the special occupational features of career-mindedness and company loyalty. In this chapter we will produce evidence to justify this understanding of self and society which for descriptive purposes we have called 'collusive'. As a label, the term 'collusive' draws attention to the element of game-playing which enables the worker to survive the unpleasant realisation of his inability to control his circumstances. The 'game' may be played with varying degrees of awareness but however openly played, it is a positive strategy for reconciling a potentially hostile environment and it contrasts strongly with the resigned dependency of the steelworkers. The term is also fortunate in expressing the dynamic, interactive quality of consciousness which we have tried to reflect in all our description and analysis.

The interview schedule used with the clerical workers is the same as that used with the previous two samples, with minor alterations. The analysis will therefore proceed in a similar way from details of the work situation to the employee's experience and interpretation of it and thence to the image of the firm and its place in the wider order of things. To establish the context, we will make a brief comparison between the 'ideal types' which have dominated the study of office work and the most important features of clerical occupations at the present day, which include the polarisation of the labour force and the degradation of work tasks.

Clerical Occupations: From Counting House to Shop Floor

Sociological accounts of clerical work have concentrated on three main features: the growth in the number of clerical workers in absolute terms and relative to manual workers; the changing nature of office work, which has eliminated many of the 'craft' aspects of the clerk's work; and the equivocal position of clerical workers in relation to the remainder of the working class and the Trade Union movement. In his useful summary of changes in clerical labour during the twentieth century Braverman states what has occurred, 'objectively' speaking, to this group of workers.

> The problem of the so-called employee or white-collar worker which so bothered early generations of Marxists, and which was hailed by anti-Marxists as a proof of the falsity of the 'proletarianization' thesis, has. . .been unambiguously clarified by the polarization of office employment and the growth at one pole of an immense mass of *wage-workers.* The apparent trend to a large nonproletarian 'middle class' has resolved itself into the creation of a large proletariat in a new form. In its condition of employment, this working population has lost all its former superiorities over workers in industry and in its pay scales has sunk almost to the very bottom.[3]

This picture of a 'new proletariat' created by increasingly fine divisions of labour in the office and the fragmentation of tasks tied to automatic and semi-automatic office machinery including computers, has by now almost entirely replaced the rather different picture of the 'new working class' which was sometimes used previously to characterise the rapidly-growing numbers of non-manual workers who appeared to be better educated, more privileged and usually better-paid than workers in factories.[4] If this conception of the 'new working class' ever had plausibility it could not long survive the evidence of polarisation in office work, and its increasing resemblance to factory work in every aspect. It relied on extrapolation from a much earlier picture of the office as a counting-house in which 'the clerk was more of a family servant than a wage labourer' and he was taken into the confidence of his employer, acting as an assistant manager, retainer and even prospective partner or son-in-law.[5] The nature of clerical work has changed to such an extent that this picture no longer has anything but historical interest − in its 'objective' aspects, that is. However, although the changing structure of the working class may be attributable to the quite unambiguous process of capital accumulation, the same cannot be said of the changing patterns of social consciousness. There are features of social consciousness which may lag far behind or leap ahead of changes in the material condition of an individual or a group of workers, and there is reason to believe that the old identification of the clerk with his employer still has its modern counterpart regardless of its irrelevance in the modern firm.

The older image of the clerical worker therefore has continuing relevance as a source of meaning and motivation for the office worker and it should be regarded thus and not as a paradigm for sociological interpretations. At the same time, the clerk's work is changing in a way which is narrowing traditional boundaries and opportunities. This creates a demand for new meanings and explanations which cannot easily be met from the older sources within the occupation. The search may therefore be extended to other sources, including professional associations and the 'white collar' trade unions. Since these organisations are themselves motivated by partly new occupational and social images, the range of possibilities for the clerical worker to develop a sense of identity and to experience conflict is very large, certainly larger than for either the craftsmen or the steelworkers, whose occupations have been subject to fewer radical changes in recent years.

Since we are attempting to describe the construction of social consciousness among a particular group of clerical workers, who may

or may not be typical, the initial task is to describe how far this group
has been affected by the transformation of office work in general and
to discover whether there are any peculiar features of the work or
occupational milieu which distinguish this group from others. Not all
groups are equally affected by the growth in size of firms, the
fragmentation of labour and technical innovations.

The Insurance Superintendents

The medium-sized insurance company which provided facilities for the
study, had grown in twenty years from a head office staff of hardly
more than fifty to its present size of five times that number. This rate
of growth is not unusual and the firm has followed a familiar pattern
of innovative policies. Computers had been in use in the firm for eight
years before the study and three years previously the salary grading
system was extensively reorganised. This is a good example of the
rationalisation of methods and control which is not exclusive to the
largest companies and it is worth describing in some detail.

   The old salary system was based on age and to a limited extent the
category of job. The salary scales were long and only three clerical
grades were recognised so that the system was open to the objection
that it placed undue emphasis on age (which is not directly related to
experience and may be even less related to performance) and did not
distinguish sufficiently between jobs on each scale. The traditional
system was replaced by a scheme based on an eight-fold categorisation
of jobs, each with a separate grading system and salary scale. Some of
the categories (clerical, secretarial and typing, etc.) are based on
traditional jobs, others describe the new tasks associated with the new
technology (programmers and systems analysts, punch card operators).
The increase in the number of categories also reflects the increasing
division of labour within the firm. Jobs are allocated to one of eight
grades on their respective scales according to a 'job evaluation'
procedure. Points are awarded to each job for their rating on 11 criteria
which (for clerical workers) include a measure of the complexity of
the work, supervisory responsibilities, experience, education,
confidentiality, initiative, etc. Ostensibly, and according to the
management interpretation of the salary scheme, it 'offers improved
opportunities for an attractive career to all who work enthusiastically
and effectively in the Company's best interests. . .an employee can see
clearly the opportunities available to him and he has the incentive to
apply himself to the full in order to take advantage of them'. Against
this, however, it is clear that any refinement of the job measurement

procedure which removes the evaluation from the person to the position removes the job one step further away from the worker and drives a wedge between his self and occupational identity. We have already hinted that the supposedly 'attractive career patterns' which are said by management to follow from the grading system are hardly viewed in this way by the workers. They find themselves for the most part in a position where the traditional rewards associated with age and length of service have been devalued with very little to replace them. On the seventh or eighth grades of the clerical scale the 'attractive opportunities' have basically ceased to exist beyond the job itself, with its supervisory responsibilities. The attitudes to work which are expressed in the interviews can therefore be taken to signify a coming to terms with this situation and the contradictions between 'job' and 'career' which it contains.

The worker at the top of the clerical category is a supervisor or superintendent of one of the stages of the insurance process, the basic element of which is the policy. The sample of workers included proposals, policy collection, claims and pension superintendents as well as supervisors of the ancillary processes of data processing, coding and accounting. Typically, the superintendent has responsibility for up to ten workers in a small department or as many as twenty in a large department. This involves overseeing the work of other clerks, secretaries and punch card or computer operators. Although all the interviewees were men, as many as 90 per cent of the workers in these departments were women. The nature of the work brings the superintendent into contact most frequently with the clerical grades in his own department but there is at least occasional contact and sometimes frequent contact with departmental actuaries and managers. Nearly all the sample claimed to know by name all those in the office senior to themselves. All of this contact takes place within a carefully graded hierarchical structure quite unlike that of the two previous samples. In work itself there is very little routine contact with equals in this hierarchy. This is left to meal breaks, when most of the sample fraternise with their fellow-superintendents.

For all of the workers in the head office, but of course not in the branch offices, contact with the public either directly or by telephone is a rarity. However, although this job has 'more to do with systems than people' as one worker put it, there are signs that the insurance workers relate to their work not only as obligatory to management or to their own pride in work but also as a responsibility to the customer, the policy-holder. This dimension is missing from the other two samples.

The more immediate responsibility, which is felt that much more strongly by the superintendent is to ensure the speed and accuracy of the department's output. As we shall see, this is articulated by the clerical workers in a variety of ways but they all indicate a high degree of attachment to work which is equal to yet different from that shown by the craftsmen and steelworkers. It is one of the possible foci of an occupational identity which can neither appeal to easily recognisable skills of hand and eye, nor to a tangible product. Clues to this occupational awareness are found in the brief job descriptions and in replies to the question about the qualities required by the senior clerical worker.

The 'Good Superintendent'

It is gratifying in interviews to find that a question or topic evokes responses which are similar in content and expression among one social group and that a very different pattern emerges with equal spontaneity from another group. It is an indication of non-random variation and a stability of conception which, however mundane the topic may appear to be, is a more reliable guide to social consciousness than most one-dimensional attitude questions. Discussion of the topic of the 'good' craftsman, the 'good' first hand and the 'good' superintendent has this quality of clear definition, directness and richness which shows that a 'social Topic' has been activated and not just a personal opinion manufactured for the occasion.

The theories of 'commonsense' and application which the craftsmen discussed and the first hand's emphasis on level-headedness hardly figured at all in the clerical workers' replies. Their discussion of both skills and personal attributes was based on other concepts which show that they talk about work in a person-centred way, which is not altogether surprising for a group of workers whose main task is to guarantee the output of others. But it has important consequences for self and occupational identity.

The large majority of the superintendents referred to two main themes: understanding the staff in their departments and understanding their job. The first of these was given priority by three-quarters of the sample, the second was mentioned by nearly the same number. There is a consistency about these responses which is even greater than with the two earlier samples.

Firstly, you've got to have an understanding of people, of your staff. I think this is what is lacking in so many people in the supervisory

position. If you have a proper relationship with your staff they'll
work far better, the work will be done faster. Secondly, you've got
to be able to do the work yourself, have an idea of what supervising
really means — also a delegation of work.

You need technical knowledge, patience and understanding of the
people you're working with. When someone comes to you with a
query you should be receptive to that query and if you're not 100
per cent sure of the answer you should take them with you while
you're finding out. This is what I try to do.

The main thing is to have a fairly happy department under you. . .
You've got to keep people satisfied. When there's friction you don't
get the work done.

I don't know if I'm a good superintendent or not, but I would say
one has to have tact and patience. You must be firm — I'm possibly
on the lenient side — but I feel I get a fair bit out of people because
of this. . .[What about expertise?] Yes, you should be able to do all
the jobs in a department, though this is not absolutely essential. But
you should be on top.

I'd say probably a down-the-middle policy. You've got to understand
your staff, I think the days of hard discipline are over. . .and a
thorough understanding of the job.

Others gave content to the idea of 'understanding the staff' by talking
about 'being firm', 'interfering as little as possible', 'letting people get
on with the job' and so on. Except for one mention of 'accuracy' there
was hardly any reference to the performance aspect of the work itself.
Indeed, one worker denied that this was at all important.

You need personal understanding of each individual's own
requirements. Our job isn't that technical that a reasonably
intelligent being couldn't skate through the particular job they're
doing. It really boils down to keeping the staff happy.

There was only one superintendent who referred to the notion of
'commonsense' in this context. It is interesting to note, in view of the
craftsmen's stress on this quality, that this was one of the very few
clerical workers whose father was a self-employed craftsman. If this
is not purely coincidental it implies that the social Topoi of one group
of workers may carry over into the next generation in spite of upward

mobility. Of course no firm conclusions can be drawn from the present evidence.

The fundamental difference between the perceptions of work of the three samples is that the craft ideal of the craftsmen and the melter's sense of the *métier* apparently has no direct equivalent among the clerical workers. But this is not to say that they have a view of work which is any more instrumental. On the contrary, it is not the product but the work *system* and its smooth and efficient functioning which becomes the chief preoccupation. It is after all less easy to have feelings of admiration and satisfaction towards the forms, punch cards and computer print-outs which are the office worker's materials than towards a quietly-running compressor or a flow of molten steel. The administration of the labour process is not necessarily the main source of pride in work for all supervisors. For example, it did not appear to be true of the foremen in the process plant or the sample passers in the melting shop. Although they were not the main object of our study, conversation with these workers revealed closely similar attitudes to the work task, and, if anything, an even stronger reliance on job performance as a source of identity. We therefore conclude that the clerical workers' relation to the demands of the occupation is not simply a result of their being in an intermediate position in a hierarchy of authority and responsibility. Their replies could have contained many more references of the kind that one superintendent gave when he described the good superintendent as one who 'should ensure that the work is done in a proper fashion and at adequate speed', i.e. replies which direct attention to the tasks in hand. Even the workers just quoted did not elaborate on this point but went on to discuss 'communication' and 'involvement with the staff'. What the replies do indicate is that the superintendents have a relationship to the organisation, 'the company' as a social system which is not encountered in the replies from the other two samples. It is a relationship which is to a large extent a substitute for pride in work as such and it replaces occupational identity. This is why our label 'collusive consciousness' does not immediately refer to characteristics of the occupation but to a relationship with the work organisation.

We can begin to define this relationship by analysing responses to the question 'Do you think this company differs in any significant way from other insurance companies?' The main intention here was to elicit an image of the firm and to see whether it relied on distinctions between small/large, traditional/modern, etc. or whether it was more personally based. Firstly, the replies on the whole indicate a rather low level of comparative knowledge and awareness of other insurance companies as employers. Two thirds of the sample did not believe in or did not know of any differences in rates of pay between their own company and the local insurance offices. The remaining third thought that their own salaries were marginally lower than they would get for equivalent jobs in some of the larger companies in the vicinity. It is clearly not an important point of comparison for the worker who said 'I've no idea and I'm not interested in what anybody's paid in another office' nor for most of the others. However, size is a more significant variable and most of the sample drew favourable comparisons between their own relatively small company and one or two large neighbours. For example,

> I don't think I'd like to work in a huge company. . .I think you're very much more than just a number. Here they still do try to treat people as individuals. I don't think I'd like to work anywhere very much bigger than this.

> I wouldn't like it to get too big; I feel it's big enough already. There has been quite a change in attitudes in the twenty-seven years I have been here but I feel once it gets too big, management starts getting too remote.

> To walk into [a large general insurance office] is a shattering experience — to see the way people are herded in.

There is little in these replies so far to indicate any close identification with the company. In fact in the whole discussion of relationships within the firm there is markedly less use of the possessive pronoun than in the previous sample. On the other hand there is much greater fluency in discussing these questions. This is not only because the firm itself is smaller than the large complexes from which the other two samples were drawn but because the clerical workers (like a few of the craftsmen who had worked in the process plant in its early stages) have an image of the firm as a social organisation, not just as a job provider or as the site of a production process. Just what this means can be seen in the following statement about developments in the head office in which the company is referred to as 'we' and an organic analogy is used.

> There has been a lot of change. When I came there were about seventy staff and the company then prided itself as being a friendly

organisation. That has disappeared, inevitably, though nobody is
to blame. We're now in a transitional period being neither a small
nor a large company — hence the growing pains.

Even more explicitly, some of the replies used the family analogy, but
as a thing of the past or in a rather apologetic way.

Partly because of [the smaller size] you probably have more of a —
and I don't like using this — 'family unit' here. I don't go along with
this 'family' business really but comparing the large companies this
is true to a certain extent.

Years ago, when I joined, I knew everybody in the company but
not now. There used to be talk in the company of us being a 'family'.
It's definitely not like that now. They're gearing themselves more
and more to an efficient business system — which is all to the good.

These statements are noticeably different from those of the craftsmen
and melters when they discussed changes they had experienced in their
firms. In their case, the change was seen in terms of technology — new
processes, labour-saving machinery, greater precision and so forth. The
fact that these changes are introduced as a direct result of management
policies is only incidental in their explanations because technology is
identified as the key to industrial development. Whatever the benefits
or otherwise, the worker submits to technical change as destiny rather
than as something to be accounted for in terms of social action. The
clerical workers, in contrast, are more likely to perceive their company
as a social system, as a means for exerting more or less effective control
over people and processes. This is a key difference and one which is
likely to be associated with a strong awareness of 'totality' in social
consciousness, provided that it can be generalised from the work
organisation to society as a whole. The analogies of the organism or
the family are not the only ones which occur here. The 'efficient
business system', 'the company' and the frequent references to
problems of 'communication' all reveal an understanding of the
organisation (and their role within it) as an instrument of social change.
It is impossible for the manual worker in the large corporation to think
of his relation to the technical system in this way.

The Company: Conflicts and Loyalties

The question (Q.23) which we eventually abandoned in the sample of

steel melters because it was either misinterpreted or not understood at
all, received the most positive responses from the clerical workers, who
for the most part took up the distinction between the 'unitary' and
'dichotomous' models of the organisation and were able to elaborate
on them at some length in the light of their experiences. This is not
because the clerical workers are particularly articulate in comparison
with the manual workers. It applies to this question in particular and
not to the interviews in general, which reveal similar ranges of fluency
both within and between samples. To find that one question receives
an especially active response from one group and not from another
is therefore to have found a significant variation in social consciousness.
In our view, the clerical workers' ability to handle this question with
relative ease and sophistication is further evidence of what might be
called their organisational rather than occupational identity.

Discussion of the two models of the organisation had an either/or
quality about it but at the same time it was far from being non-
committal. The two-sidedness of course follows partly from the way
in which the question is put but not entirely. The craftsmen were much
less evenly balanced in their responses, for they saw the firm
predominantly as a sphere of harmony in work yet opposition with
respect to its rewards. The clerical workers, while recognising the
relevance of both models of the organisation, made a greater effort to
give them equal weight. That is, they do not just give general assent to
the unitary view and then proceed to describe instances of conflict;
nor do they differentiate between the intrinsic and extrinsic aspects
of the work. Instead, the superintendents generally associate themselves
with the unitary interpretation but go on to stress its ambiguity in
practice for those like themselves who occupy an intermediate position
in the hierarchy of the firm. Thus:

> It's partly one and partly the other. In my position I obviously
> have a responsibility *for* my department and a responsibility *to* the
> people who work in the department. But I've also a responsibility
> to the company and if the company doesn't prosper, nobody will.

In view of the hierarchically graded structure of the organisation it
is not surprising that the vocabulary of dichotomy (us/them, workers/
management, etc.) is generally lacking from the responses. But this
does not mean any shortage of perceptions of conflict or divergent
interests. These can be grouped according to three main themes: age,
education and membership of the head office or branch offices. The

first of these was the most common and in several of the interviews it
follows the pattern which we observed in some earlier replies.
According to one worker (aged 51),

> This is a very difficult question. . .I'm of the old school, of course,
> most of us in my age group feel that whatever happens you're
> working for the company and not yourself. On the whole the
> company are paying you and your loyalty is to the company and
> you do your best from the company's point of view. Most in my
> age group are brought up in this way. I think the youngsters are
> definitely interested in themselves. I think there should be a happy
> medium.

Another stated that whereas the unitary model was applicable ten years
ago it was now superseded because of the number of young people
joining the staff and the rapid turnover.

> This company always had a family type image about it, everybody
> knew everybody, but now it's just bulging a wee bit. . .The young
> people are only here for the money; they would change jobs.

> The past Chairman had a great thing about 'the family', family
> feeling. He didn't work here! I think there's a tremendous amount
> of 'them and us' situations (Pensions like a separate company,
> field vs. inside staff). . .There are breakdowns in communications
> between divisions.

> I think the lower echelons, comprising most of the staff — their
> main loyalty is to themselves. I would say that most of them aren't
> interested in the job. They're working because it is a job and nothing
> more. . .But for my own group, you obviously can't work for 15
> to 16 years with a company and not have some sort of loyalty
> towards it.

There is a general and quite strongly held feeling that the main changes
which have occurred in clerical work (increasing size of organisations,
routinisation of tasks and the influx of female labour) are more
appropriately described by the conflict than the unitary model of the
organisation. However, the above replies show that the superintendents
cling to both conceptions because their own assertions of loyalty to
the company do not necessarily exclude sympathy for the younger
workers who are subjected to 'an awful lot of terribly repetitive and

boring work'.

The same is true of the other sources of conflict, between professional and non-professional groups in the company and between head office and branch office personnel. The conflicts are spelt out but they are guided by an image of the organisation as a whole rather than a sectional interest. For example

> The first [unitary] view is more what I'd expect from a professional-run organisation, management who know exactly what they are doing. In here we're run by actuaries who have no real management training. They fall down on this, they're on a completely different level from the ordinary working clerk. . .The thing I don't like about the set-up is that the person in charge at the moment tends to look upon you as a bloody ordinary clerk.

In a similar criticism, one worker finds the conflict view the more accurate description of the company but in the phrase 'they don't realise. . .' appeals to the integrative principle.

> I would tend to come down on the side of the second [conflict view], I think, putting it at a fairly high level, the actuarial side — they tend to stick together. I suppose this is fair enough. This is what insurance is about. You've got to have actuaries. . .[Can you illustrate the problem?] This again has a lot to do with the mechanisation of the whole system. The people in management, actuarial types, are so far removed from the day-to-day work they're still thinking in strictly actuarial, strictly mathematical terms. They don't realise how much is involved in our own particular sphere. . .One finds such attitudes frustrating'.

This last sentence, which is by no means unique, is revealing. It sums up the emotional response to a view of the organisation which has two contradictory elements which cannot be resolved. On the one hand there is a version of the unitary model which may or may not be expressed in terms of 'loyalty' or 'company-mindedness'. It does not have to be, because all that it need involve is a reference to the organisation as a totality (this dimension was entirely absent from the previous two samples, discussion). On the other hand the clerical workers recognise sectional interests whether these are illustrated by reference upwards to the professionals in management or downwards to the lower grade clerical workers. The superintendent is in a position

to appreciate and articulate both views of the organisation but has no
means of resolving the tension between them either in theory or in
practice without positing an alternative mode of organisation. Hence the
expressions of frustration. One of the workers quoted above went on
to spell this out more clearly. Referring to what he called the
'breakdown in communications', he said

> It didn't exist here for competitive purposes, it wasn't that we were
> all competing for top jobs. It was more a situation caused by
> frustration. It was because people weren't encouraged to make
> decisions. . .Frustration is the greatest killer of all in modern society.
> In my opinion, I have skills much bigger than my job demands.

The problem is one of reconciling the often incompatible demands of
the job (interpreted as keeping a 'happy department' with a low
turnover of labour producing accurate and efficient work) and the
demands of the company as a whole (described by many in terms of
the application of efficient business organisation and methods, job
evaluation and work measurement). The solution which the majority
of the clerical workers arrived at was to collude in the management's
rationalisation schemes as being in the company's interests and to play
down its effects on their work and on them as individuals.

> The control as to what goes on within a company, this is dealt with
> purely by management. I think the management look on it as what
> is best for the company and if the individual benefits as a result of
> the company benefiting then they probably should. But the main
> consideration from the management point of view would be what
> is going to benefit the company and not necessarily the individual.

This ability to see and argue from the management's point of view,
though without necessarily identifying with management or approving
of what they do, is what we mean by 'collusion'. It is the habit of
according legitimacy to the social control and influence of management
even when this is felt to be personally detrimental. The need to do this
(e.g. to accept the job evaluation scheme even when it curtails career
prospects) is one of the costs of commitment to the company. Yet, as
we have seen, few of the superintendents were keen to move or to
abandon their self-identity as loyal workers. Only one of them (aged
46) took anything like an 'instrumental' view and even this was
tempered with a rhetorical question implying that there were other

considerations.

> People aren't terribly concerned about working for the company —
> they're working for money. . .If they can earn more money
> elsewhere and conditions are okay, they'll go. Obviously, somebody
> in my position: you're not going to move away, are you?

The next stage in the analysis is to see if the holistic view of the
company (which need not be unitary) is an equally strong guiding
theme for the responses to questions about representation and
membership of the staff committee. For the other two samples, of
course, membership of trade unions and association with the wider
trade union movement potentially provided a base for opposition as
well as consciousness of identity. In the event, the potential for
opposition was not at all far developed among the craftsmen and the
steelworkers. However, the so-called 'white collar' unions have grown
rapidly and have more than kept pace with the increasing size of the
non-manual labour force. Some of these unions have also been among
the most active and aggressive in promoting their members interests.
It is reasonable to predict that these trends might impinge in some way
on the clerical worker's consciousness even to the extent of providing
an externally-derived source of oppositional ideas.

The Staff Committee

Analysis of the topic of unions and individual versus collective action
begins with the staff committee, which is the only formal representative
body within the company. It was formally established after the
Industrial Relations Act for representation of workers' interests. This
opened up new areas of discussion, including salaries, and proceedings
were formalised and minutes were kept. Previously, the staff committee
which met once a month was regarded by all those involved as little
more than a means of disseminating information and as a 'talking shop'
or forum with no real power or effectiveness. The staff committee even
in its more structured phase is far from having the powers of a staff
or professional association. At this time none of the clerical workers
belonged to a staff association, a professional association or a trade
union and none had been a member previously. Neither was there any
immediate prospect of a staff association being formed or of trade
union recruitment taking place in the company studied although unions
and, more frequently staff associations, were already active in most of
the larger local companies. These questions were nevertheless a

preoccupation of some managers, who appeared to feel somewhat threatened by the progress of unionisation in the banking, finance and insurance industries generally. We therefore investigated attitudes towards both staff committees to see if there were any signs of change towards a more positive or aggressive view of representation. In effect we were asking whether there was, even in embryo, a consciousness of identity or opposition which could eventually be expressed in concerted social action to transform the situation of a group of workers or to change the direction of the organisation.

Almost without exception the clerical workers had each spent some time as a representative on the staff committee in its less structured form. Three superintendents were also currently sitting on the five-man senior staff committees set up after the Industrial Relations Act. The responses generally follow the 'unitary' interpretation of employer-employee relationships which, according to Will, is espoused by six of the seven largest staff associations in the insurance industry in their constitutions.[6] What we are dealing with, however, is a range of much less considered views in a much less formal organisation and our task is to identify the rationale of this unitary perspective as well as its existence.

Descriptions of the work of the staff committee were most frequently couched in terms of its role in information and communication. For example,

I think the main object [of the staff committee] was to act as a platform where the staff could air any points — about the running of the company, points of clarification. . .

The idea was that [the committee] could put forward views from the staff to senior management who could then answer them.

Our hope is to try and get the viewpoints of the people we represent across to the management. We don't intend to make it all one way, in that 'we want, we want'; we also hope to get something across to management that we're willing to try and do.

Others argued that the staff committee existed to help the 'upflow' as well as the 'downflow' of information and 'to put forward valid suggestions to management'. In all of these replies there is a strong sense of the terms of reference of the committee and its appropriate task. No-one suggested that it should become involved in the negotiation of salaries, for instance, and most explicitly rejected this

suggestion. The rationale for this appears to rest on the recognition of
the management's authority to make all the significant decisions
affecting employees.

> The committee's work was mainly to do with details. There was
> very little point in discussing the salary structure in a company like
> this because it is decided by the directorate and that's all there is. . .
> more the organisation of the office as such.

> The main subjects up to now have been mainly on systems and
> conditions, not salaries. We feel this is outside our terms of
> reference at the moment.

> Salaries should be taken care of in the system — although there are
> apparent anomalies in the job grading. If the grade seems wrong
> you just have to try and prove this.

This sense of participating in a 'system' whose legitimacy is taken for
granted is the outstanding feature of all these replies. It follows that
all the 'grievances' which are mentioned and examples of the staff
committee's successes refer to matters which are peripheral to the
basic workings of the system. Anomalies in job grading, the publication
of salary scales, additional holidays for long-serving employees, seating
and lighting were mentioned as examples of topics discussed in the staff
committee. Small improvements in overtime pay and holiday
entitlements for junior staff were mentioned as staff committee
successes. There is a similar rationale to those replies which, in one way
or another, dismiss the committees altogether as having no practical
relevance. One worker said 'it's a mystery in practice and theory' why
the staff committee exists. The same worker did not think that it was
the committee's job to concern itself with salaries.

> I don't think [salaries] should be discussed. But it depends on the
> attitude of management towards the question. If management are
> playing the game, there's no need for that kind of approach.

The idea that these matters are 'taken care of in the system' and that
by and large the system works smoothly is so prevalent that further
discussion of the topic brought rapidly diminishing returns. Even the
one superintendent who appeared to have an appreciation of some of
the wider issues of representation seemed to accept the unitary view
of the organisation, albeit a more complex one. It is worth considering

in greater detail, because it throws some light on the question of how
the unitary view might develop to incorporate an element of partisan
thinking.

The superintendent in question was the secretary of the senior staff
section of the staff committee and referred proudly to his father, a
postal worker, and grandfather as being 'very strong' trade unionists.
He deplores the lack of unionisation in insurance and argues that it
would be 'in most people's interest'. The general aversion to unions,
he claims, has to do with 'a pseudo-professional-class element' by which
he means the (unjustified) identification of clerical workers with the
professionally qualified groups above them in the status hierarchy.
However, he does not argue that the clerical workers should identify
with manual workers or with lower status groups instead. The rationale
is that each group has its own problems and interests but that so far
only senior management has this 'realistic' view.

> Senior management work and think in terms of self-interest. Also,
> management techniques tend to emphasise the separateness of
> clerical staff. There is a definite need for a staff committee because
> the middle management (including junior officials) are left wallowing
> in the middle.

Therefore, the main function of the staff committee is 'to provide a
bridge between senior management and staff – an ever-growing gulf'.
In other words, it is not an argument based on sectional interests alone.
It refers to the organisational system as a totality and assumes that
there is a common interest which is best served by each group playing
a full, responsible role. Within this scheme the industrial relations
legislation is welcomed as an opportunity to educate members of the
organisation into what at times looks like a version of 'self-
determination'. This example of the 'committee-minded' superintendent
is instructive because it demonstrates that collective representation may
be based as much on awareness of totality as awareness of identity or
opposition.

This is evidence to support the view of white-collar unionisation
which argues that the ambiguity of the clerical and lower managerial
worker's position in relation to capital and labour is most likely to lead
to a variety of alternative strategies and behaviour.[7] It seemed highly
improbable that the sample of clerical workers would embrace
collective representation|and collective action in the forms offered by
the trade union movement, especially in view of the hostile and

dismissive attitudes which were expressed towards unions such as
ASTMS. It is quite feasible that the conflicts and loyalties which are
felt within the company — sometimes quite strongly — could be
channelled into some form of staff association. At least half of the
sample thought that staff associations were a good thing in principle
but that they were not really necessary in a smaller company where
less formal methods were more appropriate. The circumstances which
were seen as creating suitable conditions for trade union activity were
condemned and unions themselves were seen as fundamentally alien
organisations. Asked whether they would like to see a more formal
structure of representation, some of the superintendents replied in
terms akin to the rhetorical question, which precludes further debate.

> No, I think you're verging on the trade union movement here.
> Personally, I don't approve of it; I wouldn't like to see it happen
> here.

> I think there is possibly a case for a staff association. I certainly
> wouldn't go as far as a union. I wouldn't like to see a union coming
> in. On the other hand, with job evaluation and work measurement,
> timeclocks, etc. one is beginning to feel that one is getting more like
> a shop floor. This might be paving the way.

It might indeed. But all of the workers in this sample rejected trade
unions as a means of collective representation. Clearly, they regard
unions as a threat to the mutual interests and goodwill which they, in
their capacity as men in the middle, feel they have a duty to preserve
as far as possible. This tenacity in seeing the organisation from the
'system' point of view, despite awareness of changes which makes it less
of a relevant description and more of an article of faith, is characteristic
of the clerical workers, as we have already seen. Their position is
becoming increasingly ambiguous as they find their work becoming
more routinised, more like 'the shop floor' and their access to higher
managerial positions effectively blocked through lack of education
and professional qualifications. However, their tendency to identify
upwards rather than downwards, and not to assert their own identity
as a group is consistent with what we have learned of their desire to
control and ensure the smooth functioning of the work process, for
ultimate control resides with management. In a larger organisation the
sheer size is likely to preclude this understanding of work as a system
and will consequently encourage a group identity born of isolation

from lines of communication and control. We therefore agree with
Crompton:

> That some white collar workers should see their interests as being
> best fulfilled by co-operation with management (or the capitalist
> function) – for example, in staff associations – and others in the
> same occupation see their collective interests as being best served
> by identification with the labour function – in trade unions – is
> perfectly compatible with their ambiguous class situation.[8]

We would also agree that 'the protagonists of neither view can be said
to be "falsely" conscious of their class interests', because our non-
representational view of consciousness does not allow judgements about
its truth or falsity, only the nature of its relationship towards an object.
However, there is an important question here, namely whether or not
the clerical workers' consciousness is related to the social system in a
way which parallels its relation to the organisational system of work.
This was the case in both of the previous samples because the
craftsmen's and the steelworkers' awareness of identity was carried over
from the circumstances of work to the occupational community and,
less consistently, to the wider society. In view of the importance of
'totality' in the clerical workers' consciousness so far, it is a question
of how this element might be articulated in the larger social context,
if at all.

From the Organisational System to the Social System

There is one immediate difference between the clerical workers and the
two manual workers samples which needs to be clarified before any
further comparisons are made. Both the craftsmen and the steel melters
inhabited local communities which, we argued, could rightly be called
'traditional' because of the continuity of residence through several
generations and the predominance of certain occupations in one or a
few main industries and plants. We were careful to point out that this
did not necessarily support the thesis that these are the circumstances
which give rise to a traditional or proletarian workers' consciousness –
at least, not in the case of the craftsmen. However, the clerical workers
do not share this community context to any significant degree. Like
the majority of office workers they are metropolitan city dwellers,
separated from informal contact outside work by time and distance.
Whereas the steelworkers and, to a lesser extent, the craftsmen had
networks of friends and social acquaintances who shared their

occupational experience, hardly any of the clerical workers placed the same emphasis on social contacts with fellow workers. This is not to say that the superintendents avoid or dislike engaging in non-work activities with their fellow workers: it is simply that these activities take a different form. For example, nearly all of the sample played golf more or less regularly with the company club. This, and other activities like bridge and badminton, were organised to help create a 'community' of workers rather than being spontaneous expression of shared interests and experiences in work. This is in sharp contrast to the steelworkers' social contacts with workmates outside work which were typically habitual, unarranged encounters in a small selection of local pubs. We conclude from this, and from evidence of where the clerical workers live, that they do not constitute a social network or have a common basis of experience outside work. They do not relate to an independent occupational tradition by which they can judge their own experiences. It follows from our earlier argument that the clerical workers as a group are likely to be more open to the ready-made social images and explanations which derive from established institutional sources than are those still in close touch with an 'alternative', community-based tradition. For the moment we regard this as a hypothesis to be tested.

In our discussion of the criteria used by the clerical workers to interpret careers or 'getting on', we noted the high priority given to 'luck' as well as to the personal factors of ambition and intelligence. This emphasis on luck, expressed almost universally in the cliche 'being in the right place at the right time', makes this the closest approximation to a social Topic that we found among the clerical group. In view of the general lack of close associations at work which carry over into leisure activities, this is a significant indicator of common consciousness of work which might otherwise be underestimated. Although neither Popitz nor any other commentator has applied the concept of the social Topic to any but manual workers, there is no reason to doubt its appropriateness among the clerical workers. In spite of, or perhaps because of, the variety of personal experiences and the relative complexity of their paths in the occupational structure, 'the commonplace and the catchphrase take over as soon as the conversation switches to general issues'.[9] If, as Popitz argues, the propensity to adopt certain Topoi is a guide to relatively enduring interpretations of personal experience, phrases like 'being in the right place at the right time', 'having a face that fits' or 'circumstances beyond anyone's control' are noteworthy. These phrases embody a view of the organisation as an impersonal, even arbitrary, system. This conforms with the general tendency we have noted for the clerical workers to orientate themselves towards the organisation as a totality but it casts some doubt on the otherwise generally positive evaluation of the organisation as an efficient and beneficent whole. 'Luck', can of course be either 'good' or 'bad' and most of the superintendents recognised both possibilities. It can account for opportunities as well as obstacles to advancement. However, we can predict that as career paths are increasingly curtailed and as the recent rapid expansion of the company slows down, the chances that 'luck' will come to mean 'bad luck' will grow. There is a possibility that this Topic might become an element of oppositional consciousness if the superintendents ever came to feel that they had lost touch with the effective controlling function in the company. At present we can only say that there are implications of a common consciousness of work and that this is based neither on closely-knit groups of workmates and friends at work nor on an occupational community in the usual sense of the term. In fact it is consciousness of an individual rather than a collective confrontation with 'the system', i.e. the company and employment generally. This is where it differs most radically from the consciousness of the other two groups whose work-related identity implied that what happened to one would happen to all. Further questions about social background provide responses which help to explain how the clerical workers relate their occupational experiences to the varieties of occupational and social differentiation.

It will be remembered that the clerical workers, like the craftsmen and the steelworkers, were almost unanimous in rejecting 'social background' as a factor relevant to personal advancement. This clear response provided a useful opportunity to discover which aspects of social background the clerks were referring to and to explore the implications of the social 'theory' they were using. In nearly every case social background was taken to mean a combination of family circumstances, friendships, and schooling which are connected with the way people speak, where they live and their outlook on life. It is what we refer to when we 'place' people in a casual encounter. At the same time it appears that social background is something a person can leave behind if he has drive and intelligence. 'It's up to your own individual outlook on life' is one of those statements which seems to rely on an open mobility theory. This, the most common interpretation, had a historical dimension which contained the view that if social background was once an important factor in getting a job and in building a career, it no longer applied. Two of the superintendents did think that it might be an important factor 'at a higher level', where the 'old school tie' or education at a private school might be an asset. It is clear from these replies that the clerical workers do not have a ready means of interpreting the changes in their personal situation at work by reference to any social processes beyond the organisational sphere or outwith themselves. They do not make any connection between a person's social circumstances (status or class position) and their occupational progress. In claiming that 'it's not where you've been, it's where you are that counts', they can only regard their own lack of progress or prospects as a sign of personal inability. Yet at the same time, many of them feel that their capacities are being under-utilised, which results in frustration. The only solution for those who are not prepared to move is to collude with management in the process which they find increasingly restricting – though to a somewhat lesser extent than the junior clerical workers they supervise.

The nature of their own social background was put as a question to the clerical sample. The responses to this question show how far the ideas which are used to describe the occupational sphere can be applied generally to other social relationships. It emerges quite clearly that social circumstances continue to be rejected as an explanation of personal standing or progress. This places the superintendents in a dilemma because they recognise that the system which they claim is based on equality and personal merit in fact has a distribution of the deserving and the undeserving which fails to match. The way out of this is to dismiss aberrations as the results of 'class bias' or 'snobbery' and not vice versa. This problem is illustrated quite clearly in several of the replies and is hinted at in others. For example, the worker who claimed that 'social background is superfluous, as far as society's concerned, it's up to your own individual outlook on life' was quite prepared to describe class in the same terms.

Q. Which social category would you say you belong to?
A. Middle class, I suppose.
Q. Is social background the same as social class?
A. I'd think so. It's funny you should ask that question. We once got a pro forma that was produced with these categories on it. I must admit I laughed at it because of the definitions – money and so on.
Q. What is it that makes a class a distinct category?
A. I would think it's basically the environment you're brought up in and educational standards. You can arrive at your own social level.

This was the dominant understanding of social class and it is not
surprising that nearly all the clerical workers located themselves
without hesitation nearer to the middle than to either end of the class
or status hierarchy. The labels most commonly used for self-
identification (always without prompting, because we wished the
discussion of social class to follow the terminology which was most
familiar and meaningful to the respondent) were 'middle class' or
'lower middle class'. Another version of what could be called the
'cultural' model of class based on attitudes and life styles occurs in the
following description.

> I was brought up in a working class background. Now I think I've
> gone a little above that. . .but it's very difficult to say. It depends
> on your housing even, things like that. I'd say I've moved up rather
> than gone down. You can distinguish between social classes by the
> way you live, how you conduct yourself.

To prevent any misinterpretation of this as a 'biased' or 'snobbish'
view, this worker went straight on:

> I'm not saying all working class people conduct themselves in a
> different way from middle or upper middle class people. When I'm
> talking about working class − my own problems − we had problems
> of finance all the time, a constant struggle, never any extra money.
> Well nowadays I certainly haven't the same problems. . .I know a
> lot of people − of working class tendency − and they live from
> week to week rather than form any definite plan. The working class
> type person doesn't think of it this way. It's a week by week
> existence, 'get what you can' − and do as little work as possible
> for it sometimes.

The aversion to class feeling, to illegitimate trading on social
differences which have not been earned, is expressed rather more
strongly by some of the sample.

> I don't like to try and put people in compartments. I've always
> tended to take people as I find them. . .I don't think class is a valid
> way to describe. . .Someone from the poorest slum can be a hell
> of a nice person and a person from the top drawer can be a so-and-so.

> You may have a person with working class background but socially

he may fit in.

At the 'low' end of the social scale you get the good, bad and
indifferent just as you do at the other end.

The problem of these interpretations is that unless some mechanism
other than attitudes or personality is introduced, it cannot account
for the ideas about class among the clerical workers. Their interpretation
does not, of course, make social class a basis of collective identity any
more than did the other two groups. They are not 'class-conscious' in
that sense of the term. But class is interpreted as the expression of a
basic 'totality' principle, namely: a person's place in the social system
is the outcome of their personal efforts and abilities and the system
provides for the exercise of these abilities. Some of the references, to
the obsolescence of class attitudes and the difference that money makes
for example, are echoed in the other samples, but this particular view
is not. Although the data from interviews alone must be regarded as
incomplete because they artificially invoke a pre-selected range of
topics, there is evidence here that the clerical workers are more inclined
than either the craftsmen or the steelworkers to approach society as a
system of action rather than as an aggregate of social groups. However,
their relationship to the problem of control in society is no less
ambiguous than their relationship to the problem of control in the
organisation.

The discussion of politics provided a way of focusing on the question
of social control which is of course the defining issue in a society
conceived as a system of action. The pattern of voting, which is a
preliminary guide to any sense of allegiance or identification, is quite
strongly in support of the Conservative party. Sixty-eight per cent of
the clerical sample had voted Conservative at the previous general
election and had always voted Conservative. Only 2, or 11 per cent
were 'loyal' to Labour, in the sense that they had always voted for that
party. The remainder were equally divided between the Liberal Party
and the Scottish National Party. This pattern is dissimilar from the
craftsmen's, who were more likely to vote for either of the main parties
and who showed the strongest tendency of any of the samples to
support the SNP. In fact, the degree of consistency in voting compares
very closely with that of the steelworkers, although the loyalties are
reversed. This could mean that the clerical workers, like the first hand
melters, tend to vote out of a sense of what is natural or proper for
someone in their position, i.e. out of a sense of tradition. We argued

above that this is the rationale of the first hands' approach to voting. There are some indications that the superintendents start from a similar position. For example, one described Labour voters as 'the backbone of the labour force in the coal-mining and industrial areas' and Conservative voters as those 'people who know a little bit more about it in finance, those who read the financial pages rather than the sports pages'. These comments appear to rely on stereotyped views of manual workers ('they're only interested in themselves, what they can get out of it') and better informed and more altruistically motivated people like himself. However, even these stereotypes contain a hint of an approach to the political system which is not purely habitual or traditional. Thus, 'Labour encourages the trade union movement to the detriment of the country. . .the Conservatives inherited a bit of a mess'. This approach is more fully elaborated in those replies which judged political performance as 'good' or 'bad', replies which occurred only very rarely in the other two samples although the questions were identical.

Some of the superintendents made explicit comparisons between the organisational system and the social system. For example, one argued that

> The Conservatives have a more flexible outlook (the government party should be like a manager). Generally, one will be better off financially — everybody. But Labour never seem to do anything, they've no hard and fast policy.

Another, who had earlier shown support for but some scepticism towards the 'unitary' conception of the organisation, spoke in very similar terms of the country as a whole.

> The attitude of management versus worker. The solution to the malaise would be a change in attitudes — seeing the overall aspect of the country, not your own small system.

Comparison with the other samples shows that the clerical workers are unique in their use of the unitary view or management analogy. Even when 'traditional' criteria are used to make political judgements they are criteria of performance in system terms, i.e. what is good for the country in general rather than for oneself or a sectional interest. This is not the place to assess whether these judgements are 'correct' or not but simply to illustrate the grounds on which they are made.

In the clerical workers' schedule there was one additional question which they alone were requested to answer (Q.42). It was designed to provoke a discussion about social change which would give data of more dynamic ways of looking at society. We were in some doubt as to whether the rather static view of structures rather than processes which we discerned in the previous interviews might have arisen from the interview method itself. In the event, the question posed was not entirely successful because it appeared to take some of the respondents a long way beyond their normal horizons of thinking about society. Of course, this in itself is useful information but the lack of comparative data from the other two samples must make any conclusion highly tentative. What we can say is that, as far as they go, the replies continue to use a model of society as a system of action rather than as an object of 'blind' technical or economic forces. In fact economic factors were most frequently chosen as being most important in accounting for social changes. When respondents were asked what they took this to mean, it became clear that for the majority, economics were the basic control mechanism and politics simply a question of more or less efficient use of these controls. For example

My theory is that the state of this country today can be traced back to World War II. . .we took a terrible hammering 28-30 years ago and that set us back terribly. But, social attitudes are rather unfortunate. . .perhaps it's because the leadership isn't there (and you get small minorities who don't care, like the communists in the trade unions).

Is it not the politicians who have — or should have — the answers to the economy? But I'm not sure they're capable.

Technical and (party) political factors were usually placed behind economic and social (usually interpreted as attitudinal) factors. There is therefore nothing to suggest the 'technocratic' approach to social change which is sometimes assumed to be synonymous with a view of society as a system of action. In our view, further questions designed to elicit generalisations about social processes would continue to provide evidence for the consciousness of society as a totality — signs of which we have been observing continually in our analysis of these replies. Such generalisations undoubtedly occur in natural conversations at work and elsewhere and ideally analysis should include such material. However, within the limitations of the present method we have encountered and set out the properties of a social consciousness which is both consistent within the sample and which differs systematically from the social consciousness of the other two samples.

There remains the problem of whether the forms of consciousness of society which we have been describing can properly be called 'occupational'. That is to say, is there a parallel between the 'craft' consciousness of the fitters or the steelworkers' sense of *métier* and the clerical workers' view of themselves in society? It is clear from our analysis that this is not the case in any strict sense. The superintendents do not, it seems, assert their identity through the performance of their work tasks because there is no tangible product and efficiency is as likely as not to be achieved through self-effacement. On the contrary, the process of self-identification is a process of harmonising with the organisational system, becoming part of it. Taking the three samples together, the less the consciousness of 'craft' or occupation, the greater the consciousness of work as a system. This conforms with the general tendency in the evolution of work which is moving from occupational systems to technical systems. We find that the sample which is closest to the technical system (i.e. the sample of clerical workers) has a consciousness of work and society as more or less complete systems. It has been argued by Touraine and other theorists of 'post-industrial' society that these circumstances will lead to new social conflicts and especially to competition for control of the organisational and social systems. In reply to this we can only say that however applicable it may be to more highly qualified groups, it does not describe either the dominant consciousness or the action of the superintendents in our sample. None of them were making claims on the organisation or on society which went beyond the claim to be recognised as a contributor to the smooth functioning of these systems. The ultimate direction or control of organisations and society was never questioned but was regarded as the legitimate sphere of those already in the commanding positions. It is because of their active approval rather than passive acceptance of this state of affairs that we have applied the term 'collusion' to the clerical workers.

If the organisation rather than the occupation is the main formative sphere of social consciousness it follows from our argument so far that the clerical workers should be more vulnerable to external sources of ideas and imagery about society than either of the other two samples. From our evidence this does not seem likely, because the interviews do not contain noticeably more terms, phrases or cliches which can be traced directly or indirectly to media or other public sources. On the other hand, there is a noticeably greater consistency in the replies from the insurance workers. For example, there is no equivalent to the inconsistencies of perspective which we noted in the craftsmen's discussions of trade unions. This is to be expected to the extent that the totality view of the organisation which the clerical workers generally have is in close harmony with the frameworks for interpreting society which are used in the media, in government pronouncements or in education. They share the basic assumption that there is a common interest and that to reject this is to be an outsider, an 'extremist' and a threat. To change from viewing society in this way to developing a sense of opposition would involve a far greater transformation of social consciousness than among either the craftsmen or the steelworkers. And at present there are no signs that this is occurring or is about to occur. However, the foundations are being laid as these and other clerical workers find the career patterns they once thought to be open and available being curtailed with every new application of office technology and organisational technique.

Notes

1. D. Lockwood, *The Blackcoated Worker* (London, 1958), p.7.

2. See for example E. Mumford and O. Banks, *The Computer and the Clerk* (London, 1967); R.M. Blackburn, *Union Character and Social Class* (London, 1967); G.S. Bain, *The Growth of White Collar Unionism* (London, 1970); J.M. Shepard, *Automation and Alienation*; R. Lumley, *White Collar Unionism in Britain* (London, 1973); R. Crompton, 'Approaches to the Study of White-collar Unionism', *Sociology*, 10 (1976).

3. H. Braverman, *Labour and Monopoly Capital* (New York, 1974), p.355.

4. F. Zweig, *The Worker in an Affluent Society* (London, 1961) and R. Millar, *The New Classes* (London, 1966) are among those who helped to popularise this latter view.

5. H. Braverman, *Labour and Monopoly Capital*, p.294 quoting F.D. Klingender.

6. G.J. Will, 'Staff Associations in the Insurance Industry', unpublished thesis, Ruskin College, 1972, quoted in R. Crompton, 'Approaches to the Study of White-collar Unionism'.

7. See R. Crompton, 'Approaches to the Study of White-Collar Unionism'.

8. Ibid, p.422.

9. H. Popitz *et al.*, *Das Gesellschaftsbild*, p.71.

8 CONSCIOUSNESS AND ACTION IN INDUSTRIAL SOCIETY

Social consciousness, however fragmentary or confused it may be, can only be understood properly as part of a wider system of social action. Our analysis so far has been restricted to the field of action described by work and the local community. In this chapter we situate our findings in the wider context of industrial development, class relations and culture.

The assumption which in one form or another has guided nearly all the studies of social consciousness we have referred to, as well as our own study, is the assumption that work experience is the key to social consciousness. The use of the term *social* rather than *occupational* consciousness does not exclude the possibility that religious commitment, national feeling or class consciousness, for example, may become more pronounced under certain circumstances or that these may transcend the boundaries of the social division of labour. However, industrial society by definition subordinates or harnesses religious, ethnic, class and other sectional considerations to industrial production and accumulation. Direct experience of work is therefore an appropriate starting point for an interpretation of social consciousness. The amount of variation in social consciousness which can be explained by reference to work experiences we take to be further justification of this choice.

One of the chief problems has been to find a model of the evolution of work in industrial society which is neither too general nor too detailed to apply to the range of occupations we have analysed. On occasions we have had recourse to the very general model used by Touraine which relies heavily on a simple distinction between the 'occupational system' of work and the 'technical system' of work — i.e. the slow evolution from the pure *métier* to advanced automation. This is useful as a rule of thumb but little more; it is open to some of the criticisms which have been levelled at Blauner, for example, who argued that historically there has been a movement from craft production through factory production to process production and that degrees of 'alienation' have varied with each type. In practice the movement from one type to the next is neither complete nor does it follow an abstract technical imperative. Rather, as Braverman has shown, the 'logic' is that of capital accumulation which has shown a

174

historical tendency to remove the control of work (through skills and experience in production) out of the hands of workers, whatever the system of production.[1] This process is to be seen in all three of the samples we studied. For example, the craft workers were being called upon increasingly to simply replace rather than repair faulty parts in the process plant; the steelworkers had experienced innovations in furnace instrumentation which made redundant some of their traditional skills; and office mechanisation had done much the same for the clerical workers. Braverman deliberately avoids any discussion of the possible effects of 'de-skilling' on workers' consciousness, but he clearly believes that the process he describes has profound consequences for states of consciousness. He also believes that they are ultimately class-related. For us the problem turns on whether we have been observing the recognition of, and response towards, a particular system of production or whether we have tapped a more general reservoir of class attitudes. Wishing to leave this question open we made a distinction between social consciousness and class consciousness.

In our presentation of the results of the interview study we emphasised the differences between the three samples. If we follow Touraine, variations in consciousness will be interpreted as responses to particular phases of industrial development — these being more salient in the individual worker's experience than the collective experience of labour under capital. On the other hand, following authors like Braverman, we might seek signs of a growing similarity of consciousness among workers as their subordination to capital becomes more and more obvious. Since the interview method did not allow for the observation of changes in consciousness through time, there is a built-in bias against the second mode of interpretation. In this chapter we intend to go some way towards correcting this bias by comparing our results with those of researchers who have used alternative interview and survey methods.

There is a further problem arising from the limitations of our method. It is a consequence of the deliberate emphasis we have placed on the work sphere: namely, a tendency to limit analysis of workers' consciousness to this sphere and to underestimate or ignore social relationships in other spheres, including the family, the community and the state in all its forms. All of these relationships provide materials for the construction of social consciousness and not only relationships at work. Therefore, just as we initially require a model of the evolution of work in industrial society to understand the role of labour as the foundation of social consciousness, so we eventually require a model of the evolution of culture to understand some of the

particular forms which consciousness takes. In our view such a model
is unavailable at the present time but, in their various ways, cultural
studies, public opinion research, media sociology and semiology are
engaged in the search.[2] They all address the problem of why, in a class
society, social consciousness and class consciousness are not
synonymous.

These are some of the general considerations which guide this
summary and contextualisation of the interview findings. More
specifically we are concerned to resolve a methodological difficulty
which has become apparent time after time in investigations of social
consciousness. This arises from the often neglected but substantial
proportion of interviewees who are virtually 'written off' as having no
discernible image of society. Their attitudes and interpretations are
intelligible and they are no less important a group than the very small
minority who espouse well developed world views, like a Jehovah's
Witness and a Communist Party member in our study. Another
associated task is to state what is left unexplained by the present
method.

Beyond Class Images

The numerous studies which have tried to clarify the relationship
between technology and workers' consciousness have naturally
emphasised the variable 'technology' or the technical division of labour
and have developed more and more sophisticated typologies of technical
systems. However, since the three samples in our study are drawn from
very different work systems, the most detailed typologies of production
are of little direct use except in the case of the steelworkers who are
direct producers of a tangible commodity, steel. The others are not
directly involved in the handling of materials, the transformation or
reworking of a product. This may be one reason why maintenance
workers, clerical workers and those with supervisory responsibilities
have often been treated as 'special cases' in factory studies — they are
not the archetypal manual worker. But one group in the division of
labour is not necessarily more important than another. A close
understanding of the whole span of work organisation and work
processes is essential if manual workers, or clerical workers for that
matter, are not to be mythologised into heroes or anti-heroes of the
working class. The technical division of labour — the fragmentation
and degradation of work tasks — does divide workers from one another
as well as from their employers. For instance, the physical isolation of
the process worker and the demands of shift working have their

correlates in consciousness.[3] The increasing technical differentiation of work has certainly influenced workers' consciousness by making it less uniform. However, the relative homogeneity of the samples in our own study (which is an inevitable result of our method) automatically diverts attention away from the technical division of labour towards the social division of labour and its role in consciousness.

By 'social division of labour' we mean the distribution of labour among occupations and industries rather than the distribution of tasks within an enterprise or industry. The fact that the occupations of fitter, steel melter and insurance superintendent all include a relatively wide range of tasks, have a complex form and a measure of control over the work process allows us to speak of a measure of 'occupational' consciousness. This is what sets them apart from their contemporaries in the same industries and elsewhere who are to a much greater extent victims of the simplification of work processes. It is reflected in the above-average wages which the craftsmen, the melters and the clerical workers earn. But in the long term they are also subject to the processes of 'rationalisation' which are leading to the ascendancy of the technical system of work over the occupational system. This movement, and the tension between occupational traditions which flowered in the past and the future which is likely to suppress any further growth and development, is the common denominator of the three groups of workers.

The Craftsmen

At first sight the occupational experience of the craftsmen appears to have little in common with the occupational experiences of the other two samples. In their social origins, their education and occupational socialisation they have access to a constellation of individual and collective experiences, a craft tradition, which provides the key to their understanding of their position in the world of work and in society. This craft tradition is not something fixed and static which allows us to predict what 'craft consciousness' will look like among any group of skilled workers whatever the circumstances. It is an active tradition with origins in pre-industrial work but it has a complex history of interaction with developments in technology and changes in the industrial structure. There is no single group which has all the characteristics of the 'ideal type' of craft worker but for the fitters at least it is appropriate to emphasise the occupational qualification as something which is still largely their own property, a set of skills and a social status which they take with them even when they move.

One of the significant limitations of our method is that it does not provide a picture of the way in which the occupational qualification is changing through time. We can only make the general observation (which holds for many other skilled trades as well) that while apprenticeships are becoming shorter, the 'intellectual' component in the form of college courses in theory, is being enhanced. At the same time, there is evidence that for all but a few of the craftsmen, the tasks they perform do not exploit the full range of their knowledge and skills. For the majority, their work is becoming more routine and less demanding, while traditional areas of decision are being whittled away. It might be anticipated that such developments would provoke a defensive response or at least some nostalgia for the time when craftsmen had greater autonomy. But we found little evidence of this.

The craftsmen's self- and occupational-images were dominated by considerations which we interpreted as an appeal to individual rather than to occupational attributes. In other words, 'being a good craftsman' was said to involve natural aptitude (commonsense) and application (pride in work), qualities which are not strictly exclusive to the fitter's occupation. Some appealed to technical skill and experience but not in a way which indicated a defensive attitude towards other occupations. The fitters who did emphasise these strictly occupational attributes were those who were seeking to extend their career into more skilful applications of their craft. For the most part, however, the fitters had few reservations about the state of their trade. They were more inclined to contrast their present job favourably with jobs they had held previously in other industries. This underlines an obvious but important fact about 'craft consciousness'. It is not formed in the work situation or in work experience narrowly defined. The special features of the technical division of labour which appear to be so conducive to 'factory' or 'plant consciousness' in car assembly plants for instance, are not salient among the craftsmen.[4] For in the first instance, the craftsmen evaluate work according to the merits of one job compared with another and not according to the relative merits of employers. Of course the cash nexus is inescapable and probably the group of fitters interviewed were inclined to run together their evaluation of the job and their opinion of the employer. However, the main problem of interpretation is this: if craft consciousness is a form of occupational consciousness, not bound to a particular position or employer, how is it maintained in the wider network of social relationships? Craft consciousness may originate in the training and socialisation of young workers but it needs to be continually reinforced. In other words this is the recurring problem of the parts played by work, community, class and non-local factors in the formation of social consciousness.

The answer to the problem demands a new and more subtle interpretation of that complex of social relationships referred to as 'community' than has been found hitherto in studies of working-class communities and images of society. If it ever existed at all, the community based on a single industry was a rarity. It has less and less relevance — even as an ideal type — with the great majority of industrial work being located in conurbations with an infrastructure of communications and services spread over large distances. Therefore the emphasis of any interpretation should be as much on the divisions between industries, employers and occupations as on the homogeneity of local factors. In the particular case of the maintenance craftsmen we have already referred to the special circumstances of a grouping of modern process industries in an area with a lengthy history of industrial activity in mining, docking and engineering. This ensures a continuity of tradition (seen for example in the language of conflict used in discussing the role of trade unions) and provides a brake to any tendency for the craftsmen to re-evaluate their occupational position. Although the skilled trades may be experiencing a general decline, the fitters' standing in the one expanding sector of a region dominated by older, declining industries is unchanged; they possess transferable skills and are not immediately threatened by redundancy; and their place in the division of labour gives them considerable autonomy and hence prestige. Not least their earnings are sufficiently high for most of them to be free from the perennial problems of shift working and overtime which shape the lives of many other manual workers. This relatively privileged position is attributable to the characteristics of the occupation and, since the occupation is seen as a personal property of the worker, it is a major source of identity, pride and dignity.

The data we collected contain only a few clues to the way in which the craftsmen and their occupation are perceived by other workers in the community. One such clue is the way in which fathers were reported to have encouraged their sons to learn a trade and to avoid 'dead end' jobs. However, there is another way of grasping the problem — by imagining the craftsmen in a different context of community. There is a good example of what can happen when one community is exchanged for another in the 'northern foremen' described by Nichols and Beynon.[5] Process workers from a 'traditional' working class community in the north were persuaded to move to a new plant in the south of England by the offer of promotion and better conditions. However, these improvements did not automatically enhance their status in the community.

> To *be* somebody, the foreman needs the social backcloth of the manual working class. But these men tend to live tucked away in Wimpey houses on 'mixed' but predominantly 'white collar' estates. They work the same shifts that their manual workers do, and despite the 'office work' get dirty. Hundreds of miles away from 'home', they lack the audience required to confirm to themselves that they have indeed distinguished themselves from the mass.[6]

What these foremen lack in their relations outside work, the craftsmen have, namely a stable position in a community which is being transformed only gradually by industrial development. Whilst we cannot make any direct comparison between the craftsmen in our sample and the closely similar group of maintenance workers at 'Chemco' (because they were not included in that study) it is likely that their self-image and their image of society is affected in a similar way by their geographical mobility, extended journeys to work, residence on large housing estates and so forth. The craftsmen in our sample do not suffer the social disorientation which these factors seem to induce.

To summarise the part played by the local community in the social consciousness of the craftsmen, we can say that their occupational consciousness and any occupational consciousness in fact must be defined negatively as well as positively — by reference to other occupations, to what the occupation is not as well as to its obvious technical functions. If craft consciousness followed directly from the characteristic training, tasks and methods of working of a trade or occupation, the problem would simply be to identify these characteristics. But this fails to explain those variations which are found both within a group of workers and between groups of workers in different work situations. On the basis of our own evidence we conclude that the local community is at least as important as the research tradition allows but that the emphasis on shared experiences, especially attachments in the work group which spill over into non-work activities, is misplaced except in rare isolated cases. Greater emphasis should be placed on relationships between groups within the community and the use of local reference groups. We know from studies of reference groups that manual workers tend to make judgements about their social position by comparing their own past and present rather than by comparing themselves with other (especially higher) groups in the social structure; also that reference groups are those most closely adjacent in the social hierarchy.[7] The implications of these studies for social consciousness need to be carried through to give the community its proper weight — not just as the medium of occupational cultures but as a system of social relationships which allow the construction of a variety of interpretations of occupational experience. In our sample, the craftsman's milieu provides for a number of comparisons — horizontally as well as 'up' and 'down' — with other groups in the manual working class. Locally, apart from the petro-chemical industries, there are all categories of skilled and unskilled workers in the mining, dock and engineering industries. The other major category of worker is the process worker in the chemical and petroleum refining plants. Used as reference groups for comparing wages, skills, conditions of work and employers, these groups tend to sustain the craftsman's hierarchical interpretation of the occupational system based on personal ability and effort. The craftsmen are too much part and parcel of this predominantly working class milieu to regard the less skilled manual workers in any other way than as fellow-workers with fundamentally similar interests, aims and opportunities. The traditional exclusiveness of craft occupations is not visible to any great extent. Whether it is assumed and therefore unacknowledged or whether it follows from the historical decline of the skilled trades is a larger problem than we can answer here. However, it is clear that an answer must satisfy two conditions: it must identify the craft tradition as an active, modifying ingredient in the changes which have occurred in the history of the labour process and it must identify the special local conditions which make this process intelligible.

The Steel Melters

If we had not been alerted previously to the need to interpret consciousness in the broadest possible context of a system of social action, it would have been tempting to draw the conclusion that the steel melters are a good example of the 'proletarian traditionalist' worker. It is possible to romanticise the steel melters' work and culture and some — steel workers included — have seen fit to do this. However, the theoretical approach which we have adopted and the generalisations about the work and community relationships in the formation of social consciousness apply no less to the steel workers than to other groups. In fact they help to reveal and explain features of social consciousness which have been misconstrued in the approach through community studies.

In our analysis it has become increasingly clear that the equation
which is sometimes made between a dichotomous image of social
classes, a sense of class solidarity and a collectivist ideology has little
bearing among the steelworkers we interviewed. The equation is based
on the argument that the work situation throws workers together and
compels a high degree of fraternal feeling and that this carries over into
non-work activities in geographically and socially confined communities.
The argument is then taken further. Relationships at work and in the
community are said to be the basis of interpretations of class and
society as a whole. In our view there are two problems with this
argument. Firstly, it assumes that categories such as individual/collective,
harmony/conflict or class/status are mutually exclusive. Secondly, it is
still a one-way argument which begins with the concrete daily
experiences of work and moves towards increasingly abstract
experiences and relationships. But dominant social institutions are
powerful sources of ideas and vicarious experiences and it is
unreasonable to exclude them even from an argument about the
distinctiveness of particular groups in society. To the extent that they
are in society, participating in the labour process, the market,
consumption and politics, sub-groups are open to the influence of these
institutions. The question is not whether the political institutions,
education or the media have an effect on class or community cultures
and consciousness but what effect they have and how this is mediated
by relationships in the community.

Our data on these questions show firstly that those circumstances
which are undeniably conducive to expressions of team spirit,
fraternalism and solidarity among the steel melters do not necessarily
operate at the expense of similar feelings towards other groups. In fact
we can say that the more an occupation is likely to promote solidarity
among its members (because of conditions of deprivation or danger,
for example) the less likely this solidarity is to imply common cause
against other groups. The conditions under which these two things are
most likely to be combined are those in large assembly plants for
instance, where the workers may recognise their general subordination
to the highly detailed division of labour and experience a very different
sense of solidarity in opposition towards their employers. This is clearly
not the case among the steel melters, who were the least willing of the
three samples to identify conflicts within the workplace. They were
closest to holding the 'unitary' view of the enterprise. Both within the
melting shop and in relationships in the wider community, their most
important reference group is the hierarchically arranged group within

which they themselves had risen to a position of prominence.

The melters make reference not to just one or two strata in this hierarchy but to steelworkers as a whole from labourers to sample passers. This is shown by the melters' frequent use of 'we' and 'our' in discussing aspects of their occupation and trade union activity. These pronouns include all grades of worker. The importance of the apparently homogeneous and insulated community is that it strongly reinforces these undiscriminating expressions of solidarity. If the continuity of the tradition were broken by large-scale redundancy, urban renewal or an influx of new industries, for example, it seems likely that solidarity would assume different guises and would extend to making 'demands' on other groups. At the present time this potential for opposition is not being realised. The community supplies the context and the materials for the construction of a personal identity which can make sense of the worker's destiny. He does not as a rule have to look beyond the works, the club, the pub, the school and the home for confirmation of what he is. The question of identity can be answered within the confines of the community and its traditions. It does not require a totality view of the occupational structure, market relationships or social class.

As long as the continuity of experience remains, the steelworkers' essentially passive consciousness of society as 'static order' is likely to be undisturbed. For the next generation of workers this continuity has already been broken —hence the rumours of 'bother' at a nearby steelworks. This is a timely reminder (since we have been considering an unusually static context of work and community) that the system of historical action is in constant flux and this places strict limits on the generalisations we can make from a single group of workers studied over a limited period of time.

The data lead us to a second conclusion about the impact of the socially dominant institutions and ideas represented especially through the mass media. These are totality views but there is no evidence that they are appropriated directly by the steelworkers as ready-made images of society. The formative influences of work and community effectively obstruct this, especially in the steel melters' lack of formal education and locally-centred life style. This is well illustrated in the interviews by a recurring feature which we have already drawn attention to. That is, the steel workers were in general more reluctant than either the craftsmen or the clerical workers to cross the horizons of their own direct experience and generalise about social relationships between employers and employees, middle class and working class. This is not the same as evidence of parochialism or a deliberate refusal to contemplate these broader issues. Rather, these relationships are simply accepted as 'given', not subjects for questioning or complaint. The same quality infuses the allegiance of the majority of the sample to the Labour Party. Theirs is a traditional, even anachronistic, loyalty. Partly because of the high average age of the sample and partly because of the unity of their occupational experience, the melters do not need to seek confirmation of their identity outside the traditional milieu. Their occupational consciousness does not contain the negative element which we discerned to some extent among the craftsmen. The steelworkers' social consciousness can actually be said to have a totalising element because its firm occupational basis leaves no significant part of the melter's career unaccounted for. Even social relationships which lie outside this totality do not pose a significant problem. It takes an 'academic' exercise — like an interview — to bring these relationships into the foreground. And even then, the replies tend to confirm the lack of salience that these topics have.

The Clerical Workers

The absurdity of a phrase like 'the occupational community of the clerical worker' shows the limitations of the concept of 'community' as used in typologies of working-class consciousness. With its emphasis on face-to-face contact, cultural isolation and patterns of work and leisure *imposed* by certain occupations and industries, it effectively precludes any understanding of the social consciousness of groups who do not share these characteristics. Clerical workers in large metropolitan business centres are almost automatically excluded. They live in relatively large and heterogeneous urban 'communities', they rarely meet their fellow workers outside the office and their life styles are constrained more by their income and education than by local tradition. Short of abandoning the concept of community altogether, social relationships outside work could be classified instead according to criteria of difference as well as similarity — i.e. which groups do clerical workers associate and identify with and which groups do they use to define themselves negatively?

For the interviews and observation of the insurance company we found that there were few if any of those features present which are assumed to promote solidarity among workers in traditional occupations. The organisation of departments and the firm as a whole is hierarchical, with more vertical than horizontal contact. This, despite the close similarity of the superintendent's function in different departments, forces attention on individual or departmental performance. It was nonetheless true that a particular version of the idea of mutual interests was quite strongly developed. This 'solidarity', if it can be called that, embraced the organisation rather than the occupation. The relatively small size of the company may help to account for this because it is easy to define 'the company', its offices and management numerically, geographically and historically. However, 'company loyalty' or feelings of solidarity are not simply a natural and spontaneous product of such circumstances. To a greater or lesser extent they are cultivated through a range of social and sporting activities and through an ethos conveyed by management informally and through channels such as staff association meetings.

Criteria of occupational similarity are therefore likely to be unimportant in relationships in the wider community. To be employed as a clerical worker is less crucial for personal identity than to be an employee of the company, whereas for the steelworkers the fact of being a first hand melter was paramount. It does not necessarily follow from this that the clerical workers — who almost invariably call themselves 'middle class' — rely completely on a negative self-interpretation. They are in fact reluctant to define themselves as 'not working class', for this would be incompatible with their belief in the openness of social mobility. Many of the sample saw themselves as having come up from the working class and held their origins in high regard. Instead, the 'community' or social relationships outside work which may span a variety of social and geographical networks are regarded in the same way as work itself, as an organisational system. This 'systems' thinking is more conducive to hierarchical interpretations than class interpretations of social structures.

Thinking of the community in this way, primarily as the sphere of social action rather than as a source of identity, has the following consequences. Firstly, it does not presuppose the relatively stable and close-knit relationships which are often used to give content to the term 'community'. On the contrary, relationships may be quite short-lived and superficial but none the less meaningful. Secondly, it enlarges the sphere of potential social relationships. The significance of the steelworker who claimed never to have met someone socially from the middle class is that his self-understanding does not routinely require him to entertain these thoughts of social relationships outside the habitual sphere. They do not contribute positively to his self-image and understanding of society. However, for the clerical worker with a hierarchical, 'systems' interpretation, every conceivable social relationship can have meaning and can contribute to self-understanding. For example, where you live, your standard of living, your children's education, your cultural and sporting tastes or the model of car you drive are not then only matters of personal preference, social background or what you can afford. They can take on a wider meaning as they signify performance or achievement in the totality of social relationships in the city or community. One of the important differences between states of social consciousness based on traditional occupations (represented in our study by the steel melters) and those based on clerical occupations is that the latter are bound to make more use of generalised if not 'universal' (i.e. society-wide) symbols of personal ability and worth. Where a traditional occupation and its associated community exist, social consciousness needs no other central signifier of personal identity than the occupation itself. Conversely, where the occupation has no tradition comparable to the craft tradition of the skilled trades and is exposed to the technical division of labour, social consciousness will be constructed from other materials — from the social division of labour and from outside the sphere of employment. We have suggested that materials from both of these sources tend to enlarge the sphere of social consciousness and at the same time bring it closely into line with the totalising interpretations of the dominant cultural institutions.

For the clerical workers, the importance of 'community' is that, far from being an independent and potentially critical source of occupational identity, it is the sphere in which a personal and social identity can be constructed which is free from the limitations imposed by the division of labour. At present, the cost of this freedom is 'game-playing' with management in the sphere of employment and uncritical acceptance of an analogous 'systems' view of society. It must be measured against the fact that, without a critical or oppositional identity, an awareness of the totality of social relations can only mean acquiescence in their prevailing forms, even where there is a strong awareness of identity.

Social Consciousness and Action

In this summary of the relevance for social consciousness of the occupational community or localised social networks, it is apparent that a simple division between 'factors' affecting consciousness at work and outside work cannot be made without distorting the relationship between these two spheres. Neither of them can be reduced to a catalogue of factors like skill, danger and deprivation in work or geographical proximity and cultural isolation in the community. These are not factors which exert an influence independently of each other or independently of the consciousness of the worker. For instance, the decline of traditional skills may be a challenge to one worker and cause resignation or despair to another. If these factors were autonomous, their absence — the absence of occupational traditions and community in the narrow sense — would imply an absence of social consciousness. However, social relations in local milieux are important because the work situation alone cannot account for the variety of social consciousness either within or between groups. An attempt to understand the significance of different milieux therefore needs to include a wider range of community structures than has hitherto been considered. This is not simply a question of extending the typology or making allowances for geographical mobility, for instance. It is more a question of showing how, according to the circumstances, social relationships can furnish the elements not only of identity but of opposition and totality awareness which have equal weight in the movement of society. The focus of attention is then the 'historical subject' or the system of historical action and the community ceases to be only the conservative, retarding force which it sometimes is, but one part of a system of social action which is effective in the production of society as well as the reproduction of its past states. The community is not only a mediator of sectional or parochial ideas and interests. As part of the system of historical action it is also a mediator of the cultural model controlled by the dominant class.

Placed in this context, the circumstances which we call community can, like work itself, be described according to the way in which they embody the principles of identity, opposition and totality. The essentially static community of steelworkers embodies the first principle almost to the exclusion of the others. The craftsmen also participate in a milieu which, though more diversified, gives almost equal weight to the recognition of skills and achievement in work. The urban milieu of the clerical workers is almost certainly more complex in terms of networks but we have seen from the interviews that social relationships outside work are perceived, above all, in terms of their totality as a sphere of action. Viewed in this way, communities do not cease to have importance as soon as they stop being isolated or structured around a single occupation. Whether rural or urban, open or closed, the community is a sphere in which personal identity can be upheld or destroyed, demands can be made on others and social relationships defined as a field of action, and not just adaptation. That is to say, relationships in the community are a means of participating in social change and movement, whether this is directed towards sustaining or modifying prevailing structures.

To complete this review of the findings as evidence of occupational and community consciousness we can now comment upon some of the recurring themes in the images of society tradition of research. The first of these is the problem of the fragmentary, even confused, nature of social imagery among those groups of manual workers who have been studied. It appears that consistent, unambiguous and all-inclusive 'images of society' are increasingly hard to find and that interpretations of class inequality, for example, typically combine attitudes and beliefs about status, occupational attributes and income which together cannot provide a single, coherent action orientation. We referred earlier to evidence that judgements about social questions are increasingly uncertain and inconsistent. It may be that this is simply a result of more sophisticated research techniques but in our view this is unlikely. The method of extended interviewing and observation remains the most appropriate in spite of its limitations. It is more likely that inconsistencies within and between workers' accounts of their experience and social relationships is evidence of the growing difficulty of constructing a coherent social consciousness in a world of work in which the technical and social division of labour has become unimaginably complex. If this is so, the most important consequence for social consciousness is that awareness of collectivity (either occupational awareness or identification with workers as a whole) will be diminished. Only at times of crisis like large-scale redundancy or a major strike is the awareness of the collective fate of the working class likely to be regained and then only temporarily.[8]

According to Popitz the routine expression of consciousness of achievement and collectivity is best seen in the Topoi of the working class. If this is correct we should then find it easier to identify social Topoi among groups whose experience of work is 'occupationally' based than among groups whose experience of work is fragmented. The results of our interview studies show that certain statements in the form of Topoi occur in each of the three samples. Among the craftsmen we found that the occupational tradition and experience was referred to in predictable, patterned ways with a close similarity in the language used. This is to be expected, for the occupational career is structured in the same way for all the craftsmen, however differently they may interpret it or their own place within it. For similar reasons, we found that both the steel workers and the clerical workers had stable, though different, conceptions of their work and career which were spontaneously expressed in commonplace and catch phrases. However, the importance of the social Topic is not simply that it expresses a set of direct, shared experiences among a group of workers. It becomes most significant as evidence of a shared consciousness when it is not limited to common experiences of work but goes beyond this to encompass general issues. The important assumption is that social consciousness is formed in the common experience (the occupational career, especially) of a social group and that this common experience, expressed in Topical forms, allows a person to make sense of himself and society.

At this point we find less evidence to support the idea that there is a catalogue of Topoi appropriate to each social group. The idea entails a differentiation of social groups according to criteria of 'location in the social structure'. However, as soon as these criteria are spelt out, whether they be those of occupation, education or residence for example, it becomes clear that there are further important aspects of experience which are shared by the same groups. Even the criteria of occupation and education are ambiguous. Very diverse occupational groups are united in a similar condition of wage labour and a variety of educational achievement is possible within a single educational system. Moreover, the mass media of information and entertainment provide vicarious experiences on a society-wide basis. Our own evidence therefore brings us to the following conclusions. Topoi are not necessarily declining and they are by no means limited to 'traditional' workers. In each of the samples the discussion of general issues was structured in a way which became predictable as more interviews were conducted. And there were distinctive emphases among each group. For example, the craftsmen's insistence on 'equal opportunity' is distinct from the steelworkers' acceptance of the occupational system of work and this in turn is very different from the clerical workers' functional interpretation. It is appropriate to refer to these as Topoi because they guide each group's interpretation of wider social issues. But they are not the only basis of interpretation – which brings us to our second conclusion. To the extent that general issues (of class or status differences, social and political management, etc.) are not amenable to Topoi based in occupational experiences, interpretations of these issues will be governed by the assumptions and propositions of the 'dominant meaning system' which are mediated by national cultural and political institutions.

Evidence to support these conclusions is found, for example, in the answers to questions about trade unions and management-worker relations. It has often been argued that manual and white collar groups diverge in their interpretations because they rely on contrasting Topoi or images of the social structure. Thus, manual workers are attributed with a 'class' or dichotomous image and white collar groups with a 'status' or graded image of social differences. In our investigations we found no evidence of a sharp divide between these two types. On the contrary, all three groups showed an ability to use *both* class and status models in their discussion of social inequalities, though with different emphases. The analysis showed that these differences were too small to justify a typology of 'class' or 'status' images. Neither were accounts of social inequalities so restricted to occupational histories as to justify an interpretation based on immediate, direct experience. The answers to questions about industrial relations (and other questions) therefore have to be interpreted with reference to the essentially undifferentiated normative system of values and the largely consistent frameworks of interpretation which constitute the 'dominant value system', as Parkin has called it.[9] In arguing thus we are following those who would deny that sub-groups in the social system have autonomous or relatively independent values and patterns of behaviour. On the other hand we reject the strong version of the argument that all social groups hold values in common which are controlled and manipulated by a dominant class in their own interests. To accept this would be to abandon the possibility of understanding the complex unity of social action. The problem lies in reconciling the evidence that social consciousness is formed and re-formed in social action (i.e. labour or any process of the creation of values), and the fact that this occurs in the context of a system of historical action which is a unity more or less under the control of a dominant class.

To make some headway with this problem we have to go beyond the limitations of our own evidence to consider studies of 'public opinion' and its long-term tendencies, together with assessments of the role of the mass media. In particular, we are concerned to find out whether these other lines of evidence lend support to the idea that class consciousness was historically specific and is now being replaced by other forms of social consciousness which correspond with new kinds of social movement.

Trends in Class and Social Consciousness

In recent historical perspective there have been two important trends in class and social consciousness which the majority of observers agree are beyond dispute, although their interpretation is a matter for debate.

Firstly, there is the trend towards greater social and cultural diversity which is to be seen in the decline of bi-partisan politics, the rise of the 'counter-culture' and the expression of a wide range of interests and values in pressure groups and less organised social movements. This has sometimes been interpreted as a sign of the demise of 'traditional' classes and class attitudes. At other times it has been taken to indicate the emergence of a new class or classes based on something other than the ownership of property or the distribution of income and wealth. In the study of workers' consciousness, as we have seen, most current interpretations of this trend emphasise the fragmentation of culture and consciousness. They point to a general lack of coherence and consistency in beliefs, attitudes and images of society.

The second important trend which it is usually agreed can be traced to a watershed in the late 1960s, is the tendency for organised opinion in the form of 'official' accounts and mass media messages to emphasise the commonality of social and political interests. This is therefore a trend towards greater, not lesser, consistency and coherence. Thus Burns' conclusion to a survey of the historical development of public opinion is

> that although it has been manifest to everybody that political, social, economic and cultural interests, values and opinions have appeared to become more and more disparate, and this disparity more and more organised, the kind of opinions and attitudes and values and, above all, information, conveyed by broadcasting and the press has tended to become more constrained and more internally consistent.[10]

If these are indeed the dominant tendencies in the organisation of public opinion in the past two decades we can assume that they have some repercussions in the social consciousness of workers including those in our samples. For example, the 'organised disparity' which Burns refers to might be reflected in a heightened sense of identity, and the narrowing range of opinion available to consumers of the mass media might be reflected in an increasing awareness of totality. These are empirical questions which require further research before they can be fully answered. However, there are indications that the varieties of social consciousness which we have described may in part be subject to these conflicting tendencies. In fact, certain of the apparent 'inconsistencies' become meaningful within this context, i.e. within the system of historical action rather than the action of the individual or the group.

The inconsistencies which we observed included, among the craftsmen, the beliefs that the trade unions were superfluous or ineffective and that they had too much power. Another example was the denial of class because of 'equal opportunities' in a speech which made easy use of the term 'class' to refer to contemporary social differences. Among the steel workers there was an inconsistency between the use of the term 'class' for defining social status or predicting social behaviour and its use in explaining personal achievement or destiny. The clerical workers' replies, we noted, were generally more consistent than among the other two samples but there was similar evidence of aversion to class feeling at the same time as familiarity with a class vocabulary. In each sample there is some evidence of the tendency towards greater social and cultural diversity. One of the best indicators of this is the denial of 'class' as a basis of social identity. It is predictable that the sample with the greatest degree of dependency on the occupational system of work, the steel melters, is the sample with the least ambiguous understanding of class. Conversely, the awareness of (class) identity is weakest among the clerical workers, who are farthest removed from the occupational system of work. At the same time as this general weakening of the sense of social identity based on class there has been a strengthening of the sense of totality. This was most strongly developed among the clerical workers. At present it cannot be said that this counter-tendency which brings greater consistency of social consciousness has developed so far as to replace class identity and in any case there is no reason to suppose that they are mutually exclusive.

The problem of reconciling these two aspects is seen in two divergent accounts of trends in 'class' awareness. The first is the account based on opinion polling and it appears to show quite a high degree of 'class consciousness' and moreover a high degree of conflict consciousness based on class identity. Moorhouse has assembled some of the evidence, including that shown in Table 5 from the Gallup Poll.[11] From this evidence it is difficult to escape the conclusion that a majority of people believe that, in a political context at least, class conflict is important in this country and that there has been no decline in this view in the medium term. Moorhouse interprets this account quite literally and argues that the main conclusions of sociological research into images of society have been mistaken because they are based on inappropriate concepts and inadequate empirical methods. He argues that they have overstressed the cognitive and verbal understanding of class and have assumed that intellectual understanding is a prerequisite

Table 5: Class Struggle and Politics

Replies to the question:		'There used to be a lot of talk in politics about the "class struggle". Do you think there is a class struggle in this country or not?'					
	July 1964	June 1972	January 1973	April 1973	December 1973	February 1974	May 1974
Is	48	58	53	60	57	62	60
Is not	39	29	33	29	29	27	29
Don't know	13	13	14	11	14	11	11
	100	100	100	100	100	100	100

Source: Gallup Polls

for radical action. On the basis of opinion poll data and his own survey evidence he claims that the majority view of the class system is a dichotomised one which contains little trace of dominant values. The alternative view, which Moorhouse criticises, points to the disintegration of traditional communities and cultures and appeals to evidence of limited, 'economistic' understandings of class relationships. There is a divergence of interpretations here which cannot be resolved without a better understanding of the dynamics of social consciousness than either of these two superficially plausible but incompatible accounts contain.

If social consciousness is itself a complex set of relations with a variety of objects, it is reasonable to expect a certain degree of flexibility and even inconsistency in the relation of consciousness to such multi-faceted objects as 'class' and 'society'. The problem of analysis is to trace these objects and their paths of influence as well as their place in consciousness. It appears that, depending on the questions asked and the context in which they are asked, the majority of members in the surveyed groups are capable of articulating both views which use class and views which deny class as the basis of social differentiation. This is not necessarily because of any fatal flaws of method or interpretation. Many of these apparent contradictions can be resolved.

Changes in the labour process and especially the decline of the occupational system of work account for the passing of what has been called the 'traditional' occupational community. Whether or not this is the best term to describe a nexus of social relationships which could never have been exclusively occupational, our study points towards two empirical generalisations. Firstly, to the extent that the worker is dependent on the occupational system of work he will tend to define himself and his social position in relation to that system. The technical system does not provide the same possibilities for recognising occupational roles or *métiers*. This is not a simple reiteration of the idea that craft or skilled workers automatically take more pride in their work. It can apply to any worker, skilled or unskilled, who can relate to the job as a secure personal investment instead of a doubtful asset. For this reason, the steelworkers, despite their inferior skills, had a higher level of occupational awareness than the craftsmen. Secondly, variations in the strength of identity are likely to be inversely related to awareness of the totality of existing social relations and the perception of conflict between social groups. The clerical workers, who more than any other group are subject to the increasing technical division of labour can hardly be said to exhibit a common occupational identity. Instead, their social consciousness is dominated by a conception of the total organisational system — a 'systems' view which can be generalised to the social system as a whole. In the cases we have studied it appears that neither the emphasis on identity nor the emphasis on totality is associated with a definition of fundamental conflict between social classes. However, the analysis at this level does not exclude the possibility that such conflict may be recognised in abstract terms, as in the opinion survey responses. Since we did not uncover any evidence from the workers' own experience to account for antagonistic interpretations we therefore assume that the views which appear in the opinion poll data (i.e. views which cannot be dismissed *a priori* as views pertaining to the groups in this study) are 'externally' derived. That is not to say that they fail to connect with any elements in the workers' experience or with the residual ideologies of the labour movement. It is simply that the majority's unqualified agreement with the view that Britain is a class society in which conflict or class struggle is present is fundamentally out of character with all the in-depth responses to questions about personal and occupational experiences.

The problem of analysing external influences on social consciousness is that opinion-forming and consciousness-creating institutions are no more static than social consciousness itself. They are not simply neutral channels for conveying sets of beliefs or bodies of knowledge. However, the relative movement of social consciousness and organised public opinion on social questions is almost certainly non-random. If, as seems to be the case, the movement away from the occupational system towards the technical system of work brings a loss of identity based on achievement and performance, we can postulate a general problem of social integration. At another level, a similar diversification and separation of spheres presents itself as a problem of 'legitimation'. Thus with the growth of the state and the separation of the economic and administrative systems there is an increased possibility of inconsistency and conflict between them. It means for example that economic crises appear less and less 'natural' and more a problem of inadequate management and regulation. Reintegration of the social system can be achieved up to a point by the propagation of a totality or consensus view of society. We can predict that at least some of these integration needs will be met by the key institutions of culture and communication and in fact there is considerable evidence to show that such consensual interpretations dominate the output of the media whose task is to provide information and comment on social questions.[12]

It is consistent with this understanding of the media as formative of public opinion that *political* issues should be presented in terms of 'class' and 'class struggle'. It is only a short step from the metaphor of the fight to a class identification of the opposing sides. Significantly, the opinion polls quoted above prefaced the question with a remark about 'talk in politics'. The context of electoral politics and the rhetoric of recent political debate greatly reduces the relevance to these polls for general questions of class attitudes and social consciousness. The attitudes expressed cannot necessarily be generalised to social relationships in the broader, non-political sense. In his discussion, Moorhouse argues that the opinion poll data provides evidence of opposition to dominant social values and specifically that the majorities who believe in a class struggle in Britain are opposing the dominant value that classes are either not important or that they are positively based on mobility and achievement. It is unfortunate that the opinions expressed are not combined with further evaluative data but this is not essential. Despite their plausibility, we are sceptical of Moorhouse's conclusions because they cannot be reconciled with the evidence from our own more detailed investigations. Our evidence does not reveal any substantial opposition element in the social consciousness of the three samples. We are therefore inclined to interpret the opinion poll data as lending further support to dominant values in the following way. The view that class struggle exists is not difficult to find in political speeches and in commentaries in the media. Usually, however, this view has been used as a negative gloss on interpretations of industrial action and opposition to government policies (e.g. resistance to the Industrial Relations Act). Furthermore, this usage is not limited to one or other political party. 'Class struggle' amounts to a slogan or social Topic lifted from its roots in labour history and re-applied to connote 'outdated', 'politically irresponsible', 'insincere' and 'ideological'. Used in this way it serves dominant values by presenting the alternative to the consensus view of politics and society in a negative light. Therefore, it is only partly true that 'few agencies promote a view of the structure of society as composed of classes in conflict'.[13] Versions of this view are promoted for the purpose of discrediting it and defusing the opposition which it could represent.

We have used this example from public opinion surveys in some detail in order to highlight the relative independence of 'public opinion' from social consciousness formed in the experiences of productive activity. We have pointed to the dangers of interpreting one (images of society) in terms of the other (opinions about class). As a general conclusion we can state that as occupationally-based social identity declines, so the external influences on social consciousness are likely to become more important. As a hypothesis it is more soundly based than those which have so far guided both studies of media influence and studies of images of society.

There is, however, an important qualification which needs to be made, namely the circumstances under which an element of opposition might arise and even become dominant in a group's social consciousness. The fact that none of the groups in our study showed a significant awareness of fundamentally opposed groups or classes does not close the issue altogether. Rather, it is an indication that claims on the social system are being met or at least the possibility of their being met is perceived to exist. The twofold need to create and control within the occupational system of work leads to the defence of a particular status or role in work — that is, to claims based on identity. If these claims are not met, opposition will be expressed towards the system, 'industrial society' or 'class society', which defines the distribution of work and its rewards. In this sense it is correct to speak of 'class consciousness', a specific form of social consciousness which is merely residual among the manual workers in this study. Increasingly, as far as these groups are concerned, but especially among the clerical workers, claims are based less on identity and more on totality, on views of work and organisation tied to a societal value system. In practice this means that claims are made on the management of social and economic development. There is potential for conflict here based on competition for control of social organisation rather than on defence of a role in the work process. It is inappropriate to call this opposition a form of class awareness because it expresses a relationship to the social system and its control rather than to the means of production. This potential for conflict, though latent and occasionally evident at the personal level in expressions of frustration and dissatisfaction among the clerical workers, has not yet been realised in action and there are few signs that it is about to be. In fact the evidence submitted here leads to the conclusion that talk of new forms of social consciousness prefiguring the forms of the post-industrial society is premature. The analysis does not negate the view that occupational and therefore class consciousness is in decline. Rather, it shows that where this process is occurring it is very slow, both because the transformation of the labour process from the occupational to the technical system is very far from complete and because the transformation of social consciousness proceeds even more hesitantly.

Notes

1. H. Braverman, *Labour and Monopoly Capital.*
2. Behind all of these approaches is the idea that 'consciousness', 'ideology' or 'symbolic systems' are distanced from the social reality which they represent, reflect or signify and that consequently they involve an effort to control or transform the system of action. In a complex and hierarchical society this control can never be complete or free from tension and ambiguities. We therefore reject any unidirectional model of cultural influence, whether the unqualified view that experience 'determines' consciousness or the view that the ideological and cultural hegemony of the dominant class is so complete that social consciousness is, so to speak, 'one-dimensional'.
3. See T. Nichols and P. Armstrong, *Workers Divided*, pp.28 ff.
4. For an example of the concept of working class 'factory consciousness', see H. Beynon, *Working for Ford* (London, 1973), p.98.
5. T. Nichols and H. Beynon, *Living with Capitalism* (London, 1977).
6. Ibid, p.56.
7. See especially W.G. Runciman, *Relative Deprivation and Social Justice* (London, 1966).
8. See for example R. Martin and R.H. Fryer, *Redundancy and Paternalist Capitalism* (London, 1973); T. Lane and K. Roberts, *Strike at Pilkingtons* (London, 1971).
9. F. Parkin, *Class Inequality and Political Order* (London, 1971), especially Chapter 3.
10. T. Burns, 'The Organisation of Public Opinion', in J. Curran, M. Gurevitch, J. Woollacott (eds), *Mass Communication and Society* (Open University, London, 1977), pp.67-8.
11. H.F. Moorhouse, 'Attitudes to Class and Class Relationships in Britain', *Sociology*, 10 (1976), p.477.

12. See for instance the Glasgow University Media Group's study of broadcast news, *Bad News* (London, 1976) and *More Bad News* (forthcoming).
13. H.F. Moorhouse, 'Attitudes to Class', p.478.

APPENDIX: THE INTERVIEW SCHEDULE

Interview no._____   Date_____

1.   Age
2.   Marital status
3.   No. of children
4.   Educational qualifications
5.   Occupation/job title
6.   Hours worked
7.   Father's occupation

JOB HISTORY

8.   How long have you been working for the company?
     Have you always worked for the company?
9.   If NO: where did you work before?

	Type of firm	local/not local	occup.	years
i.				
ii.				
iii.				
iv.				

FOLLOW UP: reasons for moving

10. Can you explain why you came to this company and not to any other?
11. Did you know anything about the company before you came here?

FOLLOW UP: were any of your friends or relatives working here?

12.   How did you find out about the job?
13.   Which of the following was the most helpful in getting you into
      your *first* job?

      Hand list: FATHER   YOUTH EMP. OFFICER   FRIEND
                   RELATIVE   NEWSPAPER ADVERT   TEACHER
                   (NONE OF
                   THESE)

      FOLLOW UP: which of these is the best method for a young
      person looking for a job today?

THE WORK TASK

14.   What is the title of your present job?
15.   Would you describe briefly what it involves?

      FOLLOW UP: position in the structure of the firm
                 steadiness of work flow
                 special problems encountered
                 responsibilities for work/personnel
                 do you take work home?
                 what are the main changes you have experienced?

16.   What do you consider to be the most important qualities required
      by a person in your position?
      i.e. what does it take to be a good_____?

SOCIAL RELATIONS AT WORK

17.   Does your work involve you in personal contact with the
      following people (specify)?

      FOLLOW UP: who are you responsible to/for?

18.   With whom do you usually have lunch?

19. Do you have any (social) contacts with company employees outside hours?

THE COMPANY

20. Do you think this company differs in any significant way from other companies you've worked in?

    FOLLOW UP: does size make a difference?
    is it more traditional/modern?
    are salaries higher/lower?
    has nationalisation made a difference?

21. Have you ever considered moving in search of a different job?

    If YES: for what reasons?
    do you have any definite plans?

22. Do you expect either to change jobs or receive promotion within this company?

    FOLLOW UP: is the path predictable?
    what are the main obstacles?

23. The next question is a more general one. Popular ideas about work organisations tend to have one of two main emphases — EITHER: all the members of the organisation have a common interest and what benefits the organisation benefits each individual, OR: organisations contain groups with different aims and interests and each group looks after itself first. Which of these two views is nearest to your own view of this company?

    FOLLOW UP: if there are different groups, what are they?
    why do you think this?
    can you give an e.g. of what you mean?
    would you say this company differs from others?

UNION/ASSOCIATION

24. Are you a member of a staff association/trade union/professional association?

25. Would you call yourself an active member?

     FOLLOW UP: extent of involvement and attitude.

26. What is the staff association/trade union/professional association (or staff committee's) job?
     What would you say are its main functions?

     FOLLOW UP: salaries, work conditions, security, etc.
                          if not mentioned spontaneously.
                   do you think it is doing its job?
                   have you ever been on strike?

27. Do you regard your present earnings level as a direct outcome of formally negotiated agreements?

28. Do you consider that you personally can exert any influence on company policy —
     (a)   in your department?
     (b)   in the company as a whole?

29. If applicable: have you used the Suggestions Scheme?

_____

WORK AND SOCIETY

30. Have you ever been made redundant?
     If YES: how long out of work?

31. Do you think this could happen (again) to you in the future?

32. Hand list: AMBITION   CHARACTER
                 EDUCATION   HARD WORK
                 INTELLIGENCE   KNOWING THE RIGHT PEOPLE
                 LUCK   SOCIAL BACKGROUND

     Which of these would you select as being most important for a person to get on in the world of work?

FOLLOW UP: clarify meanings

relate to own experience

reasons for dismissing other qualities

33.   Is your present occupation what you've always wanted to do? Have you (ever had) any other ambitions for a job?

34.   (Cf. 'social background' Q.32) Which social category would you say you belong to?

35.   What is it that makes this a distinct category?

36.   People talk of 'social classes'. What do you think of this?

FOLLOW UP: do classes exist?

meaning of 'class'

relate to experience

POLITICS AND IMAGE OF SOCIETY

37.   A general question about politics. Do you think there is any significant difference of principle between the two main political parties: Conservative and Labour?

38.   Have you voted in previous general elections? If YES: which party did you vote for last time?

39.   Have you always voted for the same party?

FOLLOW UP: what are you looking for when you decide to vote?

40.   If there were a general election tomorrow, which party would you vote for?

41.   In general, what sorts of people vote   (a) Conservative
                                                   (b) Labour?

42.   Societies are constantly changing, in different aspects and at different speeds. We can account for these changes in terms of a number of factors. Arrange the following in order of importance:

ECONOMIC   SOCIAL
POLITICAL   TECHNICAL

43.   Looking ahead to 5 years from now, what do you expect to be the main changes in your life?

Finally, are there any questions you would like to ask me, before we finish? Are there any topics you feel we should have discussed?

BIBLIOGRAPHY

Ackermann, W., Moscovici, S., 'La Sociologie existentielle d'Alain
Touraine: Note critique', *Sociologie du Travail*, 8 (1966), pp.205 ff
Andrieux, A., Lignon, J., *L'ouvrier d'aujourd'hui* (Paris, 1960)
Bain, G.S., *The Growth of White Collar Unionism* (London, 1970)
Banks, O., *The Attitudes of Steelworkers to Technical Change*
(Liverpool University Press, 1960)
Bannister, D., Fransella, F., *Inquiring Man: the theory of personal
constructs* (Harmondsworth, 1972)
Bannister, D., Mair, J.M.M., *The Evaluation of Personal Constructs*
(London, 1968)
Bell, C., Newby, H., 'The Sources of Variation in Agricultural Workers'
Images of Society', *Sociological Review*, 21 (1973).
Bensman, J., Lilienfeld, R., *Craft and Consciousness: Occupational
Technique and the Development of World Images* (New York, 1973)
Berger, P.L., Berger, B., Kellner, H., *The Homeless Mind*
(Harmondsworth, 1974)
Beynon, H., Blackburn, R.M., *Perceptions of work, variations within a
factory* (Cambridge, 1972)
Beynon, H., *Working for Ford* (Harmondsworth, 1973)
Black, E., *Rhetorical Criticism: a study in method* (New York, 1965)
Blackburn, R.M., *Union Character and Social Class* (London, 1967)
Blauner, R., *Alienation and Freedom* (Chicago, 1964)
——, 'Work satisfaction and industrial trends in modern society', in
S.M. Lipset and R. Bendix (eds), *Class, Status and Power*, 2nd ed.
(New York, 1966)
Bott, E., *Family and Social Network* (London, 1957)
Boulding, K., 'The Place of the Image in the Dynamics of Society', in
G.K. Zollschan and W. Hirsch, *Explorations in Social Change*
(London, 1964)
Bowen, P., Shaw, M., Smith, R., 'The Steelworker and Work Control:
a sociological analysis and industrial relations case study', *British
Journal of Industrial Relations*, 12, 2 (1974)
Braverman, H., *Labour and Monopoly Capital* (New York, 1974)
Brook, E., Finn, D., 'Working Class Images of Society and Community
Studies', *Working Papers in Cultural Studies*, 10 (1977)
Brown, R.K., Brannen, P., 'Social relations and social perspectives

amongst shipbuilding workers: a preliminary statement', *Sociology*, 4 (1970)

Bulmer, M. (ed.), *Working Class Images of Society* (London, 1975)

Burns, T. (ed.), *Industrial Man* (Harmondsworth, 1969)

——, 'The Organization of Public Opinion', in J. Curran *et al.* (eds.), *Mass Communication and Society* (London, 1977)

Centers, R., *The Psychology of Social Classes* (Princeton, 1949)

Coulthard, M., *An Introduction to Discourse Analysis* (London, 1977)

Cousins, J., Brown, R.K., 'Patterns of paradox: shipbuilding workers' images of society', in M. Bulmer (ed.), *Working-Class Images of Society* (London, 1975)

Coxon, A.P.M., Jones, C.L., *The Images of Occupational Prestige: a study in social cognition* (London, 1978)

Crompton, R., 'Approaches to the Study of White-collar Unionism', *Sociology*, 10, 3 (1976)

Crozier, M., *The World of the Office Worker* (Chicago, 1971)

Dahrendorf, R., *Class and Class Conflict in Industrial Society* (Stanford, 1959)

Davies, A.F., *Images of Class* (Sydney, 1967)

Dreitzel, H.P., 'Selbstbild und Gesellschaftsbild', *Arch. europ. sociol.*, 3 (1962)

Dubin, R., 'Industrial Workers' Worlds: a study of the central life interests of industrial workers', *Social Problems*, 3 (1956)

Dumont, L., *Homo Hierarchicus* (London, 1972)

Durand, C., *Conscience ouvrière et action syndicale* (Paris, 1971)

Durand, C., Durand M., *De l'ouvrier specialisé à l'ingénieur: carrière ou classe sociale* (Paris, 1971)

Eldridge, J.E.T., *Industrial Disputes* (London, 1968)

Finsterbusch, K., 'Demonstrating the Value of Mini Surveys in Social Research', *Sociological Methods and Research*, 5, 1 (1976)

Fox, A., *Industrial Sociology and Industrial Relations* (HMSO, London, 1966)

——, *A Sociology of Work in Industry* (London, 1971)

Geertz, C., 'Ideology as a Cultural System', in D.E. Apter (ed.), *Ideology and Discontent* (New York, 1964)

Giddens, A., *The Class Structure of Advanced Societies* (London, 1973)

Glasgow University Media Group, *Bad News* (London, 1976)

Goldthorpe, J., Lockwood, D., Bechhofer, F., Platt, J., *The Affluent Worker in the Class Structure* (Cambridge, 1969)

Goldthorpe, J.H., 'L'image des classes chez les travailleurs manuels aisés, *Revue française de sociologie*, 11 (1970), pp.334-8

Gray, R., 'The Labour Aristocracy in the Victorian Class Structure',
   in F. Parkin (ed.), *The Social Analysis of Class Structure* (London,
   1974)
Hamilton, R.F., *Affluence and the French Worker in the Fourth*
   Republic (Princeton, 1967)
Hiller, P., 'Social Reality and Social Stratification', *Sociological*
   Review, 21 (1973)
Hinton, J., *The First Shop Stewards Movement* (London, 1973)
Hobsbawm, E.J., *Labouring Men* (London, 1964)
Hoggart, R., *The Uses of Literacy* (Harmondsworth, 1957)
Hunter, L.C., Reid, G.L., Boddy, D., *Labour Problems of Technical*
   Change (London, 1970)
Ingham, G.K., *Size of Industrial Organisation and Worker Behaviour*
   (Cambridge, 1970)
Jackson, A., *Modern Steelmaking for Steelmakers* (London, 1967)
Kern, H., Schumann, M., *Industriearbeit und Arbeiterbewusstsein*,
   2 vols. (Frankfurt, 1970)
Kohn, M.L., *Class and Conformity: a study in values* (Homewood,
   Illinois, 1969)
Kornhauser, A., Dubin, R., Ross, A.M. (eds.), *Industrial Conflict*
   (New York, 1954)
Laing, R.D., *Self and Others* (Harmondsworth, 1971)
Lockwood, D., *The Blackcoated Worker* (London, 1958)
——, 'Sources of variation in working class images of society',
   Sociological Review, 14, 3 (1966)
Lumley, R., *White Collar Unionism in Britain* (London, 1973)
Mackenzie, G., *The Aristocracy of Labour* (Cambridge, 1973)
Madge, C., *Society in the Mind* (London, 1964)
Mallet, S., *La nouvelle classe ouvrière* (Paris, 1963)
Mann, M., 'The social cohesion of liberal democracy', *American*
   Sociological Review, 35 (1970)
——, *Consciousness and Action among the Western Working Class*
   (London, 1973)
McGeown, P., *Heat the Furnace Seven Times More* (London, 1967)
Mercer, D.E., Weir, D.T.H., 'Attitudes to work and trade unionism
   amongst white-collar workers', *Industrial Relations Journal*, 3 (1972)
Millar, R., *The New Classes* (London, 1966)
Moore, H., Kleining, E., 'Das Bild der Sozialen Wirklichkeit', *Kölner*
   Zeitschrift für Soziologie und Sozialpsychologie, 11 (1959),
   pp.354-76.
——, 'Das Soziale Selbstbild der Gesellschaftsschichten Deutschlands',

Kölner Zeitschrift für Soziologie und Sozialpsychologie, 12 (1960),
pp.86-119.

Moorhouse, H.F., Chamberlain, C.W., 'Lower class attitudes to
property: aspects of the counter-ideology', *Sociology*, 8 (1974)

Moorhouse, H.F., 'Attitudes to class and class relationships in Britain',
Sociology, 10 (1976)

Mills, C. Wright, *White Collar* (New York, 1951)

Mumford, E., Banks, O., *The Computer and the Clerk* (London, 1967)

Nichols, T., Armstrong, P., *Workers Divided* (London, 1976)

Nichols, T., Beynon, H., *Living with Capitalism: class relations and
the modern factory* (London, 1977)

Ossowski, S., *Class Structure in the Social Consciousness* (London,
1963)

Pahl, J.M., Pahl, R.E., *Managers and their Wives* (Harmondsworth,
1971)

Parker, S.R., *The Future of Work and Leisure* (London, 1971)

Parkin, F., *Class Inequality and Political Order* (London, 1971)

Platt, J., 'Variations in answers to different questions on perceptions
of class', *Sociological Review*, 19 (1971), pp.409 ff

Popitz, H., Bahrdt, H.P., Jueres, E.A., Kesting, A., *Das Gesellschaftsbild
des Arbeiters* (Tübingen, 1957)

——, 'The worker's image of society', in T. Burns (ed.), *Industrial Man*
(Harmondsworth, 1969)

Price, H.H., *Thinking and Experience* (London, 1969)

Pugh, A., *Men of Steel* (London, 1951)

Ramsay, H., 'Research Note: Firms and Football Teams', *British
Journal of Industrial Relations*, 13, 3 (1975)

Reynaud, J.D., Bourdieu, P., 'Is a sociology of action possible?', in
A. Giddens (ed.), *Positivism and Sociology* (London, 1974)

Runciman, W.G., *Relative Deprivation and Social Justice* (London,
1966)

Salaman, G., *Community and Occupation* (Cambridge, 1974)

Sartre, J.P., *The Psychology of Imagination* (London, 1972)

——, *Search for a Method* (New York, 1968)

Scase, R. (ed.), *Industrial Society: Class, Cleavage and Control*
(London, 1977)

Scott, W.H. *et al.*, *Technical Change in Industrial Relations* (Liverpool
University Press, 1956)

Sennett, R., Cobb, J., *The Hidden Injuries of Class* (New York, 1973)

De Soto, C.B., 'The Predilection for Single Orderings', *Journal of
Abnormal and Social Psychology*, 62 (1961)

Seeman, M., 'On the Meaning of Alienation', *American Sociological Review*, 24, 6 (1959)
Shepard, J.M., *Automation and Alienation* (Cambridge, Mass., 1971)
Stinchcombe, A.L., 'Bureaucratic and Craft Administration of Production', *Admin. Sci. Quarterly*, 4 (1959)
Sykes, A.J.M., 'Some differences in the attitudes of clerical and manual workers', *Sociological Review*, 13 (1965)
Touraine, A., Ragazzi, O., *Ouvriers d'origine agricole* (Paris, 1961)
Touraine, A., *Workers Attitides to Technical Change* (OECD, Paris, 1965)
——, *Sociologie de l'action* (Paris, 1965)
——, *La conscience ouvrière* (Paris, 1966)
——, *The May Movement* (New York, 1971)
——, *Production de la société* (Paris, 1973)
——, *The Post-Industrial Society* (London, 1974)
——, *Pour la sociologie* (Paris, 1974)
——, 'Social Identity and the Formation of Social Movements', in W.S. Dillon (ed.), *The Cultural Drama: modern identities and social ferment* (Washington, 1974)
Turner, H.A., *Trade Union Growth, Structure and Policy* (London, 1962)
Vidal, D., *Essai sur l'ideologie* (Paris, 1971)
Walker, C.R., *Steeltown* (New York, 1950)
Warner, W. Lloyd *et al.*, *Social Class in America* (Chicago, 1949)
Warren, N., 'Social Class and Construct Systems', *British Journal of Clinical and Social Psychology*, 5 (1966)
Webb, D, 'Some reservations on the use of self-rated class: Research note', *Sociological Review*, 21 (1973)
Wedderburn, D., Crompton, R., *Workers' Attitudes and Technology* (Cambridge, 1972)
Westergaard, J., Resler, H., *Class in a Capitalist Society* (London, 1975)
Wilensky, H.L., 'Work, careers and social integration', *International Social Science Journal*, 12 (1960)
Willener, A., *Images de la société et classes sociales* (Bern, 1957)
——, *The Action Image of Society* (London, 1970)
——, 'Payment Systems in the French Steel and Iron Mining Industry', in G.K. Zollschan and W. Hirsch, *Explorations in Social Change* (London, 1964)
Willener, A., Gajdos, C., Benguigiu, G., *Les cadres en mouvement* (Paris, 1969)
Williams, R., *The Long Revolution* (Harmondsworth, 1965)

——, 'Base and Superstructure in Marxist Cultural Theory',
  New Left Review, 82 (1973)
Williams, W.M. (ed.), *Occupational Choice* (University of Keele, 1974)
Zijderveld, A., *The Abstract Society* (Harmondsworth, 1972)

INDEX

212   *Index*